PRAISE FOR
THE IMPERFECT PARENT

"Successful journeys typically start with a road map and plan. Very successful journeys also include an experienced guide who has been there, done that. *The Imperfect Parent* has both. Kate has invaluable advice for all parents, and her sons are the proof of her wisdom. Loving your kids is the easy part. Raising them requires an entirely different set of muscles. Kate's book is the thoughtful, hard-earned insights that can make the difference for anyone who wants world-class clues for the hardest job in the world."

—KEITH CUNNINGHAM, entrepreneur, international speaker, and author of *The Road Less Stupid*

"If all parents read Kate's book, it would change the course of humankind. Whether we like it or not, our children are the next leaders of the free world. They are coming. Nothing affects the future of the human race more than how these kids are raised and developed. They need great parenting so they can soar with their strengths."

—JIM CLIFTON, chairman of Gallup

"Kate's ability to help parents acquire the mindset needed to raise their children successfully, no matter what their parenting situation may be, is nothing short of amazing. She shares many parenting stories that send home the messages of listening to understand, staying curious when communicating with your children, and staying aware of the human nature response. The way she encourages parents to lead by example, to be comfortable examining their own flaws, and to trust their intuition is game-changing."

—SANDY HEIN, instructor and coach with the Black Swan Group

THE
IMPERFECT
PARENT

THE IMPERFECT PARENT

A Nonjudgmental Guide to
Raising Children in the Modern World

KATE HAMILTON

GREENLEAF
BOOK GROUP PRESS

Published by Greenleaf Book Group Press
Austin, Texas
www.gbgpress.com

Distributed by Greenleaf Book Group

For ordering information or special discounts for bulk purchases, please
contact Greenleaf Book Group at PO Box 91869, Austin, TX 78709,
512.891.6100.

Design and composition by Greenleaf Book Group and Teresa Muniz
Cover design by Greenleaf Book Group and Teresa Muniz
Cover images used under license from ©AdobeStock/lunglee
and ©AdobeStock/Oranuch

Publisher's Cataloging-in-Publication data is available.

Print ISBN: 979-8-88645-203-7

eBook ISBN: 979-8-88645-204-4

To offset the number of trees consumed in the printing of our books,
Greenleaf donates a portion of the proceeds from each printing to
the Arbor Day Foundation. Greenleaf Book Group has replaced over
50,000 trees since 2007.

Printed in the United States of America on acid-free paper

24 25 26 27 28 29 30 31   10 9 8 7 6 5 4 3 2 1

First Edition

This book is dedicated to both of my future daughters-in-law. It is my hope that this book gives them even more insights into how my sons were raised—my failures and my successes. I want them to start where Charlie and I left off, add their unique perspectives, and create a family life with my sons that is uniquely theirs.

CONTENTS

PART V: FOCUS ON WISDOM

INTRODUCTION

MY PURPOSE

My mother used to break her pasta in half before she cooked it; I grew up assuming that was how you did it if you were Italian. After all, my mother copied Aida, her Italian mother-in-law. Then one day in an Italian cooking class, the teacher stood in front of the room and asserted, "You never break your pasta when you cook it. If you do, you're not Italian."

To say that surprised me would be an understatement. I was taught *you always break pasta before you cook it.* The next time I saw my mom, I asked her about it. She shrugged and said, "That's the way my mother-in-law taught me. She's Italian. I figured she should know."

A few days later, I was cooking spaghetti beside Grandmother Aida. So I asked her the same question after she broke the pasta and placed it into the boiling water. She cocked her head slightly and looked up, thinking back to her own childhood.

"Because my mother did it that way," she said.

Confused, I put down my wooden spoon and looked into her warm brown eyes. "But my cooking teacher told me that Italians *never* break their pasta before cooking it."

She smiled and said, "Your teacher's right, Kate. My mother only had one pot that she used for everything. It was smaller than the pot one would usually cook pasta in. So my mother broke the pasta to make it fit. I break the pasta because that's what I learned from my mother." It was simply a habit.

We learn from our parents. Right or wrong, they pass down habits and patterns for a variety of reasons, and if we never question these habits and patterns, we'll continue to use them and pass them on to our children. I wrote this book in part because I would like my sons to know the *reasons* for my parenting actions. I want them to take what I did as a parent, understand the reasons for it, improve on it, and even break unsuccessful patterns passed from one generation to the next. Ideally, my children will understand the past so they can apply correct reasoning to the present so their children's future will be full of even more opportunities than their parents had. The bottom line: I want my sons to find a bigger pot so they do not have to break their analogous pasta. And who knows? Maybe their kids will invent a better pasta pot in the future.

I hope this book helps parents avoid some of the bad habits that have been passed down through generations in their family. It is one way I feel called to give back. I have been blessed in life and have always believed that those who have been given much have the responsibility to share their good fortune. I realized it was time to share my parental triumphs, as well as my failures, with others openly and honestly. My parents were wonderful, and they did the best they could with the information they had. They made mistakes, like I did—like we all do. Even their errors made me a better parent.

I expect that my boys will make errors raising their kids. When they acknowledge those errors, they will grow and learn. I did. Growth is the silver lining to the cold, hard reality of failing. Anyone who thinks they can live an error-free life is just kidding themselves. Children require a playground for learning, complete with obstacles to overcome and struggles that cause pain. That's why I always say it's a blessing that no one's childhood is perfect; we learn the most through our struggles. So, for every parent reading this, if you feel like you're messing up, allow me to be the first to congratulate you. You're doing it right. If you observe the parents who supposedly know what they are doing, you'll discover that no one is truly prepared for parenting.

No one can be prepared because no two kids are alike. They will not react the same, understand things the same, or feel emotions the same. Some kids will seem to glide through difficulties. Others will need to battle through problems to become an adult. This can be difficult for the parent; what may seem a monumental battle to you may be a minuscule one to your child—and vice versa.

My hope is that in reading this book and given the suggestions provided, parents learn from my mistakes and triumphs. Each reader may take away something different from my errors, observations, and successes: that's the beauty and magic of the parenting process. After all, there's no one right way to parent. Just as there's an art to making lemons into scrumptious lemonade, each parent paints their family portrait with unique strokes of love, patience, and creativity.

Please remember that your lemonade will be different from mine because you and I have different preferences. It's up to you to interpret my suggestions the way you see fit and then apply that advice to your family. If you're picking up this book, that means you're interested in learning. You want to improve. It also means you're ready to act, and hopefully you have fun doing so. I applaud you for that, for we are all learning. Thank you for joining me on this learning journey. In the remainder of this introduction, I introduce myself and my boys and then give you an overview of what the book covers.

WHAT TO EXPECT

The Imperfect Parent isn't about following specific rules; instead, it is about applying certain general concepts to your life. It outlines what I did to teach my boys, along with pertinent, humorous, and sometimes poignant examples from my life and stories I've heard over the decades from friends and family. The examples are based on what I did that worked, what didn't work, all kinds of mistakes, and what I learned from others. Of course, you will need to use your own good judgment to decide how to apply these concepts to your child. I don't know your children as well as you do.

For some, a person's life story can grant them credibility and foster trust. To others, such narratives seem inconsequential. No matter where you find yourself in this spectrum, know this: my past is not only the fuel that ignited my desire to pen this book but also the foundation that shaped my perspective.

From an early age, I recognized the patterns in my life—the same patterns that appeared in the actions of my parents and those around us. This observation and my inherent knack for systematizing paved my way, changing my life forever. I firmly believe God endowed me with these abilities and experiences to share my insights, in this case ensuring other parents don't inadvertently perpetuate cycles of hurt and trauma.

My parenting philosophy wasn't born out of textbooks; it was reflected in the pain, the struggle, and the resilience of my own family history. I saw, with painful clarity, the patterns passed down from my grandparents to my parents, and to me. I understood the toxic legacy of unaddressed trauma, control, and expectations.

> I recognized a crucial truth: we have the power to change our narrative.

Most importantly, I recognized a crucial truth: we have the power to change our narrative. My decision to raise my children differently wasn't rebellion; it was evolution. I chose to learn, to grow, and to heal, ensuring my children would be nurtured in an environment of understanding, empathy, and conscious decision-making.

My earliest memories are of Columbia, Maryland, where life was filled with adventure, mischief, and occasional misfortunes. Throughout these experiences, from the nerve-wracking search for my brother when he was lost in the woods to the stark contrast between my siblings' accolades and my academic struggles, a mosaic of resilience was taking form.

Life propelled us from Maryland to Arizona, marking my first real encounter with loss and adaptation. It was there, held back a grade because of my struggles with reading, that I first understood how we all progress at our own pace—a lesson I've carried into my parenting philosophy. These foundational memories were merely the beginning. Moving across states, facing health challenges, confronting the dark menace of a stranger trying to kidnap me three times, and absorbing the shock of my brother's near-fatal accident when a car hit him while crossing the street—each event crafted a narrative of survival and grit.

My experiences moving as a child helped propel my husband, Charlie, and me to talk more openly and honestly about moving with our sons. We addressed their fear of the unknown and the disruption of their life routine together. We gave them a voice and a vote in our family decisions. We had many family conversations where their concerns could be validated. This formula and my learning grew with time. Coupled with my early responsibilities due to my younger sister's drug addiction and my father's failing eyesight, a variety of experiences, such as managing household finances as a teenager and witnessing my brother's and sister's tumultuous journey through addiction and recovery, bestowed on me maturity and experience far beyond my years. When I saw my sister's addiction relapse, I learned a hard lesson. My parents were enablers. Despite what the experts advised, they did what they thought was needed, providing food, shelter, and financial resources. They knew no different.

I saw no change or progress in my sister, I realized my parents were doing what they saw their parents do, and I knew there had to be a better way. I analyzed my past experiences, read numerous books, and attended expert lectures, learning invaluable lessons: to listen actively, to avoid judgment, and to own my actions. I learned to discern patterns in behavior, devising systems to comprehend and tackle them. This was only possible because of God's grace and plan for me and because I listened to a person tell their story at a Narcotics Anonymous meeting I attended with my brother when I was in high school. The story was compelling and I vowed not to go down the same path. While others might view my childhood adversities as horrifying, I see them as powerful lessons that equipped me to navigate life's most intricate mazes.

My credentials do not come embossed on a certificate or highlighted on a resume. They were earned through lived experiences, through the trials I faced, and through the resilience I fostered. My experiences mirror the testimonies of countless others. My children, now well-adjusted adults, are a testament to the efficacy of my approach. While I won't attribute their successes to my parenting, I credit the conscious choices I made—decisions rooted in introspection and the urge to break generational cycles—that gave my sons a multitude of choices. They also learned at a young age that their choices matter, and they had to live with the consequences of their choices.

I'm not claiming to have all the answers, but my life has been an extensive course in resilience, adaptability, and change. I've listened to numerous experts from a variety of disciplines related to parenting and personal growth, amalgamated their wisdom, and applied it uniquely to my family's context. Years of work researching and applying hard-won lessons are interwoven throughout this book. Today, I stand as a trusted advisor not only to my grown children but to several friends and their children too.

This book is not about dictating how to parent; it's about sharing the wisdom gleaned from a life lived fully, with all its bruises and its grace.

It's about showing that we can break cycles, that we can learn from our past, and that we can choose the legacy we leave for our children. I invite you to join me on this journey, to explore the depths of your own experiences and perceptions, and to embrace the beauty of doing things differently. Together, let's navigate the intricate art of parenting fueled by love, learning, and the courage to grow.

My message to you, dear reader, is simple: Trust in your instincts and your capabilities. While my life's lessons form the backbone of this book, your own discernment and adaptability will allow you to harness its wisdom. Learn from my journey, take what resonates, and use it to create a better future for your family. Your children deserve the best version of you, and with conscious effort, you can ensure they receive just that.

The book is divided into five parts, each focusing on important lessons on parenting shared with experiences and possible recommendations for applying the general principles drawn from those experiences. Part I focuses on the family structure in relation to parents' responsibilities to children, to other guardians, and to the family unit. Part II focuses on the larger context of the family, its values and influences, and your children's passions. Part III bridges the gap of getting to know the importance of the context in the first two parts to focus on the microenvironmental influences of how we communicate with our words and emotions. Part IV moves outward and explores how parents create a system in which kids can thrive through the parents' oversight. The final part focuses on the most important task of all: learning and teaching wisdom—for us and our children. Now that you have a sense of the book's structure, let's dive into the structure of the family.

PART I

FOCUS ON FAMILY STRUCTURE

CHAPTER 1

THE PARENT'S DUTY

I think you'll agree that parenting has changed from when we were kids. When I was young, my parents would let us play outside whenever we wanted all weekend. Nothing was planned and nothing was expected—just fresh air, nature, exercise, and fun. Today many kids spend much of their weekend participating in scheduled activities.

Have you ever seen the craziness involved with parents trying to get their kids into the *perfect* preschool? Then, when high school comes, parents are jockeying for the school with the best of everything. What about the complicated college admission process?

There's no doubt about it, raising kids can be scary. The pressures parents face today can be overwhelming. Even something as simple as knowing how many activities to enroll our kids in so they don't miss out can tie us in knots. Knowing what our duty as a parent really is can be difficult.

Are we doing the right thing by pushing our kids so hard?

Or are we erring if we don't push them at all?

Sure, some of the baseline expectations are obvious such as keeping clothes on their bodies, food in their stomachs, and roofs over their heads. But when considering one's duty as a parent beyond basic survival, there is no one right or wrong answer. It's a matter of absorbing all the information you can and forming your own conclusion.

PARENTING IS A RESPONSIBILITY

> There is no one right way to parent all kids, and most parents will make mistakes.

Parenting is an amazing responsibility that every caring parent wants to get right. My most important words of advice are that, ultimately, there is no one right way to parent all kids, and most parents will make mistakes. Don't be afraid of mistakes; they are opportunities for you and your kids to learn and grow.

The first step a parent takes is the decision to *be* a parent. *You* are the person who will set the tone for your family, *you* will influence your child's beliefs and desires. It will be *your* worldviews, religion, and cultural norms that will be taught. This can be challenging whether there are two parents or not. In co-parenting or guardian homes, you each bring values from your childhood and then blend these to create a value system for your family. Whether you choose to bring a child into the world or to adopt, you must decide what is important to pass on to your children, how to pass it on, and what will influence you.

In a co-parenting home, each parent will have strong views on certain topics. Your challenge is to come up with a workable plan on what is important and what is not. Your friends, your family, and the outside world will offer their opinions. If you don't discuss parenting with your partner or don't have a clear plan in mind for yourself, others will exert their influence without you realizing it's happening.

Let me give you an example from my own life.

I grew up Roman Catholic and believe in Catholicism and Jesus

Christ. When I was in college, I took a class called World Religions and another class called Catholic Social Thought. Through these studies, I found that at the heart of all religions around the world, people are collecting information that makes up the basis for the rules, rituals, traditions, and meanings of each religion. I believe some of the books and teachings by humans are divinely inspired while others are not. Humans can create a religion that inspires, teaches, and leads followers to God or one that leads people away from God. After all, free will gives us the ability to learn, consider, and choose our path.

My husband, Charlie, grew up in a Methodist family, and he became a practicing Christian when he was in college. As we were preparing to get married, my parents stressed the importance of our being married in the Roman Catholic Church. As an obliging daughter, I thought nothing of this request. However, Charlie was a little resistant because of his lack of knowledge of Catholicism. In addition, we had to meet many requirements of the Church to be married.

In the end, Charlie honored my family's request. We both took the marriage preparation classes offered by my church and did what was asked of us to get married in the Roman Catholic Church. This was my parents' influence on our relationship. As a result, when we started our lives together, we were following someone else's plan. It took us several years to figure out that this interference was pulling us apart.

As a couple, Charlie and I decided that what was important was our faith in God, not the branch of Christianity. We chose to attend a church service based on what was being taught, what we would learn, and what we could contribute to the community and those in need.

It was our choice to do what was best for us. My parents were not happy at first, but I explained that my desire to please them was causing a rift in my marriage. My mother agreed to stop interfering; she even visited the church we attended and asked many questions. In the end, she realized that even though our church wasn't Roman Catholic, it held the same core beliefs that were non-negotiable in her mind.

You, and if co-parenting your partner, will encounter many situations where you will need to make decisions that might contradict the advice of your parents, friends, or culture. It's important to make decisions based on what is best for you and your children, not to please others or earn their approval.

Of course, not all advice is solicited. When unsolicited advice is offered, I like to listen to it with an open mind. It's good to hear what others believe; however, I don't argue with them. Most of the time the person is just looking out for me and I appreciate that. That's a good time to take the high road and show gratitude.

Inevitably, there are times when I can't just smile and say *thank you*. My friend Nancy can be very opinionated. Her children attended a school that she was passionate about. She'd constantly extol the virtues of this school and try to convince me that Conrad and Carson should attend as well. I could tell from her description that it wasn't right for our family, but she continued to praise its virtues. Eventually, I had to stand strong and tell her that not every school is right for every child, and I felt her school was not right for my sons. Then I walked away.

Though she thought I was rude, I never explained the reasoning behind my decision. After some time and much prying by her, I told her my explanation would not serve our friendship. I firmly believe there are times to remember a wise quote attributed to President Ronald Reagan: "If you're explaining, you're losing." If I were to explain my decision, Nancy would see that I thought her perfect school had a flaw. Then, someone would have to be right and someone would have to be wrong in her mind. By not explaining my reasoning, I was being gracious. I chose not to mention the attributes of the school that didn't fit my family, even if they did for her children. Not all friends are like Nancy, yet those friends who have strong opinions and see things in black or white might need a strong, gracious walk away. Nancy and I are still friends, and good friends will respect your choices.

My advice in parental disagreements with unsolicited advice is to be firm, take control, and parent the way you believe is best for your family. Be informed about what the experts you respect say, but remember you don't have to follow their advice. Not every action the experts recommend will work for your family. Experts usually operate off what has worked in the past for a group of people. They are not always innovators, willing to try new concepts and grow. Consider breaking past routines. Even though experts (or friends) think their way is best, original ideas can open new doors for you and your family.

THREE STYLES IN PARENTING

I have a good friend, Ricky, who from a young age groomed his three children to go into his family business. His wife, Lucy, supported him throughout the process. They taught their children valuable lessons and provided a fast track to success. The kids fully understood the expectations of the parents and acquiesced. While the path laid out by the parents appeared to be a good one, and they are kind and giving people, Ricky forgot one important factor: he didn't ask his children what they wanted. Instead, he continued to direct his children's decisions into their adulthood.

One day the eldest son, Jim, a productive adult, brought a girl home, Pam, to meet his parents. Ricky didn't like Pam and made his feelings known. Jim was hurt and defended his girlfriend. The parents pushed Jim to break up with Pam, but he stood firm in the face of their opposition for the first time in his life. Jim made his own decision to do what he felt was right, which was to marry Pam. Eventually, the parents chose to accept Pam and they, too, grew to love her. Was this easy for the parents? Absolutely not, because they had to let go of their expectations and hope for their child. They had to accept their son's plan including the struggles they believed he created. Protecting him from hardship could have ended in no relationship with him. In the end, they chose to be there for him through his struggles. They couldn't bear not being a part of their son's life.

There are many ways to raise a child, each of which derives from one's understanding of what it means to be a parent. Parenting is also something about which there are many opinions. To me, a parent is not simply someone who produces offspring and is beyond being a caregiver. Parenting is about giving unconditional love and support to the child. This definition is not confined to the traditional idea of *father* and *mother*. It encompasses anyone who takes on the role of caregiver, who chooses to love a child unconditionally. Many people in your child's life can be a part of your parenting team, and each may have a different way of parenting. Experience has taught me that there are essentially three different styles in parenting, and a parent might use each style in different situations: the assertive parent, the negotiating parent, and the curious parent. These styles are adapted from Diana Baumrind's work. Baumrind was a developmental psychologist at the Institute of Human Development, University of California, Berkeley, known for her research on parenting styles.

STYLE ONE: THE ASSERTIVE PARENT

The assertive parent requires their kids to follow directions, do what they say, and follow in their footsteps. There is a list of rules, spoken or unspoken, and the parent expects those rules to be followed. This parenting style will have specific outcomes and goals for the kids. Praise is given when rules are followed and accomplishments are achieved. The parents have experiences and expertise to share. They spend time with their children doing things of the parents' choosing, passing on their interests, hobbies, and proficiencies. Their children often go to the same schools as the parents did, play the same sports, participate in the same extracurricular activities, and sometimes even dress like the parents. These parents want their kids to be even better than they are and help them achieve this by pushing their kids down a path they know how to navigate.

STYLE TWO: THE NEGOTIATING PARENT

When using this style, the parent will get what they want from their kids by negotiating. If the child wants a snack, the parent makes the child clean up the toys first. Perhaps the parent wants their child to eat dinner, but the child wants to play video games. So the parent lets the child play video games after dinner. This parent gives money or rewards for good grades. Almost everything is a trade of some kind.

STYLE THREE: THE CURIOUS PARENT

In the third style, a parent strives to support and develop their child's unique talents. They delight in the differences as well as the similarities. They attend their child's baseball game even though they know nothing about the sport. They let their child make a mess when working on a creative project and then teach them to clean it up. They try to understand their child's needs and to figure out the best way to meet them while maintaining the child's sense of self and independence.

The story at the beginning of this chapter is an example of a parent using the assertive style in the relationship between parent and child. This style can be associated with first-born children; these are the kids destined to take over the family business. First-born children tend to want to follow the path their parents lay out for them, and parents naturally want to do what they know works and what they think is best for their kids. However, with this style, the parent must watch that their own desires don't overshadow the desires of the child. While the assertive parent style can be negative, it might be needed to push the child to a place where the curious style becomes effective. For instance, the assertive style can be helpful in setting boundaries for very young children. The parent tells the child the rules and expects the rules to be followed. The shift then comes when the parent sets a consequence for not following the rule. The curious style lets the child know that he has a choice and what will happen based on his choices or the consequences of his actions. Some kids will still touch the hot pot even if they know they will get burnt. Some kids need the assertive style of parents when they are young to keep them safe.

I think my sons were born negotiators, and often I found myself using the second style of parenting. I will never forget our early grocery shopping adventures when the boys were around two and three years old. I was always losing Conrad, and Carson would be screaming to get his way. I'd have a screaming kid and/or a missing kid. Not ideal. Each time before we entered the store, I'd negotiate with Carson that he could be in any place inside the cart as long as he stayed in the cart. Conrad, on the other hand, had to touch the cart or me at all times. My strategy was to run like a crazy woman through the store filling up the cart as quickly as I could and finishing my shopping before *they* were done.

I got so good that I often made it all the way to the checkout line before Conrad stopped following or Carson started screaming. The checkout line was where things fell apart and all bets were off. The impulse items called out to my boys, so I found myself getting into endless negotiations just to leave the store.

Our grocery adventures finally changed when Carson and Conrad began earning their own money. It started when I paid them to do little jobs for me that lay outside their normal familial responsibilities. The distinction was clear for them: I'd pay them if they did something extra for me or their father, but I'd never pay them for doing their personal and family chores. Having said that, sometimes I'd give them an incentive to be the first out of bed, dressed, and to pick up the newspaper from the porch for their dad, Charlie. For this, I paid them a penny. They saved their pennies; Conrad would buy bubble gum, and Carson would purchase bouncy balls.

At first, that was all they could afford, and they quickly learned that they needed more money if they wanted higher-priced items. That's when they decided to start a lemonade stand and found ways to sell other items. I also created a system where they could earn money by doing good deeds. I go into more detail about these activities in the "Reward Problem-Solving" section in chapter 11.

After they started earning their own money, I tried something new when we were grocery shopping. In the checkout line, when Conrad and Carson begged for candy bars, I replied, "Sure, if you spend your own money." I remember that Conrad really thought about that idea and decided against buying the candy. Carson, on the other hand, asked again to use my money and tried to negotiate. I shook my head and told him he'd have to spend his own money.

After a moment Carson said, "If it's your money, I want the candy. If it's mine, I don't need it." Conrad agreed. Simple words, but I'll never forget them.

That day I learned that Conrad's and Carson's actions in the grocery store came from their need to be in control of their choices. Making them pay for the candy allowed them to express what they wanted, feel heard, and make a choice. Prior to that, I'd been too busy trying to make it out of the store. I'd been too caught up in negotiating.

Understanding this, I was able to shift from the negotiator style to the curious style and give them the opportunity to make their own decisions. After that, grocery shopping became an enjoyable experience, I could even direct the boys to help me collect items off the shelves. The day Conrad asked me what a pineapple tasted like, we bought one, and he loved it. That success came because I included my children in the shopping process. We were working together as a family.

It is easy for parents to get stuck using one style of parenting. We can become comfortable handling our children in a particular way, but the truth is that at different stages and ages of your child's life, you will naturally flow in and out of these styles depending on which is most appropriate to your child's needs. Your context and personality help you decide which style will work best for you. And possibly, as your parenting experiences grow, so do your parenting styles change. When my boys hit high school, I found that my style was overwhelmingly curious. The more I knew about them, the easier it was to say yes to what they wanted to do. I suggested the family make dinner together a priority. It was hard not only for the boys, who had football practice from 6:00 p.m. to 8:00 p.m. four days a week, but also for my husband, whose schedule is ever changing. We made it work because the discussions at dinner were worth it for everyone. Many nights my boys' friends were at dinner too. We got to have conversations about life choices and listen to their perspectives. The give-and-take at family dinner gave me confidence that they would tell me truthfully what they were doing. It also gave me the opportunity to listen and hear the story before I judged or decided my response. My boys' dinnertime stories allowed me to align my parenting decisions and actions with their personal goals and dreams. Nevertheless, I was armed with the other styles and used them as needed.

Each style centers on teaching at a particular moment of development in your children's lives. With the assertive style, parents are the authority figures keeping their children safe, teaching them how to recognize wise choices by imitating them. In the negotiating style, parents seek to help children make wise choices by giving them something for making a wise choice. This teaches children they can speak up and ask for what they want yet also lets them know there is a cost to getting what they want. In the third style, the curious style, I've learned that parents let go of their sense of control and start leading through questions and getting kids to think and accept their own consequences for their actions. With the curious parenting style, children learn that they get more control through exercising wise choices and accepting the consequences of those choices, good or bad.

CREATE YOUR UNIQUE JOURNEY

Parents have opportunities to provide examples of choices for their children. Relentless conformity will not help you raise the children you want to raise. Stepping out, trying new things, and being uncomfortable a little or a lot from what you consider to be the norm can be a transformational experience for your family. Charlie and I have always been disruptors of the norm. When we moved from Austin, Texas, to Puerto Rico, many thought we were crazy. The language, the culture, and the environment were all different; but then again, that's why we did it. We wanted our children to learn another language and experience a different way of life. We weren't attempting to break the norms we knew because we disagreed with them; we wanted to give our children a larger perspective of what other people consider their norms. We wanted to teach our children that other people have different norms, values, and cultures. We believe learning a wide variety of norms and cultures gives our kids a unique journey that broadens their perspective.

Living in Puerto Rico had many challenges. For instance, when Hurricane Maria hit the island, we were left without electricity for three months. Most families would have bolted back to Texas, but Charlie and I knew it was an important learning experience for all of us. We knew we could survive, thrive, and help others. Hard times have a way of forging wonderful family bonds and creating lasting memories.

In fact, our family memories of Hurricane Maria include feeding thousands of people with Jose Andrés at World Central Kitchen, opening a food distribution center with Calvary Chapel, delivering medical supplies to help open three hospitals, clearing roads, and sharing our home with a family whose house was unlivable. We played lots of board games and cooked lots of food on our gas grill and a crock pot connected to solar panels. To this day, my husband often says, "No great story starts with, 'When I was staying at a five-star resort . . . .'"

While Charlie and I do our best to march to the beat of a different drummer, I've noticed that many parents stick with a routine dictated to them by the various organizations around them or succumb to loud and opinionated family members. Maintaining your own viewpoint can be a challenge when there are so many institutions and individuals bombarding us with their views on a regular basis. The racket of advice, opinions, and demands can be deafening.

> **We need to take control of our lives and forge a path that will work best for our children.**

As parents, we need to take control of our lives and forge a path that will work best for our children, even if it diverges from the advice of others around us. After Charlie and I got married, I learned that his family tradition involved spending their holidays traveling from one home to another visiting all their relatives. It was their way to stay close even though they lived in different places. I found it exhausting being pulled in so many directions and longed for a holiday plan that allowed me to relax.

That experience led Charlie and me to create a holiday rotation system that is still in place today. As you might expect from two business owners, it required a spreadsheet, but it worked; every member of the family fell into line, and everyone got to enjoy the holidays.

Why not boot mediocrity from our lives and refuse to live an average existence? Don't get me wrong, routines have their place. Without them, we'd have complete chaos. However, I find that it can be freeing to stretch beyond the status quo. Relish in the freedom to create your own routines based on the needs of your family. Two of my friends provide good examples of each choosing a different path for their family.

My friend Becky chooses to lead her family to live an unstructured life. Her outlook on raising kids is relaxed and laid-back. She has the financial resources to send her children to any prestigious private school she likes but feels that their local public school is less stressful for her kids. "There's more to learning than reading, writing, and arithmetic," she likes to say. Becky never puts limits and restrictions on her children. They can watch as much TV as they want and play video games to their heart's content because she feels children gain from these activities. As a result, they don't take advantage of the freedom and don't spend every waking moment absorbed with electronics. Knowing that electronics can be highly addictive, Becky focuses on encouraging her children to take an active and creative role with these advanced tools. Here are some phrases Becky would say to her kids to move them from passive viewers to active participants:

- I believe you can create a video as good as this one.

- What kind of video would you like to make?

- Why do you think that video is so popular? How could you make it even better?

- Do you want to make videos too? When are you going to start?

- Tell me more about your ideas for videos. Do you need any help making videos?

Her words were encouraging yet not forceful. She planted seeds and waited for them to grow. Yes, it started with her kids simply sitting there for hours on end being passively entertained. Yet with encouragement, Becky knew her kids just needed to find their own path. Becky's encouragement was in the form of questions and reassurance that they could create content too. Her confidence in them rubbed off, and the more time they watched others post and become influencers they thought they could do the same. Jacks, Becky's son, saw a video looking for people to post cat videos and get paid for the views generated. Jacks enlisted his sister, Tina, to help. They borrowed the neighbor's cat and made videos. No longer were they being passively entertained; they acted and were the entertainers. Each time one of their videos got a view on the site, they made money. When the first check arrived at the house, their parents were proud.

In addition, my friend doesn't prioritize grades or conform to the school's schedule. If she wants to pull her kids from their classes to take them on a trip, to make a video, or for a fun day with mom, she will, because she feels that these all provide valuable experiences you can't get in a classroom. Her vision for her children doesn't include college—but it doesn't exclude it either. She'll tell you that self-made entrepreneurs either didn't attend college or, if they did, it wasn't the school that made the difference.

Becky is fond of saying that these people became a success *in spite of* attending school. In researching successful entrepreneurs, I discovered that one bright entrepreneur got a C from his Yale University professor regarding his company concept, which later became FedEx. Look where he is now! There are many examples of creative people who think outside the box and become a success. In fact, Becky's son is still in high school and has earned over one hundred thousand dollars providing content for websites and social media.

My friend Terry lives by a very different philosophy. She taught her children to read in prekindergarten. They have participated in the gifted summer programs to boost their abilities in various subjects. These kids put their time in on their homework, and, as a result, they win spelling bees, math Olympics, science bowls, and have nearly perfect grades. Terry's children plan to apply to the top universities. Their resumes of achievement are perfectly balanced with experience in leadership programs, community outreach, as well as scholastic achievements. Terry's oldest was a high school presidential scholar and now attends Harvard.

This family is always active and runs on a tight schedule, which works well for them. Terry chauffeurs the children from one activity to another—all day, every day. This wouldn't work for all families, but it does for them. Of course, she makes sure to schedule playdates to give her kids an opportunity to socialize as well.

Becky and Terry have different approaches to parenting, but they are both dedicated to making sure their children are happy and thriving. So who is right? Both moms structured their lives according to their beliefs about what is best for their family and how they want to raise their children. They are both remarkably effective parents, and their children are doing well, which makes both successful.

The key is to know your foundational principles and use those to guide your decisions regardless of what the rest of society is doing. If you do not already know your foundational principles or if you have not shared yours with your significant other, then do so now. If you need help creating your foundational principles, see the appendix for a list of questions that will get you started. This is an incomplete list of questions. As you answer the questions, other thoughts and principles will become top of mind. Write down what is important to you and what you think should be the foundation of your family. Do this alone first, and then share your answers with your significant other. Together create a shared list of answers. The shared answers are your family's foundational principles.

Now that you have your foundational principles, you must seek out the environment and structure that works well for your children and you. This is done through trial and error. When we moved to Puerto Rico, we had no idea if it was going to work, and frankly, at first, it was a struggle. The first school the kids went to was wrong. We realized the aesthetics, being like our old school, blinded our judgment. Our kids were not happy and told us. We listened to them and changed schools in the middle of the year. They knew when we moved to Puerto Rico that their voice mattered. We voted as a family to move to Puerto Rico, and they knew each year we were going to vote to stay or move. Our error gave our kids a firsthand experience of their parents listening to them over what our friends were doing.

There are an infinite number of ways to structure your family's life to achieve your vision. After Charlie and I determined our foundational principles and parenting goals, I made many personal changes. I shifted my routine to working from home, delegating more, cutting back on work and lunches with friends, stepping down from boards, and volunteering less. Instead, I focused on quality time with my husband and children, which also meant that if my children were not invited to an event, I rarely would attend.

In the process, I realized that teaching my boys independence was a priority for me, so I stopped planning their events and playdates. Under my supervision, they oversaw their own socializing. We didn't let school schedules dictate our lives; we wanted travel to be a priority, and we agreed that visiting new places was important to a well-rounded education.

Teaching my boys independence meant that I strove to allow my children to take the lead in the decision-making process for things that involve them. Sometimes the choices they made turned out to be wrong, but that's okay, because not only is failure a great way to learn, but also you can always change your mind as the parent. In fact, explaining to your children why you changed your mind is a learning opportunity as well.

As I said before, when we moved to Puerto Rico, we allowed the boys to choose their school. There were two options: one school they instantly rejected because they felt it looked like a prison from the outside. They wouldn't even go inside.

The boys chose the school with the prettier campus but soon learned not to judge a book by its cover. It didn't take long for Conrad and Carson to come to us about the problems they faced at the school they'd chosen. The content being taught was controversial, there were strong ethnic biases, and there was little effort to teach Spanish to the non-native, non-Spanish-speaking kids. After two months we all saw the error in our choice, so midyear Charlie and I moved the kids. It was instantly apparent that the new school was a much better fit. To this day they call it "the best jail we ever attended."

BE YOUR CHILD'S ADVOCATE

I've had many conversations with my sons about taking a stand for themselves, especially if they ever feel uncomfortable about doing what an authority figure demands. Just because someone in authority asks you to do something does not mean you do it blindly. One should always speak up and openly discuss the problem. We are in control of our actions by the choices we make. Doing something that is wrong, regardless of who tells you to do it, is never right.

I have a great respect and admiration for educators. The majority work tirelessly and do a great job. Most want to partner with you to do their best for your children. However, just because a teacher or administrator has a master's degree doesn't mean they know more than you about your child. The teachers and administrators at your child's school are not the authority in your family. You know your child better than anyone else; trust your gut and intuition.

There may be times when you have trouble figuring out the problem your child is having. You know something is wrong because they are acting out, but you have no idea what it is. The first step is to listen to your child. The problem might not be confined to them; it might involve others around them.

My friend Olivia's son, Ralph, was behind in reading and math and acting out in class. At home, he was calm and obedient, but Ralph was misbehaving at school. The principal and teacher called Olivia in and said that he had attention-deficit/hyperactivity disorder (ADHD). Both advised her to give him medication to handle the condition. The principal had degrees in education and psychology and was quite adamant about this opinion. The teacher was also certain that medication was the answer. The school threatened her with further action if she didn't comply.

The conversation was one-sided, and all Olivia felt she could do was listen. She was cowed by their authority. These "experts" never asked about Ralph's behavior outside of school; they decided on a unilateral solution. Fortunately, when Olivia went to the pediatrician, he observed that the boy was fine in the doctor's office. The doctor explained that many other issues could be causing Ralph's learning and behavioral problems: dyslexia, dyscalculia, and dysgraphia (which are, respectively, difficulty with reading, math, and writing), to name a few. None of these would be helped by taking medication for ADHD, but these issues would be revealed through a series of simple tests.

On her way home from the doctor's office, Olivia called me. I was grateful that she was confiding in me and seeking my help. She told me how the school was pushing her to put her son on the prescription medication but that the doctor had pointed out the drugs' many bad side effects. She was worried about what would happen if she didn't follow the principal's recommendation. Bullies come in many sizes and shapes.

I listened to her and suggested that she get her son tested for the various learning disabilities the pediatrician mentioned. She agreed but was worried about the principal's potential response. I suggested that she ask the pediatrician to put his recommendations for testing in the form of a prescription.

I took a deep breath and said, "Olivia, you are your son's advocate. He needs you to stand up for him. Talk to him and find out what's going on."

Olivia and Ralph had an open relationship, yet Ralph never told Olivia how he felt in school until Olivia asked. Ralph confided in her that he would get upset when the teacher insisted that he read out loud in front of the class. He told his mother that he felt humiliated and stupid but that the teacher made him continue. On top of that, if any kind of misbehavior was going on and Ralph was nearby, the teacher would single him out from the group and punish him. The teacher seemingly had decided Ralph was a bad apple.

When Olivia told her son about the tests, she explained that not everyone learned in the same way and that the tests would help them both discover how Ralph learns best. Ralph was greatly relieved and for the first time shared with his mother that he enjoyed learning. This was the moment Olivia knew that testing—not medication—was the correct next action. She took on the role of advocate and called a meeting with the teacher, principal, and school counselor. Despite everything she said to them, the "experts" pressured her into medicating her son. This time she stood firm.

In the end, the school relented, the teacher sat down with Olivia and Ralph, and they had a real conversation. The teacher got to know Ralph for the first time and could see how perhaps the tests might reveal the underlying learning problem. As it turned out, Ralph had dyslexia. If my friend had capitulated to the school's recommendations, her son would have taken drugs that would have masked the real problem and likely created others. I commended her for maintaining her integrity and standing her ground.

Now, I want to reiterate that I have a lot of respect for educators, as does my husband, Charlie. The fact is that whenever we go to a parent-teacher conference, Charlie makes a point of saying to the instructor, "The teacher is always right, and I'll always have your back." When I first heard him say that, I was conflicted. How could we be our sons' advocates if we had the teacher's back?

Charlie explained that his grandmother had been a teacher, and he grew up in a household trusting teachers. If he ever got into trouble at school, the punishment was double at home. When he became a father, Charlie refused to be the kind of parent who wore blinders and could never see the fault in his children. I agreed with him but needed to make sure that Charlie's viewpoint didn't mean that he didn't want to hear our boys' side of the story. When I asked him, he gave me a puzzled look.

"Of course I want to hear their side of the story," he said. Charlie's support of our sons' teachers led our children's educators to welcome our input and appreciate us.

When a teacher knows you have their back, they are more willing to work with you when a problem arises. I remember a time when Conrad's kindergarten teacher created an exercise that, on the surface, sounded great: Write a nice letter to another classmate. Unfortunately, the teacher selected a boy who, unbeknownst to her, had been bullying Conrad.

Conrad refused to write a letter to the boy. The teacher had him stay in the classroom, missing recess, until he wrote the letter. He wrote a letter, but not what the teacher expected. When the teacher read my son's letter, she called me and asked me to come to school immediately. When I arrived, I found my son in tears. Conrad, the teacher, and I sat down and spoke together. The teacher explained the situation and showed me the letter. It read:

"Dear Dwain, I do not have anything nice to say about you because you're a bully. I do not like you and do not want to sit at the same table with you. Merry Christmas, Conrad."

The teacher was remorseful for what had happened and admitted that she'd been having trouble with Dwain. She went on to say she thought Conrad was getting along with Dwain even though Conrad had requested to move tables. In the end, she apologized for not having listened more attentively. Conrad learned that he needed to speak up more. He explained in detail what was going on and asked again to be moved. She nodded and thanked him for telling her. It was a great learning experience for all three of us.

This was a great teacher who felt confident enough to call me in to discuss the situation. She didn't hide her misunderstanding of the situation; rather, she sought to better understand Conrad. After all, she knew that Charlie and I respected her, and she trusted us for that reason. She was willing to have an open dialogue because she viewed us as a team.

Ultimately, you need to be your child's advocate, and the best advocate is an informed advocate. By understanding all aspects of the situation, your job as an advocate has a greater potential to be collaborative. Especially when your children are young, they need to know that you'll always love them and be in their corner. However, you also need to work with and respect their educators. If educators feel you are with them, not against them, they will often work more closely with you to help your children. And of course, you will get this wrong at times. Do what is needed to make it right and admit your errors.

Chapter Summary: The Parent's Duty

- Make a conscious decision about what to pass on to your children.

- Be flexible in your parenting style.

- Don't be afraid to go against the flow to make the right choices for your family.

- Not everything the experts say will be good for your family.

- Be your child's advocate while striving always to give unconditional love and support.

Exercises

Answer all the following questions individually, and then share your responses with your partner and kids when appropriate.

1. Write your list of family goals, values, and beliefs, including religious beliefs, your family moral code of conduct, your value of education, your views on discipline, and anything you value and

believe is important to pass on to your children. Discuss what you wrote, and create a combined list of values that you want to pass on to your children. Feel free to be as creative as you want in designing these, and perhaps print them up for later reference.

2. What is your predominant parenting style? How could you be more flexible?

3. Is there a parenting decision or family change in the status quo that you have made that you are not implementing (example: kids' bed times, who makes lunches, after-school routines, and so on)? Is there anything in your family that you want to change and have not taken the actions needed to make the changes? Why have you not acted? What makes it hard to change? Why would your family benefit from the change?

4. What are the areas in your child's life where you think they may be having trouble or conflict? Write down all the areas you feel your child could use your help as an advocate.

CHAPTER 2

THE PARENT'S GROWTH

RECOGNIZE YOUR IMPORTANCE

While parenting is a life-changing and beautiful calling, it doesn't define your entire existence. It shouldn't define *you*. Whatever your situation, remember that your children are just one big part of your life, so don't allow parenting to be all of you. Work and family are a delicate balance. Creating a life for yourself that doesn't always revolve around your children is important. One way to do this is to take an active role in pursuing your interests. One place to start is by reading books about topics that interest you. You can be a full-time parent, work, and still have time to indulge in hobbies and recreational activities.

Before you were a parent, you honed talents and abilities that contributed to your sense of self. It's important to continue to share those abilities with the world. Being a parent is rewarding, but it can't be the end-all of your existence. Go out and get involved, make a difference, and do what makes you happy. Your kids will be inspired by watching you, and a world of knowledge will open to them.

One friend of mine, Phillis, was a stay-at-home mom. She was passionate about the electoral process and enjoyed helping the politicians she supported succeed. She often researched relevant topics and made sure to keep up with current events. As Phillis gained experience, she made a point of getting to know community leaders and built a reputation as a person who gets the job done. This reputation led to her being asked to put on a fundraiser for a candidate running for Congress.

As it happened, the vice president of the United States decided to visit Phillis's small town to support this man. As the time of the visit approached, the White House called many times with logistics, protocols, and guidelines. In the end, the fundraiser was a roaring success and the presidential advisors were impressed that Phillis raised more money than anyone had ever raised at this type of event, despite not being a professional fundraiser. Phillis was a mom following her passions. Never underestimate a stay-at-home parent! The ones I know can do anything they decide to do.

If you pursue your interests, your children might get inspired to pursue theirs. Phillis was always talking about politics at her dinner table. As a result, when one of her daughters was disgruntled with what was going on in the world, she sought an internship at her state capital. The daughter wanted her voice heard and felt confident that she could take steps to influence the political process. She was inspired by her mother's success.

Your goals don't have to be huge. Do what pleases you and what makes sense. When my boys were babies, I continued to work with my husband, joined an exercise group, took various real estate and art classes, enrolled in a Spanish course, and attended interesting lectures. I didn't allow my new role as *Mom* to stop me from pursuing my passions. You never know where these paths will take you.

These solo activities helped me be a better parent. Because I learned Spanish, my kids and I traveled to Guatemala for a Spanish immersion class one summer. Conrad and Carson got involved in learning Spanish because of my interest. There was no need to force them to learn the language because it became a family bonding experience wrapped up in a trip to an exotic country. Two years later we would relocate from Texas to Puerto Rico, no doubt encouraged by our experiences learning Spanish. Today my sons are well versed in Spanish and are grateful for the early exposure to the language.

My children see their parents as people who live life, follow their interests, and seek new passions, and they are inspired to do the same. Conrad recently suggested that we all take eFoil lessons together. An eFoil is a motorized surfboard invented in Puerto Rico. We all had a blast, and now it is a family activity. If you trudge through life, doing your duty and forgetting to have fun now and then, your kids won't relish growing into adulthood. Who would? Showing that adulthood is something to look forward to and that personal growth is important can start with providing examples of rewarding communication with your parenting partner.

COMMUNICATE WELL WITH YOUR PARTNER

Throughout this book, I use words like *spouse* or *partner* to describe anyone in your life who helps you raise your children. Please feel free to substitute any word that best describes this person for you. I completely respect that family structures can be different from mine. A person's lifestyle, environment, and religion will all influence the words used to describe that special person. If you parent solo, then adapt this advice to your situation and those who help you meet your parenting goals.

Excellent communication between parenting partners is crucial. This isn't a new idea, but it's vital. A spouse will eventually communicate with you in a way that will infuriate you. Today there are countless social media videos, internet articles, and books all suggesting communication tools. Seek out what works for you. I discovered several tools that help our communication be more effective. One tool is to have the correct frame of reference to understand my partner. That means reinterpreting his words so they make sense to me in a way that I can receive his message.

In my heart, I know the words that come out of my husband's mouth aren't meant to belittle me. Still, there are instances when he says something that hurts my feelings and I wonder if he's heard what I've said. In those moments I take a calming breath and frame his words in my mind, remembering that his intention is to help me be a better person. It takes some of the edge off his harshness, and I am able to then take in his meaning instead of fighting back. Once I do that, I'll repeat back to him my positive interpretation of his words. Sometimes this means I need to twist his words to convey the message I believe he intended. This technique is often called "mirroring" in psychology, which explores interpersonal relationships.

I know this may sound a little complex; I suggest you read the short article about various forms of mirroring "What Is 'Mirroring' in a Relationship and How Does It Help?"[1] and allow me to give you an example of a conversation Charlie and I had:

> Me: Carson said I look fat.
>
> Charlie: You do look fat.
>
> Me: Are you saying I'm fat?
>
> Charlie: No, the dress makes you look fat.

---

1   Noah Williams, "What Is 'Mirroring' in a Relationship and How Does It Help?" *Marriage.com*, March 24, 2023, https://www.marriage.com/advice/relationship/mirroring-in-relationships/.

(Now, in my mind, I think he's just called me *fat* for a second time, so it's time to adjust his words and reframe my response to match. To do that, I will need to leave out the bits I don't like.)

> Me: So you're saying I am beautiful but the dress is ugly?

> Charlie (chuckling): Yes, that is what I meant to say.

My husband has learned to joke with me about this. He'll often exaggerate whatever I reframe. For instance, he might say something like, "You are the most amazing and beautiful woman in the world, and that dress is not!" It works. We both laugh, and no one has hurt feelings.

A second tool I recommend to people is to preframe important communications with their spouse. I learned about the concept of *reframing* at a Tony Robbins seminar.[2] Reframing is a neurolinguistic programming (NLP) technique that Tony Robbins teaches and uses in his interventions.[3] Chris Voss, a former FBI hostage negotiator, speaks of strategies that involve changing the context or the way a situation is perceived, which is at the heart of reframing.[4] I have modified the term to be *preframing*—preparing the audience to receive information in a certain way—and I use the technique before I talk to my spouse. Preframing is a psychological way to influence your desired outcome. I have learned not to expect Charlie to guess what I want correctly—he'll get it wrong half the time (or more). If you need

2   Team Tony, "What Is Unleash the Power Within?," *Tony Robbins*, accessed February 7, 2024, https://www.tonyrobbins.com/stories/unleash-the-power/what-is-upw/.

3   Tony Robbins, "Why Meaning Is Everything," *Tony Robbins*, accessed February 8, 2024, https://www.tonyrobbins.com/why-meaning-is-everything/.

4   Samuel Thomas Davies, "Never Split the Difference by Chris Voss," *Sam T. Davies*, accessed February 12, 2024, https://www.samuelthomasdavies.com/book -summaries/business/never-split-the-difference/.

your spouse to just listen and provide comfort or support, let them know that you're not looking for solutions to the problems you will be presenting. If you are looking for advice, be clear about that before you start.

One preframing question I use is, "Honey, do you have time for me to tell you something? I want to tell you about my day." I always make sure to get an answer to that question and accept it either way. Don't simply launch into a rant without knowing if your spouse has the headspace to hear you. If the answer is no, don't go into a tailspin; just wait until he has time or seek out a friend and vent to them. If the answer is yes, then I explain *how* I need him to listen first. Sometimes I need advice, while other times I simply need to get something off my chest or I'm looking for comfort. Charlie appreciates that. He will tell you that I'm a bit complicated, so he needs a road map to understand the best way to help me.

Before I figured this out, I would simply tell Charlie about my day and all the crazy little things that happened with the kids. I'd usually start with the most outrageous events, exaggerating them with all the poetic license I could muster to give them that special dramatic flair. Looking back, it's clear now that my embellishments were just an attempt to get his attention, which backfired miserably. He'd wait for me to take a long breath, and then he'd shake his head and give me a solution. From his perspective, he was saving time and helping me.

Naturally, I would find myself disgruntled and sometimes livid when I hadn't even finished my story. Here I was trying to connect with my husband, and he was interrupting me to tell me where I had gone wrong. The verbal sparks would fly.

Through trial and error, I learned to select my words more carefully, matching them to the ones my husband could relate to. I left the exaggerated tales for my mommy playdates (they were a more appreciative audience). This adjustment made a huge difference with my husband and opened the door to more effective communication. I also learned to refrain from getting upset when he did offer unsolicited advice, remembering his words were spoken with good intentions. When this happens now, I am playful with him or I simply thank him.

Another valuable tool I use frequently is called the Rogerian approach by Carl Rogers. I learned about this approach when my sister was in a treatment program and she asked the family to participate in group therapy. During these sessions, I would say something, and my sister would repeat what she heard. Similarly to the mirroring technique, the listener repeats what is said. Yet the Rogerian approach is different because the listener does not impose their own ideas or judgments. The Rogerian approach facilitates personal growth and self-awareness, helping individuals find their own solutions to their problems. My sister and I would repeat the words until we discovered a mutual understanding. I found it to be useful and have continued it with Charlie. Early in our marriage, I asked him to repeat his understanding of what I said, to be sure he had processed the data correctly. The practice was helpful, and I always reciprocated if asked.

We continue this approach today, and we do this with our kids as well. I am more direct with the kids, and I ask them to repeat precisely what I said. Boy is this revealing, and the self-discovery for the kids is priceless! I can tell you that sometimes I have to suppress a laugh when what they repeat back is nothing like what I said, resembling more what they wanted to hear. One time I asked Conrad to pick up his toys in the toy room before he went outside to play. He repeated, "Play in the toy room before I go outside." My husband and I could not hold back laughing because that was what he wanted to hear. At that point, I simply repeat my message and ask my son to tell it back to me again.

Repeating concepts goes a long way toward curtailing confusion, and it builds a strong base of shared understanding. With that foundation, we have a stable ground on which to build our conversations and can better understand our disagreements, which generates mutual respect.

Having a strong, healthy relationship with my husband is important to me. I learned early on not to focus all my attention on the young members of my family. When you do, you might wind up with great kids, but you'll sacrifice your relationship with your partner (or those who are partnering with you to parent). Balancing the various people in your life will go a long way toward maintaining your sanity and happiness, but it starts with working on yourself and then your relationship with your parenting partners.

PRIORITIZE THE PARENTS' RELATIONSHIP

Good communication is vital in a relationship and parenting, yet you need to do more than simply communicate. You must make your partner a priority. Early in our marriage, Charlie would never buy me flowers. Looking back, I think this was because I'd always comment on how expensive they were. Years passed, and one day he brought home a beautiful bouquet for me. I loved the flowers and told him honestly how happy they made me feel. Every time I walked past the arrangement, taking in the fragrance, I couldn't help but smile and comment on it. I could tell Charlie was pleasantly surprised by my reaction. Today, I never ask him to buy me flowers, but anytime he does, I respond like I did that first time. I love them, and since he loves me and the positive affirmations, he brings them home frequently.

After I read the book *The 5 Love Languages* by Gary Chapman, I learned that love languages are words of affirmation, quality time, gifts, acts of service, and physical touch. I recommend that everyone read more about these love languages. My husband's love language is words of affirmation. I make a point of praising all the actions he does that I enjoy. Showing praise and gratitude is effective with friends and family as well. It's good to praise what is right and to judiciously avoid drawing attention to what is wrong. When I do this with Charlie, it has the added benefit of reminding me of all the things my husband does for me and the family. This helps me not to take my husband for granted. Of course, the praise must be sincere or the person you are praising will recognize insincerity and stop listening. The converse of this idea is that there are also times when you must address behaviors that are not worthy of praise.

I do my best to show Charlie how much I appreciate him and to do so in a variety of ways. Often, I send him text messages telling him that I love him, which one can never hear too often. My partner also loves surprises and gifts, which go a long way to helping him feel loved and safe. But also, be aware of your partner's temperament for surprises as well as their other responsibilities. For example, if a spouse surprises his partner at work with a picnic basket, it won't go over well if that person has an important lunch meeting with the boss or if your partner does not like outdoor picnics. A little preparation can avoid a lot of embarrassment.

When purchasing a surprise present, I also do a little research. I notice what my husband is drawn to at his favorite stores and note what he does and doesn't like as gifts. Charlie never wants to receive clothes, but he loves toys and gadgets. I keep his wish list close at hand and ask him at times to update it.

For me, touch is a powerful force, whether it's an intimate interaction or a simple squeeze on the shoulder. I want Charlie's touch and usually want him to initiate it. It's been my experience that the more he touches me, the closer I feel to him. When prioritizing touch with your partner, keep in mind that children can try to interfere. I remember how my youngest son always tried to squeeze his body between us when I went to embrace my husband. Sometimes he'd hug my leg to get in on the action. I think Carson was thinking, "Me too!" The way I handled that was to explain to him that it was only fair that Daddy got a hug too.

I have found that when the parents are happy, the household is harmonious; and when the household is harmonious, the children get their needs fulfilled. It's a win-win scenario. In my opinion, the most important piece your children need from their parents is a loving relationship between partners. This does not mean that you will never experience conflict, disagree, or get angry at each other. It does *not* mean that everything will be perfect all the time. It *does* mean you will show a love that wants the best for the other person regardless of what is in it for oneself. Simply because you love one another does not mean you have a strong relationship. Love does not keep a relationship together all by itself. There is much more to it; you must make the other person a priority.

So that you don't take your relationship for granted, plan ways to balance the time you devote to your children and the time you spend on the adult relationships in your life. There are many ways to create and maintain a strong relationship with your spouse. If possible, do not go to bed angry with each other. Take the time you need to calm down and then the time to reconnect. Another way to develop this relationship is to learn about what grows a relationship; this can happen through research such as advice, books, and education. Learn about what excites your partner and what makes them happy. Be a student of life and a student of your partner, growing together.

A relationship needs time, attention, and work, like anything that's important. Some people expect their relationship to be easy and enjoyable all the time, perhaps because that's how it was when they first met. A marriage can be fun, but it also requires work. One's interpersonal bonds go a long way in determining one's happiness in life.

Another point to consider is that your relationship with your spouse is your children's first model of a relationship. It will set the tone for them in life. How do you talk about your partner and the relationship you have? Do you say positive things about the other person to your kids and others? You get to decide what kind of relationship you have with your spouse. Whatever you decide, your kids are learning from you.

A HEALTHY DIVORCED RELATIONSHIP

Even relationships that begin well can end poorly, but this doesn't have to destroy your children's chances to learn lasting relationship skills from loving parents. I suggest that if you find yourself in a harmful relationship, get help. If we don't work through our differences and troubles, we are bound to repeat the same mistakes. Problems in your romantic relationship most likely show up in other relationships, so be courageous to take control of your life. Be the partner who gives without the expectation to receive. Both partners need to be committed to a healthy relationship. That can start with just one partner encouraging the desires of the other. I know this is not easy, but the easy road is rarely the most rewarding road. Being your partner's biggest supporter often sets the tone and example for the other partner, who will want to reciprocate.

I really like how Brené Brown describes marriage as never being 50/50 in an interview with Tim Ferriss.[5] In her marriage, they check in with each other. As a couple, they communicate their physical and emotional ability to give to the family. One might only be able to give 20 percent, so the other takes the 80 percent. Charlie and I have unconsciously just picked up when the other needed support, yet at times one of us felt like the other was not doing their part. In a divorced coparenting situation this responsibility can be magnified. At times, one parent is doing 100 percent. Hopefully with communication and the understanding that putting in your part will never mean 50 percent, each parent can embody an even greater willingness to give more when they have the ability.

Having said that, if the relationship is emotionally or physically harmful, please seek outside support, even if that means an end to the current form of the relationship. Never stay in an abusive relationship

---

5   Tim Ferriss, "Marriage Is Never 50/50," TikTok post, June 5, 2023. https://www
     .tiktok.com/@timferriss/video/7241204908203003142.

"for the sake of the children." Your kids will not be better off if you wait until they go off to college to get a divorce. You must choose to work on your relationship in a safe way. If you wait until the kids are in college, you've given them plenty of time to learn that abuse or pretending everything is fine is acceptable in a relationship.

I have a good friend, Vicky, whose parents decided to ignore their relationship and their problems. In front of the kids, the parents made everything appear perfect. Vicky couldn't remember any times when her parents fought or argued. Then, when she was a freshman in college, they separated. Blindsided and devastated, Vicky never knew her parents were having problems in their relationship. It took Vicky years to process her parents' divorce. When she got married years later, Vicky confided in me that she wondered if any marriage could work. The experience with her parents' marriage left deep wounds.

If Vicky's parents had sat her down at an appropriate age and told her truthfully about what was happening, they could have softened the blow. Had her parents been honest about their problems and gotten help, Vicky's wounds might have been less severe. Shielding her from the truth was not a healthy solution. Kids often benefit from seeing the mess that we parents create; they can learn from difficult adult situations. When we pause and ask if our kids are developmentally ready to handle discussions about conflict, we might find they can understand more than we give them credit for.

If you are divorced, the relationship with the other biological parent still matters. You can be divorced and still set a great example of a positive relationship. Show your children that you have a respectful and caring relationship with each other. How you speak about your ex-spouse and how the two of you handle the responsibilities of caring for your children sets the stage for your children's future relationships.

Your divorce does not destine your children to failure in marriage. Divorce or another family difficulty has the potential to strengthen or destroy. Just as fire is used to forge metal, so can a divorce create greater awareness and insights from which your children may learn. I am by no means advocating divorce, but I am advocating discussions with your children about why you and their other parent are not together. Your children need you to be honest and introspective about what really happened to your relationship. You have an opportunity to teach and to hopefully spare your children the same heartache you went through. Showing your children what a good relationship looks like is as important as feeding them. All your interactions with your parenting partners help determine your children's views about relationships.

ACKNOWLEDGE YOUR FLAWS

We all have fears and insecurities; it's part of being human. We teach our children by our actions—by what we do and what we don't do. We give them clues by the things we praise, condone, or dislike. Our kids are learning our idiosyncrasies—good and bad; however, they do not always understand which characteristics are good or bad. Yes, *good* and *bad* can have subjective elements, so let's define *bad* as those traits you don't wish your children to emulate.

> We teach our children by our actions—by what we do and what we don't do.

For instance, my grandmother yelled to be heard in her house, so my mom yelled in our house. Now I, too, yell sometimes. I don't even recognize it as yelling; I just see it as being passionate about what I am saying. It's important to me that my sons know this isn't something I admire about myself, and it isn't a trait I want them to carry forward. Let's not teach our children the bad habits that we're still working on unlearning. It may be that your parents made some of the mistakes that their parents made before them. And it's a chain that can be broken.

I was sharing a cup of coffee with my friend Jessica one day and she was lamenting over the way one of her teen daughters had been treated. Shelly was invited to a birthday party while her twin sister, Jill, was excluded.

"It was awkward because my girls are very close, and I thought they had all the same friends," Jessica said. "I'm not big on excluding people, kids especially. But inviting one sister and not the other was horrible." Jessica went on to explain that she finally decided to ask the mother of the birthday girl if Jill could also be invited. The mother's response was a definitive and curt no.

Jessica described her dilemma to me. "Now what? I'm not sure what to do. What do you think? Do I let Shelly go, or do I keep her behind?"

I didn't want to become Jessica's decision-maker; rather, I wanted to help her find her own solutions. To that end, I chose to ask more questions instead of telling her what I thought she should do. I've learned that if I tell others what to do, my solution might not be the best for them. So I try to avoid doing that whenever possible. I explained this to my friend Jessica and added, "All the answers you need are within yourself. I am just going to ask you some questions."

She nodded, so I continued, "Why did you ask the mother if Jill could go?"

"I was put in a difficult situation. I couldn't stand the thought that one of my kids might be excluded and hurt. And I also didn't like the idea that Shelly could be part of excluding her twin sister."

"Would you like it if another mother pushed you to invite someone to your daughter's party?"

Jessica hesitated at this point, blushed, and said, "No."

I then leaned in and asked, "Why do you feel like you needed to have Jill invited?"

Jessica admitted that she had been excluded a lot as a child and was sensitive about the subject. She felt bad for Jill because she was not invited. It was then that she realized that she was trying to shield her daughter from the possible pain of the situation.

I asked, "What does Shelly want to do?"

"She wants to go to the party."

"What does Jill think?"

"I never asked."

My friend Jessica has a heart of gold and the best intentions for her girls. She assumed Jill would want to go to the party, but by not asking Jill's opinion, Jessica was projecting her feelings onto her daughter. After our interchange, Jessica had a meaningful conversation with both girls and started to see that this was *her* issue, not her daughters'. Shelly and Jill had already talked and were fine with it. Jill admitted that she was surprised at first that her sister had received an invitation and she had not. But then they both realized that Shelly had received an invitation only because her boyfriend was friends with the birthday girl. Suddenly it all made sense to Jessica. Jill never cared about the situation until her mom started making it into an issue. It was eye-opening for Jessica to realize she'd almost taught her daughters her own insecurity.

If you want to avoid passing on your flaws, you must be willing to examine them. They can be hard to spot, so if you have difficulty spotting them on your own, start by noting habits your friends and family members have mentioned to you over the years. These might have been pointed out with little quips or subtle comments. Your priority should be to own up to the areas where you influence your kids in an undesirable way. Once you find these, you can begin to break the patterns.

If you're not aware of any issues, it's time to take action to learn what they are. Be an exterior observer of your own life, and work to view your family objectively. Seek out areas that might need improvement. If you can't do that, try filming your family over a period of a week or two. See if any identifiable issues jump out at you. How does your family communicate? Can you spot any patterns? The purpose of filming is to catch you in a natural setting. Before long you'll forget the camera's there, and you'll just be yourself. When you're done, erase the video. It's only a tool to help you observe objectively. This tool works great for learning many skills. Professional musicians, for example, film themselves when they practice and watch those videos to see how they might improve. Teachers film classes, and speakers film speeches. You get the point.

Another way to examine areas you need to grow is to ask those closest to you—and have a thick skin to listen for the loving answer. Find people whom you trust, like your spouse and parents, and ask them to be honest and polite. Once you have some areas to work on, hunt for resources that might address those concerns or seek out expert help from therapists.

Once you're aware of your areas for growth, don't be shy about sharing them with your children. Be open about your weaknesses. Let your kids know that you're not without flaws—they already know this anyway—and then explain that you could use their help to improve. Conrad and Carson politely let me know when I am yelling. They say something like, "Mom, you sure are expressing yourself passionately about that" or "Mom, I can hear you. Please talk more quietly." It's a safe bet that your children won't mimic flaws they have been tasked to help you discard.

Not only do we pass on our many traits and mannerisms, but the little sponges in our midst also absorb the words we use, including our intolerances and our viewpoints on current events and politics. I find I need to always be mindful of what comes out of my mouth around my children. Being aware of your flaws and willing to identify them will go a long way toward making sure your children don't copy them and will teach your children to be reflective about their own behavior. Your desire to help your children and become a better parent is a great motivator for change. Wouldn't that be a legacy to pass along?

WORK ON YOURSELF, AND YOUR KIDS WILL LEARN TOO

Parenting is hard because we cannot control our kids' actions, and yet we must control our own actions and reactions. You do this by observing unwanted or unacceptable behavior in your children and then stepping back and honestly assessing whether any of your parenting actions con-tributed to this.

My boys developed a pattern of screaming when they didn't get what they wanted from me. One day I asked my kids to set the dinner table and then, as often happened, I yelled at them when they were not coming to set the dinner table fast enough. Then it hit me: their screaming to get what they wanted was following the pattern they had learned from me, the same one I had learned from my own mother. So it shouldn't have been a surprise that when Carson wanted something and the answer was no, he would yell at me. I had taught him that was the way things were done.

Imagine with me for a moment. A family has waited forty min-utes for a table at their favorite restaurant on a Friday night. As the mom peruses the menu, her child begins to whine that he's hungry. He wants to eat *now*. The whining gets louder and louder until it becomes a full-blown screaming session. All the mom wants is for her child to be quiet so they can have an enjoyable dining experience. She searches her purse for anything she can put in his mouth, hoping that will calm him, only to find nothing edible. The people at neighboring tables stare at her with disgust, and she can tell they are as eager as she is for her child to stop screaming. She frantically flags down the server and begs her to bring crackers: anything to stop the screaming. Unfortunately, this loving mom has just responded to her child with panic and has taught the child that this behavior works. He got what he wanted, attention and food, by using poor behavior.

One day I observed a mother handle this situation quite differently. She asked her son to stop screaming and then went on to say that she would remove him from the restaurant if he continued, and this would cause further delays in him getting food. She warned him once and when he didn't stop, she took him outside. She sat on a bench with him until he stopped screaming. She remained calm and didn't allow her son to affect her mood. She didn't panic; she didn't give in. Instead, she did what was best for her child, teaching him proper behavior. It was a perfect natural consequence for his actions. This mom had decided to work on herself. I learned an important lesson that day.

To handle the screaming at a restaurant, consider a few things. For one, be sure not to push your child beyond the limits of their hunger. Kids, like adults, get angry when they're too hungry. Children often need to eat more frequently than adults, so plan ahead and bring a snack. Even without a wait time, it could still be fifteen to thirty minutes until food arrives at the table. While you're waiting for the table, pull out something for them to nibble on. If they are tired and starved, don't go out to eat that day. It won't end well.

Every kid is unique, with their own temperament and tolerances. Know your child's limits and do what is best for your family. I knew it wasn't realistic for my toddlers to sit unoccupied for long periods of time, so I would bring a portable DVD player with headphones. Today everyone has a phone with games. I also always had a ready-made pack of activities I could pull out to distract my sons. Coloring books or small toys work wonders. Knowing your values and expectations will help you decide what works in your situation.

When my boys were younger and began to scream, I'd ask them to use their inside voices and tell me what was going on. Anytime they misbehaved, I'd take them out of the situation, regardless of what was on the table. Yes, I sometimes came back to cold food. However, Conrad and Carson knew they weren't going to get what they wanted by screaming. As they got older, I would tell them what I wanted before we entered the restaurant. Then I'd hold them to that standard.

When my sons became teenagers, I would consult them about whether they wanted to go with us on an outing. Older kids respond to parents who listen to them. They are also more capable of coming up with a collaborative solution and are less likely to lash out at you. For instance, if there was an event I wanted them to go to that they didn't want to attend, we figured out a compromise, such as having them make an appearance before they left to do what they preferred to do. I can't control when, where, or why my child misbehaves, but I *can* control my reaction. I can also interrupt a child's pattern of behavior by removing him from the situation.

I realized that if I could change my actions and reactions to challenging situations, my kids would also change. While it might seem easy at times to give in to the bad behavior to make the unpleasantness end, it almost always creates greater long-term problems. I learned that calmly explaining to my sons how I was going to react to their behavior, and then calmly doing what I said I'd do, taught them in a way nothing else could.

LEARN FROM YOUR IMPERFECTIONS

Many parents spend an inordinate amount of time beating themselves up about blunders they have made. They second-guess decisions left and right, worrying they are ruining their children with their imperfections. Spending less time condemning ourselves and more time using these as learning opportunities can make for a healthy parenting style. It's much easier, and more realistic, to expect to learn from mistakes rather than try to avoid errors altogether. Knowing we won't be perfect parents, when I make a mistake, I own it—immediately or as soon as I can. My apology style is based on Becky Kennedy's TED Talk titled "The Single Most Important Parenting Strategy."[6] I say what happened, I take responsibility for my actions, and I say what I am going to do next time. My apology for yelling sometimes goes like this: "I am sorry for yelling at you. I know yelling is wrong. Next time I feel the urge to yell, I will walk away until I can control myself. I

---

6   Becky Kennedy, "The Single Most Important Parenting Strategy," TED Talk, September 14, 2023, https://www.youtube.com/watch?v=PHpPtdk9rco.

know my actions hurt you. If you want to talk about it, I am here to listen. I am not going to give you excuses for my actions or justify my behavior. I am here to acknowledge I hurt you and ask for your forgiveness." My apology, of course, doesn't get a child off the hook for their wrongdoing. We still address the problem, but I work hard to not fail to apologize for my actions that cause lapses in judgment. That's how my children can learn from my errors.

> You can lead your children in a certain direction, but in the end, they will make their own choices.

It's important to remember that you can lead your children in a certain direction, but in the end, they will make their own choices. They are their own people with their own personalities and their own goals. No matter how you teach them and what you say, they might choose to ignore your advice. Does that make you a bad parent? No. Keep trying, keep guiding, but don't beat yourself up. That's wasted energy.

Remember, no family is perfect, no matter how it may seem from the outside. Glancing at the Johnson family's Facebook page, receiving their picture-perfect portrait at Christmas each year, you might think other families have it all figured out. They don't, I promise you; they have their issues. We are all in the same leaky vessel working to overcome challenges. No one's childhood is perfect. But take heart in the knowledge that learning from perfection is difficult because it's so hard to emulate.

Our children will have trouble becoming prosperous individuals when everything is just handed to them. They need to learn from mistakes. I knew a wonderful couple who had three talented children. Both parents were highly educated, and each had a challenging vocation. To keep the household running smoothly after their kids were born, they hired a nanny, who became part of the family. The children loved her, as she did them. She took good care of the children, making sure they always had what they needed, even as they grew into adulthood. Unfortunately, these kids never learned the art of taking personal responsibility for themselves and never experienced the natural consequences of their mistakes.

The eldest became particularly dependent on others. He excelled in academics and became a leader in high school but still relied on others to help him with personal tasks. Only when he started college did he realize he didn't have the skill set that most young adults have. While blessed with a genius IQ and a wealthy family, he had never experienced the consequences of forgetting his homework or losing an important possession. This meant that he faced a steep learning curve and had quite a few embarrassing situations in college.

If you feel like your family isn't perfect and that you're messing up, congratulations! You're doing your job. Children learn from those experiences and grow. In the following chapters, I give you ideas about how to make those imperfections a proving ground for learning life lessons.

Chapter Summary: The Parent's Growth

- Don't allow parenting to define your entire existence.

- Your spouse's words matter, and how you receive the words matters more. *Preframe* and *repeat what was said* during important communications with your spouse.

- When the parents are happy, the household is harmonious. This helps the children get their needs fulfilled.

- Your relationship with the other biological parent matters. If you find yourself in a bad relationship, get help!

- If you want to avoid passing on your flaws, be willing to examine your areas of growth.

- You can't control your child's behavior, but you *can* control your reaction.

- Expect to learn from mistakes rather than avoid errors altogether.

- Apologize by naming what happened, taking responsibility, and saying what you are going to do next time.

Exercises

Answer all the following questions individually, and then share your responses with your partner and kids when appropriate.

1. What do you do for fun? What are your passions? Make a list of hobbies, activities, and passions that you would like to pursue in your free time. Pick one activity and commit to doing it.

2. Pick one topic that you want to discuss with your partner. Write down how you can preframe the conversation. What do you need to believe or understand about your partner to be able to have a collaborative and positive discussion? How can repeating what was said help your communication?

3. Write a list of personal traits or mannerisms you want to improve. Seek out others who are skilled in this area and/or who can hold you accountable.

4. Write down three typical difficult situations with your child. How can you take responsibility for your actions? How can you change your response? Do you need to apologize for anything?

5. Make a list of what you believe are mistakes or errors in raising your kids. Write down what you learned from each of your errors. Apologize for your mistakes or errors.

CHAPTER 3

THE FAMILY STRUCTURE

FAMILY GOVERNMENT

The forefathers of our country worked hard to provide us with a government that works. Because of the Constitution and the Bill of Rights, we know our rights, what to expect from our government, and what citizens can do about rules we don't like. Our government also has checks and balances so that no one portion of it has absolute power.

Your family is made up of a number of people, each of whom has his or her own viewpoint, needs, and goals in life. For your family to run smoothly, it needs a structure to govern itself. One possible structure—one that worked for us—is like the United States government where the family has a constitution, a bill of rights, and a set of laws. These can become the backbone of your family unit. The constitution will establish the fundamental values your family holds sacred. It gives structure by laying out the family's ethics and morals, as well as defining its judicial, legislative, and executive bodies.

The family bill of rights sets out explicitly what a person in the family can and cannot do. It defines the family beliefs in general terms of what is and what is not allowed. Last, there are the family laws. These are specific rules the family can apply daily to encourage good behavior and create order. Have fun creating your family's constitution. It should reflect *your* family and contains the morals, ethics, traditions, and heritage you value. These can be bundled up in a few phrases or in a long document—you get to decide. My suggestion is to have everyone that will be affected by your constitution (and held accountable to it) consent to the document before it is finalized. Your children may have some suggestions you wish to incorporate.

In simple terms, the constitution emphasizes that everyone gets a say. The parents are ultimately in charge, and when there is a dispute, a judge is chosen and everyone abides by his or her decision. You can also get into a more elaborate description that lays out the judicial, legislative, and executive branches if you wish. In our family, we kept the constitution simple. It was important that it worked for our family and was a living document capable of amendment when necessary.

In our house, the legislative branch includes all members of the family; its job is to create and update the bill of rights and the laws. There were times when everyone in our family had one vote and the right to bring forth ideas and changes, and there were times when Mom's and Dad's vote counted more, giving the parents the final say.

Our bill of rights spells out what is or is not acceptable and what is governed by our constitution. For example, one point in our bill of rights states that each child has the right to work, the right to eat, and the right to sleep. These rights are of equal value, but they can conflict with one another. During one era, my sons had a heavy homework load and felt that their bedtime got in the way of their right to do homework. They won that point, and an amendment allowing them to stay up as long as it took to complete their homework was inserted into the constitution.

In another instance, a sitter would not allow the kids to snack before a meal, so the right to eat was addressed at a subsequent legislative meeting. An additional amendment was added to give our sons the right to eat when they were hungry. Each of the points in our bill of rights was placed there for a specific reason—to clarify what is acceptable in our family.

In our constitution, my husband is the president of our family. He can veto a law, but a unanimous vote of the legislative branch can overturn that veto. For example, my husband proposed that the family buy a sailboat. Before voting, the family did its due diligence through research and an actual sailing excursion. When the proposal went to a vote, it was defeated three votes to one. Then the bill was amended to say the family would buy a powerboat. This vote passed three to one; the dissenting vote was my husband's—the president—who had the power to veto, which sent the vote back to the legislature.

On a big family decision like this, we gave time to the dissenting voter to gather more information, but my husband didn't. In this case, his veto was overturned by a vote of the legislators. My husband wanted everyone to reconsider the idea of his first choice, a sailboat, but ultimately came around to the idea of a powerboat. The process worked—everyone had their voice heard and everyone's needs were met.

This story might make it look as though my husband and I are not on the same page, but that's not the case. He and I consult one another and plan our teaching strategy before every vote. The boys do have a say, but they cannot outvote us. In the case of the powerboat, Charlie and I wanted our sons to take ownership of the decision. We wanted the boat to be a place where the entire family wanted to spend time. The legislative process helped build the boys' commitment.

For our family, this process has had some unintended but positive outcomes. Over the years, my kids have brought up topics that affected their lives, concerns that might not have been brought to light if we didn't have a constitution. Carson and Conrad both feel they have a say in family matters, and they have learned to discover and solve problems.

OUR FAMILY JUDICIAL SYSTEM AT WORK

My grandfather was a judge, and I grew up enamored with his stories about various trials he'd heard in court. It impressed me that no matter how clear-cut the case was, he'd always listen to both sides. This is a wise way to uncover the truth. Inspired, I decided that when my children were old enough, in their case around first grade, I would conduct our own courts with them whenever a dispute arose. Each son could voice his opinion and tell his side of the story. I made it a rule that they could only share testimony if they saw something with their own eyes. No speculation was allowed, just as in a courtroom. In addition, no interruptions were allowed, except by parent/judge.

I always started a family trial by hearing opening statements. Each child spoke his mind, telling me his side of the story. Just as my grandfather listened to everyone with an open mind, it was important for me to remember not to start with a decision already made. I made a point of listening so that I could understand the situation and remain unbiased. For this system to work, I needed to remind myself not to base decisions on past behavior. I also noticed that the more official and formal the mock court was, the more my sons respected the proceedings.

When they finished pleading their cases, it was my turn to ask questions. Usually, I could quickly understand what happened. Then I'd ask for closing statements, which could include any regrets the boys had or areas they might change in the future. They also needed to give a suggestion on what they could do to resolve the situation and a consequence for their actions, but they could never offer a suggestion or consequences for the other people involved. Over the years, this system worked well for our family. Here's one example of a successful mock court in action:

One day, I heard a crash and ran to Carson's room. Shattered glass was everywhere, and Conrad was cleaning up. After I determined that everyone was okay, I tried to find out what had happened. Conrad said his brother had pushed him through the glass door. For context, my boys and Conrad's friend Diego were playing rough in Carson's room. They were in the middle of a dunking competition when the glass in the door broke. The basketball hoop in Carson's room is on the back of Carson's door, which is made of solid wood with frosted glass in the center.

When I asked questions to find out what happened, my sons immediately started blaming each other. I put my hand up to silence them and told them to meet me downstairs, and that the judge would hear what everyone had to say after they cleaned up. Then I walked away. I can only imagine the surprised look on Diego's face. When the boys came downstairs, I explained to Diego that in our family, when there is a difference of opinions about what happened, I listen to both sides of the story and let my sons present their cases. I told the friend that if he wanted to give his input, he would have the opportunity; however, his testimony might not be needed.

I asked for opening statements from both sides (Carson and Conrad often played rock, paper, scissors to determine who went first). In this case, Conrad went first. He stood, while the others sat and listened. Then it was Carson's turn to plead his case. Conrad and Carson each told a different story. Conrad said Carson pushed him through the glass. Carson said Conrad fell through the glass. Conrad made the point that the glass would not have broken if his brother hadn't pushed him. Carson defended himself by saying he never pushed his brother. Conrad went on to use his friend as a witness to confirm that Carson pushed him.

I knew Diego was honest, thoughtful, and respectful, so I asked him for testimony. He spoke eloquently about what had happened and was careful not to incriminate either Conrad or Carson. I remember Diego's words exactly, "Then the glass broke." His implication was that the problem was the glass. Well, he had a point. A glass door in a teen boy's room was a disaster waiting to happen. I had warned my sons about this and cautioned them to be careful; after all, we'd bought the house with the glass in the doors.

Bottom line, the broken door was someone's responsibility to fix. As the judge, it was my job to assign responsibility. If I didn't, the responsibility would become mine, because I'm the parent. Since my boys worked, they needed to spend their own hard-earned cash to make it right. They needed to buy a new door or fix the door. So, with this trial, I taught them that no matter who was at fault, someone needed to be accountable. Life is ultimately about taking responsibility for one's actions.

After hearing everyone speak, I asked Carson if he could tell what happened from his brother's perspective. Then I asked Conrad to do the same. I refused to get caught up in semantics or definitions like real lawyers so often fight over. If I did in this case, we would have focused on defining what is a *push*. Instead, my focus was on ensuring that my sons took responsibility for the broken door. By getting my kids to tell the story from the other person's perspective, they learned to see the possibility of another point of view. This helped them understand that they also might have to take some responsibility.

My children had become rather skilled in this legal process, and it didn't take long to resolve. Conrad brought up the point that it was Carson's room and Carson needed to take responsibility for having put up a basketball hoop on his door. Carson argued that Conrad had played too rough. When everyone had been able to say their piece, I asked them both, "Do you two want to come up with a solution, or do you want me to find one?"

Conrad and Carson both recognized that neither had wanted to lose and that their brotherly competition had been in full swing as they played. When they realized this, they both were willing to take responsibility for the broken door. So they made a plan and divided the tasks. Carson, with me listening in, called places to find the glass, and Conrad, with my husband's help, went to buy the supplies needed to put the new glass in the door. The glass was delivered, and the boys, along with my husband, fixed the door so it was as good as new. Our judicial system worked, and everyone—including Diego—learned a few valuable lessons.

FAMILY TRADITIONS

In 1985, Charlie was a budding entrepreneur at age twelve and had a moneymaking brainstorm tied to the coming Fourth of July celebration: a stand that sold fireworks. Now, the sale of fireworks was not permitted in the city limits of Lubbock, Texas, but his family's house lay just past the city limits. It was the perfect place to have a fireworks stand. At the time no one realized that his hard work was the start of a family tradition.

As the years went by, Charlie passed the annual fireworks business first to his sister and then to his children, and it will likely be passed to future generations of Hamiltons. The celebration of the birth of the United States—which brings communities together with parades, picnics, and city fireworks displays—has brought a unique tradition to our family. For us, selling fireworks has been a learning laboratory, a chance to hang out with friends, and has supplied any number of amazing stories.

Traditions are important because they create a sense of belonging. One feels connected to society through patriotic celebrations and to a community through hometown and local

> Traditions are important because they create a sense of belonging.

school celebrations. In the same way, one can increase the sense of family belonging through household traditions. Celebrations and traditions teach heritage and family lore, they provide opportunities for socializing and working with others, and they help develop skills in organizing people and activities. Traditions generate positive memories that bring joy today and motivate for the future. Through them, a child obtains a sense of belonging to something bigger than themselves, which they often pass on to future generations.

A special day with a relative can bring traditions to the extended family. When I was young, my mother's cousins Bob and Thea would create a special day for us in honor of our birthdays. Having no children of their own, they would let each of us pick what to do for our special birthday outings. I still remember Bob and Thea taking me to my favorite pizza place and then a movie I requested. Special outings with family members highlight and strengthen those relationships. A mother-daughter excursion might be shopping for the first day of school or a manicure-pedicure, while a father and son might opt for the first ball game of the season, opening day of deer-hunting or fly-fishing season, or catching the local Comic-Con event. These outings can occur whenever you like and need not be gender specific, but I can tell you that kids love these kinds of traditions.

It's worth noting that you don't need a special occasion or a huge budget to create a tradition. I have a friend who used to take her kids on *night adventures*. These were often simple excursions, like a night drive or a trip to the supermarket to pick up some milk. However, since they were deemed a *night adventure*, they became fun bonding experiences.

Charlie's parents needed to be thrifty at times in their lives. However, no matter how poor Charlie's family was, they always took a family vacation. Some years they cooked on a hot plate in their inexpensive motel room to save on the cost of eating in restaurants, and they'd find places to visit that were free or inexpensive. To this day, Charlie loves to travel. When Charlie and I first started to travel with our sons, the boys flew on frequent flyer miles, and I reserved cheap hotels on the internet. We bought food at a grocery store for breakfast and lunch and only ate dinner in a restaurant.

My parents also saw the value in travel, so when I was a child we visited many different locations where we'd learn about different cultures. My grandmother would regale me with stories about Italy so often I felt as if I'd been there. If travel is important to you, it can become a part of your family's traditions without overtaxing your budget.

Traditions can be as simple as a weekly family meal. When I was in grad school, I lived in the same town as my parents. They knew I was barely getting by—paying all my bills with my savings and student loans. So they started a ritual of treating me to pizza every Tuesday evening. It was lovely: free food, great company, and a break from my studies.

As a caveat, when you start a tradition, commit to continuing the activity in the future. Children latch on to the concept and will likely hold you accountable to the implied promise. If you don't follow through, they will be disappointed. Traditions can be passed down from generation to generation or they can start today. They can continue unaltered over the years or they can adapt over time. The wonderful thing about them is that you can create fond memories that will last a lifetime.

PASS DOWN GENERATIONAL STORIES

One way that traditions are passed down is through the stories we tell each other. Stories are powerful. Tell the good, the bad, and the ugly. Don't hold back because there might be warts in the past. Your kids can learn from them all. There are so many kinds of family stories that should be shared, and these stories help children become stronger and better prepared to deal with what life throws at them. In my opinion, the stories illustrating the struggles and successes that a family works through are the most important stories because they build the conviction that if one's ancestors could survive tough times and triumph, the same is possible for oneself.

One example of perseverance we tell in my home is our firsthand experience of Hurricane Maria ripping through Puerto Rico, leaving people without electricity and safe drinking water for months. Thankfully, we had a generator, although we could only afford to run it at night because of the scarcity of oil filters, air filters, and diesel fuel. Some families didn't have a generator, and some had hardly any resources. One of our good friends and her family came to live with us for four months because their house was unlivable because of severe water damage and black mold.

This was a challenging time for everyone. My day started at 6:00 a.m. so I could shower and prepare breakfast before we had to turn the generator off at 7:30 a.m. After that, we had no water since it needed to get pumped from the cistern into the pipes. My routine included checking the level of diesel in the generator and, if it was low, to call and get on the waitlist for delivery. Once a week I'd phone my friends to get their shopping lists and plan a trip to Costco. When the kids arrived home from school (which sometimes operated without electricity) we'd head out. If we needed gas, that was a thirty-minute wait at the pumps.

When we arrived at Costco, we'd wait in line to get into the parking lot. While I waited there, the boys would hop out and get into the line to get into the store—a line that circled the building; it was at least an hour to get through the door. Once we made it into the store, one person would hold a spot in the checkout line, while the other two ran around collecting all the items on all the families' lists. Costco imposed limits on each item, so it was always important to go with three people. After returning home, we put everything in freezers or coolers to avoid opening the refrigerator until the generator could be turned back on. This became our new normal for months.

Although our situation was trying, it wasn't dire; it was tolerable. We were fortunate. Others had a tougher time. One friend had a brother-in-law in the hospital when the hurricane struck. While the hospital had a generator, it provided only enough power for the most critical tasks. Sometimes the supply of gasoline would run out before the next shipment arrived, and with the brother-in-law's life in jeopardy, a whole chain of desperate events unfolded. At great expense, my friend flew her sister's entire family to the United States so that her brother-in-law could receive adequate care. She and her own children joined them to help, but her husband had to remain in Puerto Rico to work. For four months, the kids of both families attended new, unfamiliar schools, but everyone did their best to go on.

The story had a happy ending: the brother-in-law's health improved, and Puerto Rico finally became more livable. Everyone moved back and recovered from the ordeal. Today, I'd say this family is stronger because of what they went through. This story of survival will be passed on for many generations so the descendants know that no matter what hits their family, they can unite and survive. This is part of the family's history and should be remembered.

Most families have wonderful stories of triumph and perseverance. I encourage you to find these pieces of history. Appoint one person to become the family historian. With their cell phone video, have them interview everyone in the family. Start with a list of questions to ask that are important to your family, and end with the question, "What do you want to tell the next generation about our family?" Collect pictures of people, places, and things that are a part of your family. Take more videos at every family event and continue to record the stories. Put the video in a family shared folder where other family members can add videos and view past recordings. This is one way to preserve your family history. Another way to help your children learn about their family is to create a family tree. There are many ways to compose such a tree, so let your family be creative with it. You can enhance it by adding photographs and stories and then preserve it for the generations to come. Charlie's aunt Jane created a book by starting with the family tree and writing what she knew about each person. She then asked each member of the family to provide pictures and stories. She also did research on ancestry.com and found ancestors from long ago. She made several copies of the book and gave it to each living member as a Christmas present. The book she created is treasured in our family.

DRAW ON GRANDPARENTS AS SOURCES OF TRADITION

Grandparents have an important role in a family—as elders, they have a knowledge base that parents can draw on for traditions and stories. Often, grandparents can act as sounding boards and trusted advisors to you and your children. Your children's grandparents can be a gift to both you and the next generation. They likely have skills about which they are passionate, and you can encourage them to teach your kids those skills and share their wisdom. My own experiences as a child illustrate how beneficial this can be. My grandmother was an amazing cook and would come over every Sunday to teach her grandchildren her culinary skills. The three grandchildren ranged in age from five to eleven when we started her cooking classes, and they continued for six or seven years. This allowed my parents to take a day off.

After church, Grandmother would arrive with all the ingredients for Sunday dinner. She knew what she wanted, so she laid out the tasks to be completed and told us what she expected. Then she would allow us to pick the tasks we wanted to do and let us get on with it. Sometimes everything went smoothly, while other times we bickered and fought. If our parents were around, Grandmother let them handle the discipline. She always understood her role wasn't to raise us or make the rules. She respected those boundaries.

Grandmother was a person that you knew she meant what she said. As kids, we had a deep reverence for our grandmother. She was a strong-willed woman who could have fun. When our parents weren't home, she would step in if there was an argument. She'd remain calm and ask, "Do you need help?" or "Is there a problem here?" Even if our disputes became physical, she never made a big deal about our behavior. The effect of those simple questions was amazing—often we would immediately stop fighting and break into laughter. If the disagreement continued, my grandmother would handle things differently than my parents. With my parents, we lobbied for our cases. With my grandmother, she would say something like, "It takes two to tango, and your tango isn't pretty." Then she would add, "Do you want music to tango better?" We'd say, "Yes, play the music!" and she would play something loudly or sing very loudly, and soon no one could remember what had caused the dispute. Yet, more importantly, she never took ownership of our behavior. She made it known that we always had the choice to respond positively or negatively to anything someone else does.

Whatever settled the argument, even if it was our parents stepping in, Grandmother always remained calm and cheerful. When we resumed cooking, she would often ask us how we were all feeling as a result of the argument. She'd listen attentively to our responses and then inquire about how we might have handled it if we were the parents. Then she'd give advice. I found myself eager to take her advice to heart. Even on the occasions where I felt I was right and my actions justified, Grandmother helped me to view the situation from my siblings' perspectives.

Grandmother also took the time to teach me other skills she practiced: painting, knitting, and sewing, for example. I remember one time she plucked a painting of hers off the wall and declared it was time to add color to the sunset. It was a winter scene at dusk—mostly a white sky, with just a touch of light coming through white clouds. Though her eyesight was failing because of macular degeneration, my grandmother still wanted to teach me how to improve this painting. She mixed colors and added pigment to the canvas and then asked me to do the same. After a while, she stopped and asked what I thought. I hesitated.

Grandmother laughed and said, "Even with my eyesight, it looks bad to me too!"

We both laughed and took out a new canvas and painted another scene, which again didn't come out very well. The lesson I learned that day wasn't so much how to paint but how not to take myself too seriously. If something doesn't turn out the way you expected, enjoy what you have. And I did! I learned a lot from my grandmother. She was a treasure trove of information wrapped in unconditional love. Without her teaching and gentle counsel, I would have missed out on much of the wisdom I draw on today.

SEEK ADVICE FROM YOUR CHILDREN

> Wise parents learn to listen to many perspectives— including those of our children.

Family wisdom isn't limited to our elders; wise parents learn to listen to many perspectives— including those of our children. When we first drove Conrad around one of the subdivisions that we were developing, he was five years old and interested in this venture.

"What do you think of these lots?" Charlie asked him.

Conrad looked around carefully and then said, "They look nice, but there isn't enough room in the backyard for a swing set." He was right.

To keep costs down for entry-level home buyers in Texas, these lots were purposely kept small, with the house taking up most of the parcel. While the properties were intended for new families with small kids, Conrad had a good point: they had no room for a proper play area. As a result of his feedback, in our next development project, we made the lots deeper, with room enough for a swing set. These lots sold twice as fast as the previous ones. From that point forward, Charlie and I have always made sure that our entry-level lots are large enough to hold a swing set, all thanks to Conrad's advice. Since Conrad knows his input that afternoon made a difference, I am confident that when he becomes an adult he will seek and consider the advice of people of all ages.

The idea of asking children to contribute their insight is not isolated to our family. When I was in graduate school, the CEO of Conair gave a talk in which he related the trouble Conair had initially with their hair dryers. They weren't selling. In a moment of insight, this CEO decided to consult his teenage daughter. She told her dad that the all-black dryers needed to be more colorful. He took this advice to heart, and their colorful models soon dominated the market.

Another example happened to a friend of mine who had a close relationship with her grandfather. He happened to be an advisor for two presidents and sat on the Council of Economic Advisors in Washington, DC. She described to me the feeling of wonder and amazement when her grandfather asked her opinion on a problem that was being discussed in the White House: she was ten years old at the time. It was the mid-1970s, and airlines began overbooking flights to compensate for no-shows. They needed to sell more seats than they had to fly full. Consequently, people with valid plane tickets didn't always get a seat, and this situation was becoming a national issue. Her grandfather discussed this matter with her over dinner one night. To this day she will tell you how honored she was to have her viewpoint sought, heard, and respected.

In the end, the committee assigned to the problem helped create a policy whereby airlines offered customers who volunteered to give up their seats discounts on future flights—a solution still in practice today. Even though my friend didn't come up with the answer, she was still thrilled to be a part of the process.

If you look back at your childhood, you might remember a time when someone took the time to ask for your input. My guess is that this has stuck with you and that you are still proud that an adult asked for your opinion. This can be meaningful for a child and will often give them a boost in confidence.

TEACH WHAT YOU DO WELL

If you look around, you see families that have multiple generations of lawyers, doctors, or even movie stars. Is it genetics? While genetics may play a role in our lives, parents likely love their field so much that they talk about their professions in a positive and interesting way. Raw talent can only get you so far. Children who are nurtured often go on to excel in a given field.

So often parents want to spend time with their children, but instead of planning meaningful educational experiences, they give in to something easy the kids want to do like watching a movie. While it's good sometimes to let your child pick the activity, it's also valuable to invite them to share a bit of your world. Unless you show your children that these activities exist, they won't know the possibilities available to them. Teaching your children doesn't have to involve homework, nonstop talking about your business, or sharing important life lessons. These are all good and beneficial, but teaching takes many forms. Why not share your favorite hobbies with them?

For instance, you might have your kids help you cook a challenging recipe, knit a blanket, or play your favorite board game. My husband and I started playing Monopoly and chess with our sons when they were still in preschool and kindergarten. We used these games to teach them strategy and life lessons. While many parents insist their children are too young to appreciate many activities, I say the younger you start, the better. Your children may have the potential to become great at the hobbies you show them, maybe even better than you.

In my friend Laura's case, she loved to play tournament chess. She told me that her father taught her how to play when she was nine, but only after she'd begged and begged him to do so for many years. He kept telling her, "You are too young." This inspired her to try to teach her children when they were four. Under her tutelage, all three of her children learned to play, so she went on to teach their friends. Were her children chess geniuses? No, but she told me that they all really enjoyed that time with her and she found it to be a bonding experience. Eventually, she expanded to teach classes to hundreds of children in six local schools. Today, fifteen years later, her family still enjoys this hobby with each other, their friends, and they have attended various tournaments.

Give thought to what you want your kids to love, and then teach them that skill. My family was always big on cooking, and I've carried the torch and taught my sons. When they have friends over, I teach them as well. I feel everyone should learn at least one signature dish. I love cooking and do it well, so why not pass it on? Some parents might shiver at the thought of allowing their children to use a knife or work with boiling liquids in the kitchen. Rather than shrink in fear, take the time to educate your kids to safely handle potentially dangerous situations. They need to learn these life skills. Do not allow fear to stop you from teaching your kids what you do well.

Along those lines, my husband is an excellent shot and has taken our sons hunting since they were three and four years old. I was initially uncomfortable with the idea of my young kids handling guns, but I recognized that these were *my* anxieties and I didn't want to pass on my fears to them. I trusted my husband to teach them well. As a result, both boys still love to go hunting with Dad.

If you don't have an activity or hobby to teach your children, you might consider learning a new skill with them. Charlie and I love to learn things as a family. When the boys were in high school, Charlie suggested we all learn to free dive. At first, I wasn't interested, but since I love to scuba and snorkel, I went along. We all enjoyed learning this water survival skill together. Don't worry about how to teach. You'll figure it out along the way. The important thing is to share your passion and knowledge.

Chapter Summary: The Family Structure

....

- Every family could benefit from a formal governing structure to make explicit its fundamental values and acceptable behavior.

- Through family traditions children obtain a sense of belonging to something bigger than themselves, which they can pass on. They can learn these traditions from parents and grandparents.

- Teach your children skills that your family knows—from grandparents and parents.

Exercises

....

Answer all the following questions individually, and then share your responses with your partner and kids when appropriate.

1. Outline the responsibilities and roles of each member of the family. Include acceptable behaviors and fundamental family values.

2. Make a list of family traditions and how they began. Include traditions you want to start. Why are these traditions important to pass on to your kids?

3. Write down all the things you know how to do well, and all the things other members of the family know how to do well. Include areas in which people were educated or trained, as well as hobbies. Make a long list! Have each child pick an activity they want to learn from the list and get started.

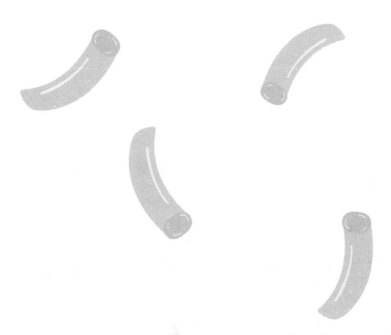

PART II

FOCUS ON FAMILY CONTEXT

CHAPTER 4

THE FAMILY'S VALUES

VALUE YOUR CHILD'S IDENTITY

Children develop their identity from a combination of genetics and environment—nature and nurture. That combination varies from child to child, even within the same household. Partnering with our children to guide the development of their identities is an important, and often difficult, task for each parent.

When we moved to Puerto Rico and our boys were in fifth and sixth grades, I was in a small child development group with another mom whose child's gender expression differed from the sex that they were assigned at birth. From a very young age, this mom observed her child's identifying with a gender different from the child's biological sex. The mother let the child do the activities she wanted. But it was only when the mother could identify herself as the parent of a transgender child that the child and the mother could really bond. The mom struggled to understand her child but learned to accept her child the way she was and accept herself as the mother of a transgender child. As time went on, the mom and the child grew close. The child knew the mom loved her just the way she was. The child knew that when her mother was disciplining her, it was not because of her gender orientation but because of her inappropriate actions.

You cannot influence your child without appreciating your child's world.

This experience showed me how powerful a role one's identity plays in the relationship between a parent and a child. That mom traded her expectations and rules for appreciation. You cannot influence your child without appreciating your child's world. Just as it is the parents' responsibility to identify their personal beliefs and values to pass on to their children, they must also strive to understand the beliefs and values of their children. Parents must work to understand how their child relates to the world around them. Relationships are the foundation for building a strong identity, and children need to believe they belong: a central part of helping them develop their individual identity, even when their perception of their identity conflicts with their experience.

Carson identifies himself in many ways. He's a great public speaker, as well as a school and community leader. When it comes to football, he identifies himself as a starting player. However, when he first graduated to the varsity team, he wasn't selected to start the games. He was tremendously frustrated by that. Since Carson identified as a starter, the reality of the situation was at odds with his own view of his identity. After some heart-to-heart conversations, I helped him adapt his view of his identity to his reality.

One of the strongest identities Conrad has is that of a leader. So, when he wasn't chosen to be the patrol leader for a Boy Scout trip, he was frustrated. He didn't understand why the adult scoutmaster hadn't selected him, as he had always performed well in a leadership role. In fact, by the time the troop arrived at the campsite, he'd forgotten his disappointment and naturally started doing what was needed to set up. Other kids pitched in and asked him for advice and direction, including the assigned patrol leader. Later the scoutmaster pulled Conrad aside and explained that the reason Conrad hadn't been selected was that other boys needed a chance to learn to lead. After all, that's a primary focus in Boy Scouts. Conrad realized that he could help this other boy learn these skills and grow as a leader himself. It aligned with his purposes and identity.

When children question their identity or purpose in a situation, emotions can run high, and children might act out. People will do almost anything to stay in agreement with their identity and fight against being forced to betray their identity. Take heed of any signs of distress that your child might be displaying. It's possible that they feel their identity isn't accepted or respected.

Here are some questions you can ask to help your older children figure out what their identity might be:

- What makes you unique?

- What skills do you have that set you apart?

- What are you so passionate about that you would not want to give up?

- Which friends, groups, and organizations are you drawn to?

- What makes you want to be friends with that group, organization, or team of people?

- How would you describe yourself to someone who does not know you?

For a younger child, keep the questions simple. For instance, you might ask:

- What do you like most about yourself?

- What are you good at?

- What is your favorite thing to do?

- What do you like to do with your friends?

- Do you like to play dress-up or pretend play?

- Who do you dress up as?

- Can you tell me about your pretend play?

Your child probably does not know their identity. Parents can help their children discover their identity through questions and guidance. This not only helps parents understand their children better but also helps the children understand themselves better. You, too, as the parent need to understand how you identify. It's worth noting that if you want a good relationship with your children, you need to at *some level* identify as a parent to your child. You might learn your child's gifts are different from yours, and you'll have to adapt to help them be themselves.

I have a close friend who is a popular mom. She's always invited to all the mom events because of her bubbly personality and willingness to volunteer. She's the kind of mom who is always at the center of the group when sitting on the sidelines at a children's sporting event or helping at school. Her daughter's personality is more introverted. She loves to read books and doesn't care to socialize. She has a few close friends and is satisfied with those; she has no desire to be the life of the party. When she was in grade school and junior high, her mom took her to all the social events. The mom would despair when she saw her daughter in a corner reading while the other girls were mingling. The daughter learned to tell her mother she had homework so she wouldn't have to go to the socials.

When the daughter got older, her mom signed them up for a mother-daughter service organization. She'd dreamed of sharing this with her child. However, she quickly realized this wasn't the path that her daughter wanted, accepted her child's identity, and they had several wonderful heart-to-heart conversations. In the end, the daughter joined the service organization, participating in the service activities, but begged off from attending some of the social events.

Everyone is capable of change, growth, and improvement. With this mindset, anyone can master what they decide to do no matter what others tell them. The mother and daughter both grew, improving their understanding of each other. It was in finding the core commonalities that the mother-daughter relationship blossomed. Every parent can connect with and build a mutual understanding with their child. My relationship with Carson is different from my relationship with Conrad because they are quite different children, and I honor their individuality.

The strongest force in any human personality is the need to stay consistent with their identity. Learn how your child identifies: ask questions and listen to their answers. Help your child develop a positive identity; part of this development means avoiding putting labels on your children.

VALUE YOUR CHILD'S GROWING EDGES

Identities are quite different from labels, and confusing the two can be detrimental to your children. Every person has growing edges, areas where we're still working on developing our sense of self, our understanding and awareness, and our control. Children's growing edges are particularly pliable. People seem to bend over backward to stay in agreement with their self-determined identity. But when they are given a label that doesn't match their view of themself, most people (kids especially) will become confused and frustrated. One reason that kids act out is that they are desperate to adhere to their chosen identity.

If an adult calls a youngster a *problem child*, they might just start behaving like one. In some cases, the kid can get so confused that they think this label *is* their identity. And who on earth can be defined by one phrase? Labels put people in boxes. That's dangerous, especially for children who are on a path of self-discovery. Even "good" labels might be detrimental because they can pigeonhole or cause discomfort. For instance, the *popular* mom in my previous story would probably be mortified to be considered that way. I'm sure she just considers herself friendly. Labels are usually gross generalizations.

When I was young, I struggled with reading and writing. I had no idea I was dyslexic, so I came up with creative workarounds. In first grade, I asked my best friend to read everything to me and found ways to get skipped when we took turns reading out loud in class. At the end of first grade, my family moved and I was assessed by the new school. The school administrators immediately spotted my reading difficulties, suggesting that I be put in a special school for kids with disabilities. Fortunately, my mother was adamant that I should not be sent there; she knew that would affix a permanent label on me. My parents hired a tutor for the summer, Sister La Salette.

Sister La Salette was so successful with me that the following year my parents enrolled me in Sister La Salette's second-grade class. She made sure to point out what I did that was right rather than focus on the difficulties. She taught me and her other students that being different was part of God's plan. "Kate," she'd tell me, "learning is important, but how you learn can be done in a multitude of ways." I made a lot of progress with her.

My third-grade teacher couldn't have been more different. Not recognizing that I might have a learning disorder, she decided I was *lazy* and wasn't shy about labeling me in numerous ways. Many days I came home in tears because of her words. One day she announced that all students were going to participate in a statewide writing competition. She explained how important this contest was for the school and for her as a teacher. I was determined to try, but it was difficult for me, and it took me more time to write than the other kids. The day before the essay was due, my teacher belittled me in front of the class by saying, "Anyone who has done as little as Kate needs to stay in during recess to finish their paper." I was mortified but put my all into completing the essay, staying up late that night.

Several months later we learned that I'd won the competition. I avoided my teacher as much as I could, sure that she'd find a way to invalidate my accomplishment. The principal personally congratulated me and then made a big announcement over the loudspeaker the next day. I was thrilled until he added that I'd be attending an award dinner with my third-grade teacher, who would be recognized alongside me. When I heard that, I ran out of the classroom sick to my stomach. The teacher had done nothing but demean me, and now she was about to be honored?

My teacher immediately called my parents in for a meeting to complain about my rudeness. She was thoroughly offended. My mom knew how many labels this teacher had given me throughout the year:

"You're stupid."

"You are so slow."

"You're just not smart."

My mother told me that when my teacher had finished complaining, she looked the woman in the eye and said, "I disagree. Kate did the most reasonable thing she could do to a teacher who never respected her. In my book, she should have done something sooner."

Later in life, I learned that this teacher told my mother she shouldn't waste an expensive college education on a child like me. She truly believed what she was saying. I find it scary to think how many other children she labeled and how many lives she destroyed.

Several weeks later, the governor of Arizona gave me the award and my essay was read to the audience. My third-grade teacher was also in attendance and was honored for having "encouraged" me. Although it might be true that I pushed myself a little harder because of her prejudices toward me, I would not call her contribution "encouragement." If I hadn't been determined to prove her wrong, and my parents hadn't been willing to believe in me and stand up for me against her authority as a teacher, I might have turned out quite differently. My parents saw my growing edges not as problems to be fixed but as opportunities to learn what I needed to be successful.

Children can fail, struggle, and even misbehave for a variety of reasons. Labels seldom help anyone. One of the best gifts you can give to your kids is the understanding that no one is defined by one learning disability, challenge, bad grade, failed attempt, mistake, or poor behavior. Help them discover their identity, keep an open dialogue with them, and respect their assessment. Then, have your children's backs and do not let others push them in ways that go against their identity.

VALUE LIFELONG LEARNING

Although I don't think the traditional university system is going away anytime soon, affordability is making it an increasing challenge for many to attend. In 1993 my college tuition was around $18,000 per year and my husband's college tuition was $7,000 per year. Today, the cost of attending those same schools has increased by more than 300 percent.

Children and parents are becoming disillusioned with traditional school systems. We know that not all kids learn the same way, and we know that only some kids do well in traditional schools. With so many ways of learning, why are we not teaching our kids with the method that is best for them? We also need to understand that college is not for everyone, and kids who do not go to college can be highly successful.

Even though both my husband and I received attractive job offers after we graduated college, only I took the job; Charlie started his own business. Today, many kids graduate with huge debt and no job prospects. Employers no longer want to teach their new employees what to do and how to do it. They want people who can hit the ground running and think for themselves, solving problems on the fly. Some businesses want internet-savvy social media experts plugging their brands—skills that are arguably learned outside of school.

Intentional learning shouldn't stop when you graduate. If you stop learning, you'll stagnate and your knowledge will lose relevance. The world you live in will become more foreign as the days pass, and it will leave you behind. That's not an environment conducive to success. If you continue to learn and show that you value learning, your children will likely follow suit. As a family, we are all lifelong learners. My husband and I recently bought a subscription to MasterClass, a platform for experts to share their knowledge. Charlie and I worked together to make the classes as practical and interactive as possible. When the four of us learned about smoking brisket Texas-style with Aaron Franklin, I bought the meat, and the entire family worked together, learning and doing at the same time. In the end, we all enjoyed the feast.

> If you continue to learn and show that you value learning, your children will likely follow suit.

These interests, developed early, can lead to larger projects. For instance, when our family became interested in eFoiling, Conrad and Carson became passionate about the sport. In high school, they were eFoil instructors and involved in an eFoil business. As a result of our family being lifelong learners, Carson became interested in metalworking. During COVID-19, Charlie and I encouraged him as he took steps to educate himself on the art. He bought supplies and built a forge, and then he asked his cousin to teach him the craft. Carson started with small projects and then took on more complex ones. He continued to refine his skills and got an internship with a metal shop.

Parents can help their children try new things, explore interesting places, and observe others. Introduce them to experts. Teach them to read about what interests them or to find educational videos and podcasts they will enjoy. It doesn't have to be work. It should be fun.

VALUE NON-INSTANT GRATIFICATION

In addition to lifelong learning, another important value to help prepare children for the modern world is to teach non-instant gratification. These days there's not much we have to wait for. However, being able to wait is an important lesson for every child. With time come some of the best rewards.

When I was little, I loved ice cream. I still do. For one of my birthdays, my parents got me an ice-cream maker. As I opened the box, I found myself expecting ice cream. I knew that was impossible, but still my mouth watered. With this tool, I could make ice cream at any time; but at that moment all I wanted was to eat some, not the hassle of making it. However, I remember how excited my mom was about getting me this gift. She knew how much I liked to cook and bake, and she knew how the frosty treat was my favorite food. What she might not have known was that she was teaching me the valuable lesson of non-instant gratification.

I picked a flavor—peppermint—and Mom took me to the grocery store to get the ingredients. Seeing how expensive the raw materials were, I quietly wondered why we didn't just choose from the vast selection of ice creams the store sold at a much cheaper price. Yet I saw my mom's excitement over making it ourselves, so with ingredients in hand, we went home. We made the base, crushed the peppermint candies, put everything into the machine, and then started the mixing process. It was fun, but I complained that I wanted the ice cream right away. Mom told me to wait and watch. Watching the machine turn so slowly, I must have asked her a hundred times when the ice cream would be done.

Several hours later Mom asked me if I wanted to see if it was ready. I wasn't sure what *ready* would look like, but I knew I wanted to taste the ice cream. I opened the lid and looked at the now semisolid treat. Unwilling to wait for Mom to scoop up a portion, I grabbed a spoon and dug in. Amazing. As anyone who has made homemade ice cream knows, no store-bought variety will ever be able to top the flavor of homemade. That day I learned that with effort and time, I could make most things better. Good things are worth waiting (and working) for.

I challenge every parent to teach this lesson so their kids can learn the same lesson I did. Now, as an adult, I know when to expect something fast and when to give something the time it needs to become delicious ice cream. Consider other ways you might teach non–instant gratification to your children and try them.

VALUE GIVING THAT LEADS TO FULFILLMENT

Teaching and demonstrating non–instant gratification pairs well with another important value, that of giving. When we give of ourselves to help others, we demonstrate acts of compassion that may not immediately gratify those whom we serve or ourselves, but the long-term benefits are priceless. Giving can lead to a sense of fulfillment.

I love it when my sons see me help others. I get so much out of these activities, and I want them to understand the joy it brings. As a family, we do service activities in our community. When Hurricane Maria devastated Puerto Rico, my boys called their friends to clear the trees in the streets and help with the clean-up. As a family we were involved with the third-largest food distribution center, helping unload trucks, organizing supplies, and distributing relief bags. Serving others during a time of uncertainty gave direction and purpose to my kids. They look back on the experience as positive, and it brought our family even closer.

When Conrad and Carson were younger, our family volunteered at our church as greeters. We went to church early and welcomed people as they entered, answering questions and engaging in friendly conversation. These simple activities might not look like they could change the world, but I knew that by encouraging my sons to volunteer, I was helping them learn to care for the people around them.

Volunteer work is important; it's a tangible way to demonstrate the value of giving ourselves. If you want your kids to volunteer, set an example by giving back to the community yourself. This is not the only way to interest your kids in volunteering, but it is powerful; they will see your actions are the standard for your family.

I recommend starting these family activities when your children are young. How young depends on the child; my sons started helping me at our church when they were five and six. When children start young, they don't question why they are volunteering. It's just what everyone around them is doing. Later, if they wonder why they are donating their time, they already understand the benefits they receive from helping others. When they're old enough, discuss it with them. Each kid will have different reasons for volunteering; ask them and seek to understand how they are benefiting from serving others.

A great place to start volunteering is with a group where you are already active. Get involved with the kids' school, help the church your family attends, or improve your neighborhood. Volunteering starts by offering to help and most organizations need it, but many don't do a good job of asking for assistance.

As my kids have gotten older, they have continued to help their community. One day the boys walked to school and saw a large section of the seawall covered in graffiti. Rather than gripe about the situation, Carson and Conrad invited their friends to come over after school to play basketball. As they walked home, my sons pointed to the seawall and asked their friends whether they might be interested in helping paint it. Everyone agreed, and all learned that many hands make light work.

There are times when it might be challenging to find an organization or group to help, but that doesn't have to stop you from making a difference. I had a friend in Puerto Rico who didn't speak Spanish, so she was hesitant to join a local organization. Still, she wanted to help. After Hurricane Maria devastated our neighborhood, my friend decided to plant new trees along the sidewalk.

She organized other families to start clearing the beds beside the roads, and then she bought new trees. Since her daughter's birthday party was approaching and she loved planting, they created a special event. Each of the friends received a tree. Each tree had a waterproof tag bearing the name of the child so that they could truly take ownership of the new sapling. At the party, the girls planted the trees. As the years passed, the girls would visit the trees and see their growth. In the end, my friend found a wonderful way to help the community and make a difference in all those girls' lives.

Giving doesn't have to become an entire family event or a community event, and it can start with something simple, like a birthday party. There are ways to teach your child that they have an abundance in their life and do not need more. One December a friend's child, Evan, was in a large store that was collecting gifts for kids who would not get anything for Christmas. Evan was also impressed by his church, which had a tree with gifts underneath, each with the name of a local child in poverty. Evan wanted to do something for those kids. Evan's mom asked him if he might like to give some of his upcoming birthday gifts to these underprivileged kids for Christmas. Evan was delighted. After the party was over, he took a few gifts for himself and gave the rest of the gifts to the church and the store that were collecting toys.

When you stop and think about it, there are numerous ways a family can help the community. Some families pick up litter in parks or collect food for the local food bank; some families give to local charities. Do what works for your family, and find what you can do for your community. Your kids will notice, and soon volunteering will become part of who they are.

VALUE TALKING IN THE POSITIVE

Volunteering is one practice that encourages fulfillment; another is to talk the positive into people's lives. I had a friend who was a happy older lady. She always smiled and loved being around her grandchildren. She wouldn't talk about her health problems. Instead, she was adamant about looking for the good in everything. She always stood out to me as different. I wondered why I always looked forward to spending time with her. One day, I asked what her secret was to such a happy life.

Her response was simple. "Kate, you must think positively!"

This concept was new to me; it meant changing my thoughts to produce positive ideas and words. It meant looking at the good in life and not getting caught up in the bad. It meant changing the way I think and not just blurting out my feelings. My friend was an elderly woman with an ailing body, yet she focused on the amazing things in her life. She focused on the words that provided positivity rather than the feelings that provided negativity. Thinking positively and focusing on positivity might seem simple. After all, who doesn't want to talk about positive things? In practice, staying positive can be difficult. As a child, my parents and teachers expected me to notice and discuss life's problems. This is usually how most kids are programmed to focus on the negative. Unfortunately, those habits follow a person into adulthood.

As an adult watching the nightly news, I found myself often repeating the negative stories about what was going on in the world to people around me. If a friend called and told me all about the bad things in her life, I'd listen and add in my own complaints. Soon, I realized that I'd been primed to focus on the negative. Once I became aware of this priming, I was motivated by my desire to set a good example for my kids: how they spoke started with me.

To help foster a positive attitude, I learned to limit my conversations with people who thought in the negative. I stopped focusing on the news, and when people talked about negative things to me, I would sometimes restate their comments in a positive way. I began doing this for myself too. For example, I have a friend who loved to call me and gossip. When we first met, I enjoyed the gossip. After I began to think positively, the pattern was hard on our friendship. I'd get frustrated with her for saying negative things about some of our friends. She'd then defend herself by saying, "But it's true. They really did that." I knew she was right and had a tough time coming up with anything positive to focus on.

Finally, one day I explained that I was working on thinking positively more often, and she surprised me by jumping in to say that it was a great idea. She embraced the concept, and now we hold each other accountable. For example, one time I was telling her about meeting up with friends at the airport who were going on vacation when I was heading out of town for work. I was a bit jealous. I sighed and said, "I so wanted to go with them instead of on my work trip."

My friend replied, "Don't you mean you *got* to attend your work event?"

My mindset shifted to one of being grateful. I realized I was happy to have challenging and interesting work to do with my husband.

I smiled and said, "You're right. And I was happy for my friends that they got to go on a trip together. Next time, I'll go with them." With that, all feelings of envy were gone.

Now when this friend calls and asks me about family members and friends, we talk all about the wonderful things they are doing. Instead of gossiping, we spread joy and are genuinely happy for the people we are talking about. Getting a close friend to hold me accountable was exactly what I needed. Perhaps you can find a friend who will partner with you to develop a positive mindset?

Of course, there are many times when I can't correct people. In those instances, I restate their comment internally to cast it in a positive light for myself. It trains my mind to think positively and to see the person in a different light, a better one. Once you make this practice a habit, you can encourage your kids to adopt this mindset and even teach their friends to speak positively as well.

Sometimes you might need to help others to restate their thoughts and see how they can make them positive. This can be tricky, so I try asking questions like the following:

- Is there another way to look at that?

- Could you be happy for your friend who gets to do that activity that you want to do?

- Is it possible that you'll get to do that activity someday?

Asking questions can help others see events in a new light. After my sons got the hang of it, I would sometimes ask them to retell a story in a positive way. It didn't take long for thinking positively to become second nature—for all of us. I still fail at times, but by working on it I am making progress with my kids. More of their conversations are positive than negative. In a few generations my great-grandchildren might be able to effortlessly speak only in the positive. How amazing would that be? But it starts with you, and it takes hard work to see the benefits.

VALUE HONESTY

With a positive mindset, we can lean into the honesty we value and not be constantly on guard to put the best face on something we've said or done. Kids tend to start out by seeing the world as black and white, right and wrong, good and bad because they are still learning that what something looks like at first might not be the whole story. Adults are the ones that see the gray associated with actions and words. Exaggerations, white lies, omissions of facts, fake compliments, and statements meant to mislead are all shades of gray. It is our job as parents to teach what is a lie and what is the truth. This is made more difficult when the person telling the truth or the lie is the only one who knows the difference.

The way I see it, it's the task of a parent to teach a child how to be trustworthy. We are honest because we want to be a trustworthy person, and we expect the same from others. Honesty is a vital component of happiness. We gain a sense of fulfillment knowing the people around us can trust the words that come out of our mouths. Trustworthiness is a virtue that many respect and admire.

We need to be careful not to teach our children the fine art of manipulation. Half-truths, white lies, avoiding the question asked by answering another question, and all the other crafty arts of deception simply help children lie better and encourage them toward dishonesty. As a child hones those skills over time, they realize that lying works, and they'll do it more often in a variety of situations to get what they want or to give what they believe is wanted or expected. Children will lie when they believe the lie is what the parents want to hear. As parents, we need to teach our kids that the truth is what we want to hear.

For young children, lying is confusing, especially since they hold adults to a strict standard and take things literally. For instance, if you say that you'll take your toddler for an ice cream and discover that the store is closed, she will get upset and say you lied. She didn't receive an ice cream: it's cut and dry. Or when you tell a child you'll take them to the playground and it rains, you've lied. The reason for the schedule change is irrelevant. You made a promise that you did not fulfill. We can teach our children early on the reasons why we didn't fulfill the promise, why our promise was not a lie, and how there will be circumstances out of our control that might lead us to not be able to follow through.

Another factor to consider is that lying can be a symptom of a bigger issue. After all, your kids might be covering something up. When confronted with an opportunity to avoid disappointing their parents (and possibly receiving punishment), many kids opt to lie. It seems like a sensible solution. At first glance, the lie immediately stops a conflict, and sometimes it gets you out of doing something you don't really want to do. Of course, with our experience in life, we know this solution can be dangerous.

When a child lies, a parent needs to investigate immediately and thoroughly. For instance, if your child gets a bad grade and tries to hide it from you, you need to act so that you can help understand the problem and make it safe for them to come to you with bad news. It's important to discuss the problems caused by lying with your kids so they can put together the perils inherent in hiding the truth from you. Lying can be a hard habit to break. If your child lies regularly, the first step would be to create an environment where your children can safely tell you the truth.

When I was young, my father had an agreement with me that if I found myself in a difficult situation, I could call him and he'd come get me. No questions asked. No consequences. This rule made it easy for me to leave a party if things got out of hand or if my ride didn't want to leave. I never got in trouble and always felt safe calling him. I carried on this tradition with my sons, with the caveat that later we'd need to go over what occurred to make sure the same situation didn't happen again. That way they could learn from the experience rather than be punished for getting in that situation.

Another area of concern is social media, where lies take the form of exaggeration. Kids get on Facebook, Instagram, and other apps and share information. It's easy to stretch the truth to try to impress one's peers. While it's fine to present your life in the positive, it isn't okay to pretend you've gone on trips you haven't or accomplished feats you didn't. These pretenses can become so commonplace that people get in the habit of lying to impress others.

So how do you help your children not lie? Be curious about your kids' lives and ask a ton of questions. If you question them from a place of genuine interest and wonder, lies will fall apart like a tissue in water. Be sure to listen and let them talk. A powerful tool is the prompt "Tell me more." Most people want to talk about themselves, what they have been doing, and what they want to do. Let your kids talk. The more they talk to you, the more comfortable they will become sharing their thoughts, emotions, and fears. They will want to be honest rather than avoid your gaze. They will know you want to listen to them and know about their true lives, not the filtered, narrated life that they show the outside world.

When your child confesses things to you, it's vital for you to be strong and loving. Don't chide them. They will not share anything of importance with you if they feel they are being judged. Your child knows what happened and is ready for a change. Just be there for them, guide them, and make sure to tell them frequently that your love for them is unconditional. My sons know that if they come to me and tell me about something, the consequences will be much less than if I find out about it after they hid it from me. When my boys come to me, I take on the role of *coach*. I don't solve their problems but, rather, give them the benefit of my experience and wisdom, sharing my hard-won lessons and asking questions. Usually there is no need for punishment, which is always a last resort. Overall, I'm not a punishment person but prefer to rely on natural consequences to teach a lesson.

Children want to make their parents happy, so I also let my children know that the truth makes me happy. Lies don't. You need to back this up with action. Kids need proof that you're serious about that. In our home, we make a game of pointing out white lies, acts of omission, half-truths, exaggerations, and well-intentioned untruths. My kids love calling me out.

"That's a lie!" they'll chirp gleefully.

It's a drill that has worked for our family. I believe that when my sons utter a lie, they'll probably call themselves out and think, "That's a lie," because they're more aware of it. We all do what we can to hold each other accountable for the truth. What are some ways you might encourage honesty in your family and help one another be trustworthy people?

VALUE WORK ETHIC

Developing our perspective on life through internal growth isn't the only area necessary for raising children. Understanding when and how to work hard is a skill that all children can benefit from as they develop into capable adults. Charlie grew up working on a ranch. He knows what hard manual labor is and knows that work on a ranch is never truly done. Hard work, perseverance, grit, and knowing that there is always more you can do has made my husband successful. His parents instilled those values, and we have instilled them in our kids.

My sons enjoy working on our ranch because they get to create something that only a few can ever say they created. For instance, they helped build our home on the ranch, as well as dig the trench and lay the water pipes going to the house. They also helped build the shooting range, plant the trees, grade the roads, and maintain the fences. Since a rancher's work is never done, they're always learning as we improve the property. As a result of this work, Conrad and Carson have learned to use equipment and tools that most adults don't know how to use. They can both operate a forklift and track hoe and can weld broken pipes. If there's a problem with the water lines, I just call my sons, and they can fix it rapidly. These skill sets are practical and valuable.

When we moved to Puerto Rico, my boys wanted to share the experience of working on the ranch with friends. They asked if they could bring a few buddies with them the next time we went to our West Texas ranch. We said yes, but I had no idea how I was going to convince the friends' parents to let them come. In true gracious Puerto Rican style, the parents thanked me for the invite but said they would need to talk it over. I completely understood this; I know I would have been worried if I had no experience or point of reference for my children's safety on a Texas ranch.

It was with complete faith in God that eight parents sent their kids to the ranch that first year. I will never forget picking them up at the airport in two pickup trucks. Charlie said to one of the boys, "Open the tailgate and put your bags in the back."

The boy looked at my husband and asked, "What is a tailgate?"

Charlie said, "It's going to be a long week for you, son, or see if you can figure things out yourself."

That was that child's first lesson: if you can figure it out yourself, don't ask. Those kids learned how to chop wood with an ax, how to use a chainsaw to cut down mesquite trees, and how to clear brush. We took them on campouts where they learned to make a fire and cook on it. In short, they learned about hard work and took home the stories of cowboys. Fast-forward to September 20, 2017, when Hurricane Maria destroyed the island of Puerto Rico. Everyone in the neighborhood was out cleaning up, but there were enormous trees blocking the streets. Conrad and Carson called their friends, and they all got chainsaws and made short work of the fallen trees.

Amid the tree clearing, one of our neighbors, Sam, received calls concerning the fact that children were using chainsaws. Sam politely asked the callers if they knew how to use a chainsaw. No one did. He told the concerned citizens that the kids knew how to use the chainsaws and that we should be grateful they were clearing the trees from the roads. The kids felt like heroes, and in my book they were. Many people personally thanked them for their efforts. Looking back, it was Charlie's commitment to teaching his sons about the rewarding feeling of accomplishment that comes from hard work that led Conrad and Carson to want to share that with their buddies. So, if you talk to your children about why you work as hard as you do, you may just hear your kids repeating those words to others. You never know when what you are taught will be used.

Chapter Summary: The Family's Values

....

- Help your child discover their identity by asking questions.

- Be patient with your child's growing edges, and avoid labeling your child.

- When your child acts out, talk to them to find out what is happening, and help them find a solution that is congruent with their identity.

- Be a lifelong learner, try new things, explore interesting places, and meet new people. If you continue to learn, your children will as well.

- Teach your child that some things are worth waiting for.

- Help your child appreciate the rewards of helping others.

- Set a good example for your child by focusing on the positive.

- Honesty is a vital component of happiness, and dishonesty can be a symptom of a bigger issue. Create a safe environment so your child can tell you anything, honestly.

- Encourage your child to work hard.

Exercises

....

Answer all the following questions individually, and then share your responses with your partner and kids when appropriate.

1. Sit down and discuss the idea of identity with your child. Help them verbalize their identity by asking these questions: What qualities describe you? What makes you unique? What do you like most about yourself? How would you describe yourself to

someone who does not know you? What skills do you have that set you apart? What are you passionate about? Which friends, groups, or organizations are you drawn to and why? What makes you want to be friends with that group, organization, or team of people? Who do you dream of becoming or who are you when you pretend play?

2. Talk to your child about and explain the concept of a label. Ask if anyone has given them a label they don't agree with. Encourage your child to change these labels or simply throw them out. Change the meaning of the label by asking your child what the good qualities are in the label they were given.

3. Hold a family meeting and discuss the importance of learning new things. Create a family list of the things everyone would like to learn more about. Write down everyone's interests and ideas. Make this list long. Pick one item as a family and set a date and time to learn it.

4. Bake a cake, make ice cream, build a climbing structure, or do an activity that your child must work hard at before he reaps the reward when completed. Potentially, the more complex, time consuming, and challenging the activity, the more gratifying the reward. Watch the pride your child will have in this accomplishment.

5. As a family, pick a volunteer activity to do. Talk about each person's talents they bring to the activity and the roles each person will play. Set a date and time to do the activity. After the activity, do a debrief and find out the highs and lows.

6. Sit down with your child and discuss the potential consequences, the dangers, and the reasons for lying. Discuss the concepts of white lies, acts of omission, half-truths, and

exaggerations. Give examples of how to use diplomacy and truth. Ask your child to give their own examples of lies and how diplomacy and truth could have been used instead.

CHAPTER 5

THE CHILDREN'S INFLUENCERS

One parenting trend I've noticed encourages parents to strengthen their bond with their child by building a friendship. While a *friend* is a coveted role, the parent role is more important. Friends are bonded by mutual affection. Parents are bonded with their children by unconditional love—and for many by blood—making the parent relationship much more meaningful than a friendship. Parenting includes responsibilities that don't typically exist in friendships like creating limits, saying no, and setting standards. Kids might not always want to be your friend when you're teaching them rules and limits, but part of parenting is teaching your kids about life.

If you are a great parent and call yourself a friend, it is possible that your child could have a skewed view of how a friend acts. It might set a standard of friendship beyond what many would consider realistic. One day I heard a seven-year-old say, "Mom, you are my best friend." The mom replied, "Yes, I am your parent first and friend second." The mom wanted to validate the friendship that the child felt for her and at the same time stress the importance of her parenting relationship over their friendship. She wanted her daughter to know that she chose to be her parent and that as the parent she would do things that a friend might not do. A parent should hold a child accountable even if the child isn't eager to be held accountable; that's a central difference. Conrad and Carson know I am parenting because I am willing to teach them what they need to learn in life regardless of our friendship.

STAND GUARD OVER YOUR CHILD'S MIND

When Conrad was nine and Carson was eight, friends of ours invited us to their house to meet a famous war hero named Chris Kyle, often known as the deadliest sniper in American history. I thought this would be an educational opportunity for my boys to hear the truth about war and what could happen to people during an international conflict. Chief Petty Officer Kyle spoke openly and frankly about what he saw during combat, delving into how heartless the enemy was. He went into detail about how children were used as bombs and explained how prisoners were brutally killed. He told us about meeting children whose perspectives were marred by growing up in a war zone. They grew up watching others being tortured and became desensitized to the violence, willing to inflict it on others without a second thought.

Chief Kyle described his own struggles with returning to civilian life and being plagued by what he had seen and experienced in the conflict. He had to guard his mind from the horrible images that might return at any moment. For the most part, he did this by staying active; and he ultimately found refuge in helping other veterans cope with their own demons. Sadly, Kyle was killed while trying to help a fellow soldier through similar mental struggles. Before hearing from Chief Kyle, I never intended to talk to my boys about guarding their minds; after his presentation, I knew it was a prime opportunity. When Chief Kyle died, it was yet another chance to discuss the issue.

I feel it's my job to stand guard over my sons' minds, to watch what they absorb and teach them why they should be careful about what they see and hear. The battlefield of our mind is also emotionally dangerous; our media rarely shrinks from gruesome portrayals of evil acts.

A memorable expression for me is "Trash into the mind will bring trash out of the mind." It's not only what children see and hear but also who they hang around with that will ultimately teach them. Kids today hold in the palm of their hands the ability to view horror movies, pornography, brutal killings, and any other harsh images they so choose. Once viewed, they cannot unsee those images. We must teach our kids not to go looking for them.

As a parent, we must remember that we get to set a good example. What you view sets the stage for your children's viewing habits. Don't watch trash. The media normalizes (and at times glorifies) atrocious situations: drug use, pornography, casual sex, and violence. By not watching this type of content, not only will you help your kids, but you might find yourself in a more positive state of mind. There's no way around it—you must keep tabs on what your child is watching. In this age of personal devices, there are tools that you can use to monitor their activity, but don't be surprised if your child figures out how to bypass them. The best thing to do is to talk to your children and keep an eye on what they view.

Unintentionally stumbling into inappropriate or harmful media has become a common occurrence. There are deceptive people and websites that can fool your children. One time I glanced over at a cartoon that Conrad was watching. Before I knew it, the whole feel of the show changed, and suddenly my young son was watching cartoon pornography. When he realized what it was, he shut it off. Then he and I discussed what had happened. By the end of our talk, he realized that he'd been lured in and that he could figure out how to avoid such predicaments in the future.

Another area to monitor is the use of foul language. If you don't want your children using that kind of language, you can't allow them to consume media that uses it. In addition, watch for songs with lyrics about killing, stealing, rape, and similar inappropriate content. This fills their minds with destructive junk. Of course, teens will experiment, peers will pressure, and culture will influence. Your child will be exposed to sights, sounds, and actions you do not agree with. That is the reason you must teach your children why it's important for them to guard their own minds. For each family, the reasons guiding your choices might be different based on your morals.

When we moved to Puerto Rico, the local kids who attended school with my sons would use English swear words, but they would never use the Spanish equivalent of these words. Their parents looked the other way when the children swore in English because they deemed these words less intense than the Spanish ones. My kids were exposed to English swear words at school and I couldn't prevent it. Since profanity was unacceptable in our family, Charlie and I talked to our sons about the bad words they heard in school, about what they meant, and how one could become desensitized by constantly using them. At the end of the conversation Conrad said, "Mom, I'm not the kind of person that speaks like that. I know better words to use instead."

If profane language is a problem in your household, code words can sometimes help. I have a friend whose daughter was using a bad word she'd learned from other friends. She and her mother worked out another phrase to substitute when she felt the urge to swear: "turtle nest." I would rather hear a substitute for a swear word than a curse word. It shows that my sons are exerting some level of control in a frustrating situation. I have heard people use *donkey*, *frank*, *shut the front door*, and *jack-o-lantern* as alternate words for popular swear words. While others might not agree, I believe that these substitutes are far less objectionable.

By using alternative words instead of curse words, your kids are taking a stand and influencing their peers. I have urged my sons to be strong in their convictions about what they put into their minds. Teach your child to be the influencer. They may not be able to influence others in every situation, but unless they take a stand and start someplace, they will not be able to positively influence anyone ever, including themselves. Teach your kids to have a say in what they allow into their minds.

KNOW WHAT CURRENTLY INFLUENCES YOUR CHILDREN

A word to the wise—never stop teaching your beliefs and views, because the other influencers of your child will never stop sharing theirs. Along those lines, always do your best to try to understand the top spheres influencing your kids. These will change over time as they grow and life changes. Kids want to learn, especially in their fields of interest. You can take the topics they are interested in and use them to help you teach your kids about what you want them to learn. Let me provide a couple of examples. Carson is influenced by sports, particularly football. Conrad is influenced by technology.

When I want to inspire Carson, I use the internet to find pro football players who are doing great things, or even bad things to use as a cautionary tale. For instance, when he wants to stay out late, I question if it will affect his game performance. I might ask, "Do the Dallas Cowboys have a curfew for their players?" He knows they have one before a game. A well-rested player always performs better. He will then connect the dots and won't fight me about staying out late. I simply remind him of his priorities.

When talking to Conrad, I know that if I relate whatever it is I am trying to teach him to technology, I'll get his attention. One day I came home to find Conrad polishing off a pint of ice cream. I asked him if a power surge could harm his iPad. He launched into a detailed and technical explanation about it. I then related this to eating too much ice cream. I asked him to turn over the container and tell me how many calories were in the pint. "Wow, I had no idea!" he said. Again, I just made him aware of how his actions affected his health. If he had no interest in good health, I would not have made an impression, and he would not have realized that moderation was key.

The dominance of social media in our lives, combined with the ever-present availability of media, is a prime influencer on our children, but it's not the only dominant influence. Other influences include our location, the people we hang out with, the language we speak, our beliefs, and the news sources we consume. Parents must be vigilant of what affects *our* lives and then be selective. You can find out what is influencing your child by taking an active role in their lives: know who their friends are, read what they read, watch what they watch, and be familiar with their activities. Talk to your child about their interests.

Also important is to share your beliefs and opinions with your child well ahead of when outside influences do. I have what I call the *eight-year rule*. It means that you teach your child your own perspective on topics eight years before you think society will do so. Share your beliefs and truths on important subjects so that when strong outside influences attack, your child will have a foundation rooted in your beliefs. *Be the first influencer on all topics.* This does not guarantee your child will adopt your views and beliefs, but at least they will be aware of them.

While we want our children to listen to and learn from others, we also want them to stay rooted in the views we taught them, the ones we believe are right. But what happens if you change your view? Or what if a child discovers on his own that a parent's view is different from what they believe?

Let me give an example from my own life. My parents were brought up Roman Catholic and married a person of the same faith. They believed their siblings raised their kids to be Roman Catholic, just as they did. So, when my cousin fell in love with a Jewish girl and converted to Judaism, my parents were surprised. I was an adult and thought nothing of it. But to my father, it was a huge deal that my cousin wanted to marry outside our faith, and he refused to attend the wedding. When I asked him to explain, he made many reasonable and even compelling points to support his beliefs and convictions. I just didn't agree with my father.

I was at a crossroads. Should I adopt my father's beliefs and wishes or choose to honor my beliefs? I respected my father and what he was trying to teach me, but I ultimately chose to stay true to my own viewpoint and attended the wedding. I believed the right response was to show unconditional love to my cousin and welcome his new wife into the family. My father had to accept that my views differed from his own. In the end, he understood my cousin's choice, and over time he came to believe that my cousin converting to Judaism was a blessing and contributed to his successful marriage.

Recognize that there are different views, perspectives, and experiences and that your children will disagree with you sometimes. Some of what you teach may be flawed or outdated. Times change. Your children's new perspective may be something you cannot reconcile with your beliefs. Just accept that they see the world differently, keep communicating and listening to their views, and respect one another.

To influence your children, parents must maintain a close relationship of love with them, which might mean respecting when they hold opinions that differ from yours. I want my sons to be independent, free-thinking, and, one day, even better than I am. That, of course, means they have something to teach me. I look forward to learning from them. We should teach our kids to voice their perspectives and listen to those of others. Banning other viewpoints hurts everyone. Having tolerance means living in peace with someone even when you disagree.

Let's not confuse listening and tolerance with a *demand* for agreement at all costs. Tolerance does not mean requiring others to believe as we do. As parents, we need to listen to the ambitious innovations, wild dreams, staunch views, and differing perspectives of our kids. If you do this, your child will have enough faith in you to share. When my sons were in high school, I kept my mouth shut and listened to their views. They told me things I would not have told my mother at their age. Listening was the prerequisite for allowing me to influence them throughout their lives.

BE ON YOUR CHILD'S BOARD OF INFLUENCERS

Similar to a corporation, your children have a board of influencers. These people have a massive influence over your child's choices because they have gained your child's trust. Your child has a relationship with them and perceives they are valuable. The influencers can include close friends, other kids your child idolizes, people they follow on social media, celebrities, friends of the family, siblings, and parents. But the influence of parents, due to their role as disciplinarians, is sometimes viewed as less valuable.

Parents must walk a tightrope to be an influencer for their children while maintaining discipline, making rules, and setting standards. Involving your children in the rulemaking process can help you negotiate this tightrope. This practice allows you to become, and remain, a part of your child's board of influencers. In this section, I discuss three more techniques to achieve this:

- Connecting with your child

- Understanding your child's world

- Helping foster a mentor relationship for your child

The first step to being on your kid's board is connecting. How you accomplish this varies with each child. You might play a game, watch a TV show, throw the football, create art, enjoy music, or lie next to your child on the couch and just listen. What you do might depend on your child's age. A youngster might want to color with you, while a middle schooler might like to take a long bike ride, and your teen may enjoy playing video games together. You know your child. Find an activity you can bond over.

Once connected, you can begin to understand your child's world. However, it is vital that once you understand it and are part of your child's board, you simply listen and refrain from doing anything else. Don't give advice, don't correct what they are saying, and don't overreact to what they tell you. Your child needs to know you will listen to them without judging and giving a lecture. Yes, I understand this might be difficult; at times this is an extreme challenge for me. My sons will tell you I'm the best lecturer ever. But now when they tell me I'm lecturing, I adjust my approach. I will stop and ask them if they want to hear what I have to share. If they don't, I don't press it. If they do, I promise them that I will try to keep it short. While Conrad and Carson know that I'm always seeking to understand their world, sometimes the answer is yes, and sometimes it is no. When they say no, I bite my tongue. By respecting the no, I am helping build our connection. They say no usually because I simply do not have enough of a connection with them at that moment.

Each time you talk to your child, you must build a new connection. Just because you connected so well the last time you talked doesn't mean this time won't require effort to do so again. It probably won't take as long to reestablish the connection, but you must find it each time you talk to your child. Then you can begin to understand them. And only when you understand can you really start to influence.

> **Each time you talk to your child, you must build a new connection.**

Convey to your kid that you understand their world. Unfortunately, it has been my observation that most parents don't understand. Our children's world is so different than the one we knew when we were young. The best way to understand your child's world is to truly be present with them (rather than mentally distracted) whenever you can. For me, medium to long car rides are ideal. I get my boys talking and remind myself to simply listen. They love this time together.

Sometimes I perch on Conrad's bed at night and wait for him to talk. A typical conversation starts with, "Mom, get off my bed." Knowing that my older son likes sympathy for all the push-ups, laps, jumping jacks, and plays the team runs in practice, I might say, "Tell me what you did in football." Conrad talks, and I listen. Soon he starts relating funny things that have happened, and I listen and give suitable responses. I'll laugh when appropriate and encourage him to continue with a gentle "Tell me more." It's important to let him know that I'm not daydreaming but really present and listening. *Tell me more* is a great phrase to use with your kids. It lets them talk to you about what they want to tell you. It usually gets my sons to open up and tell me even more than any question I could have asked. Conrad will continue to talk until he is tired, and then he'll ask me to leave—again. This time I do.

It is worth noting that I always refrain from giving advice or commenting on what he says at that time, even if he asks for my thoughts. I want him to work things out and discover his own wisdom, so I'll ask questions to help guide him. I'm just there to connect and understand Conrad's world.

There might be times, even after you've attained the status of trusted advisor, when your child will not want to learn certain things from you. In those instances, you need to find other adults who can form a connection and influence their lives. Your child will see that mentors are beneficial, and this will help them later in life. When Charlie and I asked one of our son's teachers to mentor him, the teacher was honored, and my son benefited. As a result of that success, my son has asked other adults to mentor him. When a child initiates that request, it can forge a more powerful bond between them and the adult.

With all this talk about listening and not advising or interfering, you might wonder when a parent should let go and when they should become more involved and take control. As my sons grew older, I turned over the reins to them more and more. As I gave them back the control, I continued to set standards and then allowed my kids' own actions to determine the consequences. Sometimes my boys didn't like the consequences that life dished out, but they couldn't complain because they were in the driver's seat. They also agreed to live by our family's standards.

Because they were empowered to make their own decisions, I was happily no longer pitted against my sons. Before, every time I battled their choices, I felt as if I had failed. Now I was able to give encouragement and advice and then simply turn over the reins to them and hold my kids accountable. Anything related to their clothes, their hair, their room, schoolwork, and other areas of personal choice, I made sure my sons knew they had the ultimate say. If I didn't agree, I let them know my opinions and facts supporting them and then I held my tongue. I felt it was important to allow Conrad and Carson to make their own decisions and learn to be responsible for any consequences.

My children could buy things with their own money, choose not to study for a test, or wear flip-flops on a long walk. In this last example, when Conrad then complained of getting a blister on the walk, I simply responded with, "I am sorry." He knew he was responsible for the choice he had made and that we were not cutting our walk short. I didn't rescue him, tell him what to do, or get angry with him. He was left to find a solution. Conrad toughed it out, put a Band-Aid on the blister when we got home, and learned not to wear flip-flops on long walks. As parents, we need to let consequences happen. It's in my nature (as it is in most mothers' natures) to nurture and protect. However, in this case, Conrad was not going to be permanently damaged by a blister.

If I don't allow my sons to learn when the stakes are low, they are doomed to learn when they are higher and more dangerous. If I force my boys to do schoolwork when they live at home, what have they learned? Only that mom thinks schoolwork is important and that they themselves didn't really want to do it. So I gave them a choice from a young age. I never forced them. As a result, they learned our family's standard that we all work hard in anything we do and always do our best. And I hold my children to this standard.

I remember Carson coming home from first grade and saying that he didn't want to do his homework. I told him that was his choice, but he had to find something he could practice. I explained that this was his time to practice whatever he wants to be great at. I gave him a choice between his writing homework, digging a hole, cleaning the bathroom, or mowing the lawn. Carson chose to dig a hole. I gave him a shovel, marked off a decent-sized square in the yard, and told him to come get me when the entire square hole was three feet deep. Carson started off strong and determined. Soon, he found the soil was hard, so he talked me into letting him add water to soften it. At this point, I thought he might just have a good old time in the mud and my plan would fail. But I stayed the course, telling myself he might someday be the world's best hole digger and I'd be proud.

Carson did get wet and muddy, but he kept digging. After some time, he came back into the house and asked if he could be done. I went out and examined the hole. It was only two feet at the deepest point and didn't include the entire marked-off area. Carson commented that hole digging was hard work. He then realized that if he had chosen to do his homework, he would've already been done. I told him he had picked digging a hole and had to finish it before he could go play. He was tired and frustrated but was still a good negotiator.

Carson said, "It will be dark before I finish."

I replied, "I can wake you up early before school so you can finish it."

"But my homework won't be finished for school."

CHAPTER 5: THE CHILDREN'S INFLUENCERS

"I thought you didn't want to do it."

He considered this for a while and then said, "It's a lot easier than digging this hole."

I suppressed a smile. "Do you want to change your choice of jobs?"

"Yes, please!"

"All right, but you must finish all your homework before you play, and if you do not, I will wake you up early before school."

"Okay."

"And you must agree that the next time you do not want to do your schoolwork, you will have to finish the hole you started."

"I won't. Schoolwork is easier and goes faster. I'd rather do that."

Carson learned a lesson based on his choices. Yes, there were times I did need to remind him of his alternative to schoolwork—digging the hole—but for the most part, he willingly did his homework.

Teach your child that no matter what they want to do, it will require work. Then give them the chance to choose their own path. If you have to push them, they will maintain the path you chose only when you are pushing. However, if your child chooses the direction, the likelihood is much greater that they will continue pushing themselves.

SET FAMILY STANDARDS

Each family requires standards. Standards are what we want from ourselves and each other as a family. They are the basic level for which we hold ourselves accountable. Your own family has standards, although they might not be discussed. Most of them are understood and some are assumed. It is important to write them down and to have each family member set standards for themselves. Now, when you do this, make sure you are setting down the *standards* and not the *expectations*.

For instance, one standard in our house is that we do our best and work hard. That is the level of quality that our family accepts as the norm for judging performance. Some parents might expect their kids to get all As on their report cards. However, *doing your best* is a standard, while *wanting your kids to get all As* is an expectation.

An expectation is a belief that something *should* happen in the future, whereas a standard is a measuring point for something. In the previous example, if a child does not have to work hard to get As, they might set the bar for the quality of their work at a low level. I strive to never set the bar low for my kids when I know they can achieve more. By setting expectations a parent is limiting their child to a level they believe is acceptable. By setting the standard of excellence for everything that is done, what the child can achieve is only limited by their ability to realize the standard of doing their best. When kids know they have done their best, then they take pride in their grades. My sons' final grades are theirs, not mine.

I remember Conrad not wanting to do his coloring homework in kindergarten. He scribbled with one crayon over a page and called it done. Knowing that he didn't do his best, I asked him, "Are you proud of your work?"

He hung his head and said, "No, Mom."

"Why are you coloring if you're not willing to do your best?"

"The teacher is *making* me color."

"So you mean she's holding down your arm and pushing on the crayon? That's how she's *making* you color?"

"No," he said with a giggle. "This is my homework."

"Ah," I said. "You're doing your homework and that's why you're coloring."

"Yes."

"Hmm. So you're choosing to do something. Shouldn't you do your best?"

Conrad looked a little disgruntled but finally nodded his head. "Yeah."

Good, better, best. Until good is better and better is best, never let it rest.

That's something I like to say. As the years went by, I'd hear my sons repeat this to their friends. It's good to know that they saw that my standards for excellence never changed. They understood that no matter what they did in life, I'd always be looking to see that they did everything they could to present their best work.

I don't know the life path my children will choose, and I don't want to choose it for them. That is not my job. My job is to help Conrad and Carson create standards to which they will want to hold themselves and others accountable. Parents who expect their kids to act or be a certain way or go a particular direction are bound to be disappointed. Life is never the way you expect it to be. Having expectations for your child sets everyone up for failure. This causes great sorrow. More importantly, you could miss out on an amazing present-day experience by focusing on your expectations.

In 2020, many kids missed out on graduations, proms, and being with their friends because of COVID-19. No one expected this, yet everyone had to live with the new reality. Those young people rooted in expectations struggled. Their expectation of a traditional graduation, prom, and social life in general was not possible. However, those kids rooted in standards understood that while the world had changed, their standards didn't have to. If their standard was to celebrate the completion of high school without any expectations of the manner in which they did it, then they had the opportunity to imagine a new, different kind of graduation. Having standards rather than expectations, they had lost nothing. The graduation ceremony could take place at a different place, or time, or in some different manner, or not be performed at all.

When Charlie and I first got married, we took many road trips. I quickly learned that our expectations were quite different. I feel this stemmed from my personal standard of wanting travel to be all about getting to the destination: we were supposed to get into the car early in the morning and drive the most direct route, making the fewest stops possible. Charlie's standard was quite different; he was in it for the adventure. He wasn't in a rush to leave, and if something took us off the beaten path, he was game.

One day he asked if I wanted to play bear went over the mountain.

"What's that?" I asked.

"We get into the car and drive until we find a place that looks interesting to stop at."

"Which way do we head?"

"You pick. North, south, east, or west?"

We had a blast. No destination—just heading in a random direction, talking and laughing along the way. When we hit a fork, we picked which way to go. No plan, just fun.

Midday he asked, "Are you having fun?"

"Yes!" I said. "Why do you ask?"

"Because I've tried several times to make our road trips fun in the past, but I wasn't sure you enjoyed them."

That's when it hit me: because of our different standards, our expectations hadn't been aligning. So I changed my standard for travel from getting to the destination as directly as possible to appreciation of the journey, and then I started noticing all the ways Charlie created fun and adventure.

Parents need to encourage their kids to set standards for themselves and then help them learn to hold themselves accountable for that standard. Through this process, your kids will learn and grow. This is a dance you will continue to improve on over time. I instituted the policy of working with my children to write down their standards and share them with me. Early on, Carson decided he never wanted to be late for football practice. The expectation in Puerto Rico is that it is okay to arrive late. Yet I taught Carson that arriving late to anything sent a message to the person who arrived on time or early that this was not a priority.

Carson's coach taught the same message. Even though Carson wanted to not be late, he had a habit of doing *just one more thing* before he left. This didn't work out well for him.

After he made the conscious decision to be on time and set timeliness as a standard, he set reminders and called the people in the carpool to make sure they'd arrive on time, taking into account traffic and other hiccups. Carson recognized that he couldn't blame others, so he made sure everything ran smoothly. He also asked me to be accountable on my end. He quickly realized that he could control my schedule better than those of the other parents, so he asked if I could drive everyone to practice, and the other parents could take turns driving them home. It worked, and Carson was able to keep to the standard he'd set. As a result, his teammates decided being on time was important to them as well.

Kids tend to act in their own self-interest. You need to align their interests with yours as well as with the world around them. This will not always work out perfectly. Voice your opinion kindly and directly but accept your child's choice. It might differ from your idea, but as long as these choices don't harm them, it's important to allow them to make their own decisions and learn to set their own standards for life.

MONITOR THE MEDIA'S EFFECTS ON YOUR CHILDREN

Parents can help their children set appropriate standards by providing guidelines that adjust with their children's development. One area where this combined approach is especially important is in the use of digital technologies. Digital screen technologies, in particular the cell phone that most adolescents possess, can cause difficulties such as neurological diseases, physiological addiction, behavioral problems, sleep loss, eye fatigue, headaches, and neck, back, shoulder, hand, and wrist pain.[7] The Centers for Disease Control notes that suicide accounts for 11 percent of teen deaths.[8] Risky behaviors centered on the devices that kids carry in their pockets can contribute to suicidal ideation. The time that might be spent on schoolwork and in-person socializing is now devoted to online activities like posting on social media.

The programs on electronic devices readily available today are designed to be addictive. Many apps are intentionally developed to hold one's attention and make one unaware of the passing of time. This is not a new concept. Las Vegas casinos have worked this way for years, pumping oxygen into the rooms and keeping the intensity of the lighting high. This keeps people gambling on through the night. These electronic devices aren't going away. The fact is they are becoming a necessity in our lives, so we need to teach our children to handle the potential for addiction.

In our house, we have a firm time of 10:00 p.m. when all phones are turned off for the night and placed in our room. This rule does not apply on Friday and Saturday nights. I allowed my boys to negotiate that time so they would learn to want to turn off their phones. Parents might consider having their children practice turning off their phones at a time the children themselves deem appropriate. If that sounds risky, remember that failure is a great learning tool if you ensure your child experiences the consequences.

---

7   Concordia University, Nebraska, "Examining the Effect of Smartphones on Child Development," February 28, 2020, https://www.cune.edu/academics/resource -articles/examining-effect-smartphones-child-development; "Smartphones and Health: How Your Cell Phone Affects You," *Ask the Scientists*, accessed February 8, 2024, https://askthescientists.com/cell-phones/.

8   Arialdi M. Miniño, "Mortality among Teenagers Aged 12–19 Years: United States, 1999–2006," *NCHS Data Brief*, no. 37 (May 2010), https://www.cdc.gov/nchs/ data/databriefs/db37.pdf.

The first time I let Conrad and Carson have their phones all night, my husband disagreed. He wanted them to be awake and alert in church the next day. As he predicted, the boys stayed up later than usual playing on their phones. Although they knew they couldn't sleep in the next day, they wanted to prove they could handle their phones, so they kept themselves alert at church. I also made sure we had a full day planned after the services, with no time for naps. Both kids went to bed right after dinner on their own.

I suggest that the first time you let your child keep their phone overnight you have an early wake-up time the next day and plan an activity they enjoy. They will experience the effects of sleep deprivation and associate them with staying up too late on their phone. We have all had to learn about the negative effects of staring at the blue light before sleep, and your child will learn this as well.

Another practice in our household is that we do not bring phones or screens to the dinner table. My husband and I model the standards we set for our children. When we converse with people, we put the phone down so that it does not prevent us from giving our full attention. We talk about phone usage with the boys whenever necessary.

A silver lining of Hurricane Maria was the three months without internet. My family played lots of nonelectronic games and just hung out with each other. The hurricane broke the established norm and made us appreciate life without the internet. Even today the internet goes out at times here in Puerto Rico. Each time that happens, my boys initially act as though their oxygen supply has been cut off, but they quickly adapt and start having fun with alternative activities.

When my sons were young, I paid for each of them to have a phone so I could better communicate with them. I made it clear that these phones were a privilege and that I would always set the rules for their use. Conrad and Carson could use the phones but on my terms. First and foremost, they were tools, not toys. When the boys grew older and bought their own phones, they both understood that they needed to make agreements with me about their use. Ultimately, our policies made sense, kept them safe, and prevented them from developing bad, addictive habits.

Family standards for our sons regarding the internet are based on the same standards for phone use: safety, respect, keeping their word, decency, and letting us know their whereabouts. My kids know my opinion: anything they see or post on their phone is public information and should be fit for printing on the front page of a newspaper. Kids today need to understand that what they share on the internet will follow them for their lifetime.

> Our children need to know that bad behavior on the internet has consequences and will follow them for life.

Today, many people have the tools to hack your emails, text messages, and phone calls. I emphasize to my kids that what they believe to be private on their apps and social media is not. There is no anonymity on the internet. Kids who are fooled into thinking they have privacy may participate in conversations they wouldn't normally have and visit inappropriate websites they think no one will ever find out they saw. Their curiosity, unfiltered and unchecked, can run wild and in a dangerous direction. Our children need to know that bad behavior on the internet has consequences and will follow them for life.

It is not unreasonable for parents to monitor what their kids are looking at and what they post. When my children were younger, they knew I would routinely look at all their posts, the social media content of others they were connected to, and their internet history. When I had their phones at night, I'd look at everything, including deleted information. My agreement with them was that I'd never share what I found with anyone other than them, and I would only ask questions or talk to them about things that could cause them harm. Frankly, there were only a very few times I spoke to my sons about what I saw on their phones. My role was not to interfere unless they asked me for advice or if I observed my children to be in danger, regardless of what I saw.

Conrad and Carson gave me the trusted advisor role, and I never betrayed their trust or confidentiality. They are both young adults now, and I don't monitor their phones anymore; yet I know they fully understand and agree that anything they look at, post, or follow can be observed by anyone and is never truly private.

At times, monitoring can catch and reduce the harm from internet bullying. Take it seriously if you suspect your child or anyone they know is being bullied. I know of a family whose son committed suicide because of internet bullying. Talk to your child about what they are posting and what they see posted. Others can post memes or messages about your child that are not true, and what your child posts can be taken out of context. Your kids can get tagged in pictures they don't like. Everyone has a camera, and it's easy to share pictures everywhere. I tell my kids to post less, keep their location private, and be careful about who takes a picture of them. It is sad that they must be so cautious, but pictures never go away on the internet. There have been instances where people didn't get a job interview because their potential employer did a Google search and discovered them in a compromising photo.

Some parents might try to forbid their children from joining a social media platform, but I feel this is just inviting them to do it behind their backs. In some cases, it might be better to allow your children to open an account and monitor it, with their permission. When my boys wanted to watch a movie I thought was not appropriate, I would not say no. In some cases, I would say they could watch it with me or their father. Then, if I saw something I thought was inappropriate, I would stop the movie and talk to them about what we were watching.

There was one time that Carson said he didn't want to watch a certain movie with me because he would feel too uncomfortable. I asked him if he thought he should be watching if he couldn't do so with his mom. Carson's answer was no, but he went on to tell me that his friends had seen it and he didn't want to be left out. I explained that the only way he could see it was to view it with me. Carson agreed, and we talked about what made him uncomfortable before we watched the movie. By sticking to our family standards while keeping our communication open, I was able to guide Carson to a good decision about a potentially tricky situation.

Parents can help their children understand that their digital lives are being recorded. They need to be aware of what is on the internet about them, untag themselves from questionable pictures, and monitor what is being posted about them. Social media is not all bad, but some people have tragically harmed the future of some teens. Do not let this happen to your child.

Chapter Summary: The Children's Influencers

- A parent is much more than a friend; a parent has unconditional love for their child and makes a choice to teach their child guidelines and standards.

- Stand guard over what your child is exposed to in order to prevent harmful concepts from entering their mind unexamined. Teach your kids to have a say about what they allow into their minds.

- Understand the top sways influencing your kids. You can find out what is influencing your child by taking an active role in their lives: know who their friends are, read what they read, watch what they watch, and be familiar with their activities.

- To ensure that you are your child's first influencer, use the eight-year rule: teach your child your perspective on topics eight years prior to when you think society will influence their perspective.

- Being tolerant means living in peace with someone you disagree with.

- Listen to the ambitious innovations, wild dreams, staunch views, and differing perspectives of your kids. Don't comment on them. Ask them to tell you more. If you simply listen, your child will have enough faith in you to share more.

- Each time you talk to your child, you must build a new connection.

- Allow your child to learn from mistakes when the stakes are low.

- Standards are what we want from ourselves and each other as a family. They are the basic level for which we hold ourselves accountable. An expectation is a belief that something should happen in the future. Set standards, not expectations, for your family.

- Encourage your kids to set standards for themselves, and then help them learn to hold themselves accountable for that standard.

- Kids today need to understand that what they share on the internet will follow them for a lifetime.

Exercises

Answer all the following questions individually, and then share your responses with your partner and kids when appropriate.

1. Sit down with your child and discuss the concept of standing guard over preventing harmful influences from entering their mind. Share your own personal experiences when you had to stand guard over your own mind and what that entailed. Discuss what could harm their minds and the consequences of those harmful images or thoughts.

2. Make a list with your child of what and who influences your child. Order the list from the most influential to the least. Be as specific as possible, and challenge yourself and your child to make a long, extensive list.

3. Create a list of important topics you feel strongly about or you want to be your child's first influencer on. Next to each topic write your beliefs about that topic. Share this list with your partner and your child according to the eight-year rule.

4. Learn more about your child's world, and work on building a new connection with them. Ask your child to pick an activity they are good at or enjoy doing and have them teach you about it. Spend time together doing that activity.

5. Discuss with the family what a standard is, how it applies to your family, and what you want your family standards to be. Make sure to include the unspoken, existing family standards. Have each member of the family write their own list of standards. Discuss everyone's standards and how the family will hold each other accountable.

CHAPTER 6

THE CHILDREN'S PASSIONS

IGNITE YOUR CHILDREN'S INTEREST IN ACTIVITIES

Building your children's confidence can start with building their passions. Working toward a positive first experience with any activity is one way to encourage early interest. I will never forget the time my husband asked one of our friends how they got their kids to enjoy skiing. At the time I found this question silly. I thought, *I like skiing. So I will take my kids skiing, and they will like it too.* By doing this, I have triggered their interest in skiing, right? This approach may or may not work. Charlie taught me that I needed to create a more effective strategy.

When I thought about it, I realized that I liked skiing because I'd had a fun and positive first experience. I wanted to create the same kind of experience for my sons. But I was unsure how to start. My friend suggested that we should start talking about skiing at home, sharing stories that made the sport sound fun and exciting. We followed this advice.

Next, we took Conrad and Carson shopping for ski gear. We made it a fun and positive family experience and allowed them to pick out their new ski clothes. They found crazy scarves and colorful ski helmets. Then, we made plans to take them to the slopes in March. I made sure that the weather would be excellent. After all, a positive experience must include a bright, sunny day with lots of fresh snow. It all went as planned, and the boys loved skiing and begged us to go again. Their passion for skiing was triggered from this positive first experience. Now, to be clear, some activities, no matter how good the experience might be, your kids simply won't like. Nevertheless, having your kids experience something new in the most positive way will help them develop an interest in the activity and create the potential for a passion.

Since I feel that children should learn to swim, I introduced my sons to the activity at an early age. We talked about swimming many times before we even entered the pool. I mentioned how swimming was like other activities they liked to do, such as playing in the bathtub. Once in the pool, I encouraged them to feel safe and comfortable in the water. I helped them overcome their doubts and fears about the activity by building their confidence and dispelling their illusions. These preparations for the first swimming lesson made a difference. My sons had a positive first experience with swimming and today are passionate free divers.

Not all first experiences turn out well, no matter how much you plan. The first time Conrad and Carson went out fishing with Charlie, they both became severely seasick. When I met them on the dock and saw their pale faces, I thought for sure they'd never go out on the open water again. Since Charlie and I enjoy fishing, we wanted our sons to be excited about it as well. It sure would have been easier to trigger their interest in fishing if that first trip had not been so rough.

However, it's important not to give up on the first obstacle. I talked to the boys about preventing seasickness and found some medication that would help. The next fishing trip they were prepared but still hesitant. So I went with them on the excursion to provide extra support and encouragement, while Charlie talked to the boat captain about going to a place that was calm and had fish to catch. With the attitude of not giving up, this fishing trip turned out differently. Carson and I both put our hooks into the water at the same time, and a minute later Carson was reeling in a fish, while my bait still dangled in the water. I took a picture of his fish, which was a keeper. Carson baited his hook again and—*wham!*—another fish. Again and again he reeled in the fish. All keepers. Conrad was doing the same thing all day long. Finally, I caught a tiny yellowtail snapper and had to set it free.

Carson took pity on me and offered to switch spots. "You're sure to catch one here, Mom," he said confidently.

Well, wouldn't you know it? Carson caught the biggest fish of the day in my old spot! This trip triggered a lifelong passion for fishing for my two boys because they had an enjoyable experience, they gained confidence in their ability to do the activity, and they kept an open mind that this time would be better than the last, even though they still remember that first trip and how sick they were.

There's no guarantee that your child will be passionate about any one activity, but if you set the stage for a great first experience, you have a fighting chance to ignite their passion; and if something goes wrong on the first try, persistence might be the key to sparking their interest.

I learned that igniting my sons' interest in any activity required the following:

- Do your best to prepare for a positive first experience.

- Find a way to give your kids confidence that they can do the activity, and make sure they have a positive attitude.

- Talk about the activity with your kids frequently before you go the first time.

GET OUT OF YOUR CHILDREN'S WAY

At times, your children's passions might require some thought and patience on your part. Conrad and Carson had a hankering to earn money at a young age. I almost always encouraged their natural entrepreneurial spirit. However, there was one time when I almost discouraged them from pursuing their goals. Fortunately, my neighbor helped me put things in perspective. We'd just bought a new washing machine. Conrad and Carson were fascinated by the large Styrofoam padding that had surrounded and protected the machine during shipping.

Their faces lit up when I gave it to them. They took it outside to play. After a bit, I checked on them and noticed they were having a ball creating sculptures. They proudly showed me what they'd made, and I acknowledged their creativity. It wasn't long before I received a call from a neighbor, Gladys.

"Kate, I just love what your boys did!" she exclaimed.

Not knowing what she was talking about but not wanting to seem out of the loop, I said something like, "Oh, how nice!"

"Yes, those two are just so creative."

My mind was racing, trying to catch up. "Uh-huh," I replied.

"I am so pleased to own their Styrofoam pieces to add to my art collection!"

Styrofoam art! It hit me. My boys had sold the sculptures they'd made from the packing material in our backyard to Gladys. I flushed red and was mortified.

"I'm *so* sorry," I said. "I had no idea. I'll stop them immediately and make sure they give back your money."

"Don't you dare," she said with a laugh. "I really love the works of art! Besides, one day they might be famous, and I can say I have one of their first pieces."

I thanked her and hung up the phone. My mind was whirling. Maybe it was okay. Or maybe it was better than okay. Maybe it was wonderful! I tracked Carson and Conrad down and took a closer look at their art.

It was actually pretty good. Very abstract, but quite creative. They'd put a lot of effort into it and had obviously done their best.

The boys shared their sales pitch with me and showed me the money they'd collected. I praised them for their ingenuity and sales ability. I realized that all those times they'd tagged along to our marketing meetings, they'd absorbed a few techniques. Watching their parents sell ideas to businesspeople had paid off, and now my sons were applying what they observed with success to their first business.

From this experience, I learned that sometimes you just have to get out of your kids' way. If they are on a path of their own choosing, let them continue (as long as it isn't dangerous). They will either learn by making a mistake or learn by having unexpected success.

> Sometimes you just have to get out of your kids' way.

If I'd followed my first instinct, I might have stopped them because I was embarrassed that they were going door-to-door selling the packing material from my washing machine. I was worried this might hurt my reputation in the neighborhood. Looking back, stopping them would have been silly and could have curtailed their entrepreneurial spirit. I would have robbed them of a beautiful learning experience and a victory, which most likely inspired them to be the excellent salespeople they are today.

HELP YOUR KIDS DISCERN WHAT THEY *DON'T* WANT TO DO

Our children may take to activities immediately, or they may decide what they are trying is not something they enjoy long term (or as interests change): both are learning experiences. When Carson took up metalsmithing, he sought out many experts to teach him what they knew. He got an internship at a metalsmithing shop and happily woke up at 6:00 a.m. each day to go to an unpaid job. Carson spent long hours moving heavy metal in an extremely hot environment practicing what he was taught. Even though he was physically exhausted at the end of each day, he enjoyed what he was doing. He loved learning this trade. For him, it didn't feel like work.

Did Carson plan to be a professional metalsmith? No. However, encouraging him to follow his passion will most certainly be beneficial to him in the future. It's hard to predict how, but the learning process was priceless for him. Kids need to figure out what they *don't* want to do in life as well as what they do want. By engaging in a variety of experiences of their own choosing, they discover what they want to do and will have a better shot at succeeding.

It seems that many kids have no clue what they want to do as a profession when they enter college. Some never figure it out, even by the time they graduate. But, because they must declare a major, most will pick something they think they will enjoy or that they think will make them money. Only when they start working do they realize they dislike their chosen profession. These kids will be either trapped in a job they don't enjoy or they will need to learn a new skill so they can quit and start over.

While college seems to be the acceptable next step after high school, not every graduate needs to go to college. I'd recommend that parents not force their children to go to college if they don't want to go. Let them choose. Times are changing. Many careers don't require an advanced degree.

When Carson was a freshman in high school, he had no interest in going to college. He preferred to get a jump-start in a start-up business. Charlie and I were supportive and told him it was his choice. Then when Conrad started receiving college acceptance letters, Carson began to ask questions. He interviewed a ton of people and concluded that the connections he would make in college would be invaluable. So he decided to go to college. Whichever path he chose, Charlie and I had his back.

Soon after this decision, Carson began to seriously consider becoming a sports agent. He loved sports and enjoyed teaching others how to manage their money, and the job combined both skill sets well. After all, how many articles have you read about major league athletes squandering the millions they make because they didn't know how to invest properly? Committed to learning more about the profession, Carson attended an introductory summer program at Boston College. He moved into a dorm room and attended daily classes. Very quickly he learned that sports management was all about contracts. To be successful in the field, you really needed a law degree, something that didn't interest him. If he hadn't explored this area, he'd never have known that he didn't want to pursue this field.

It's a good idea to encourage your children to try new activities at a young age when there's nothing to lose and they have all the time in the world to explore areas of interest. That way they can rule out avenues they *don't* enjoy and discover which possibilities they have a passion for. This allows your children to narrow down their options until they finally find something they ultimately love to do in life. Doing what you love in life brings happiness. People who do what they love are often successful. People doing what they are passionate about in life are not working; they are having fun.

You can help your child find their passion. Be sure you allow them to indulge in each activity for a fair amount of time before allowing them to give it up. It's been my experience that when a child wants to quit before he's given an activity a good try, there's an underlying reason. Find out what that reason is and work with your child to solve it so they can give the activity a fair shake. When my sons were young, they were on a T-ball team with a coach who was super emotional and passionate about the game. When both kids said that they wanted to quit the team, I asked many questions and learned that the coach often yelled loudly at everyone. I explained that was the way this coach felt he needed to teach and that they weren't in trouble. The coach was coaching. Conrad and Carson stayed on the team and enjoyed the rest of the season.

No one, child or adult, is an expert the first day of a new activity. Many people might not know that Michael Jordan didn't make his high school basketball team. However, Michael loved the game and had the grit to keep practicing. And now he's a legend.

It's important to note that while there is a time for a parent to push their children to try different things, one should only push so much. If, at the end of the day, your child doesn't really have a desire to try something, don't make them do it. Sure, you need to introduce them to activities on a regular basis, but your children must be willing to go for it and have a desire to gain that skill or knowledge.

REPEAT FOR MASTERY

When trying new activities and giving them an honest effort, children need to feel competent at it to stick with it. Competence requires repetition. By *repetition*, I mean *practice*. There is always room for improvement in our skills and abilities. For example, I'm always striving to be a better parent. I don't wish to repeat harmful patterns, but discovering them and weeding them out takes time, discipline, and practice. Breaking old patterns requires drilling in a replacement behavior or skill. One needs to continue practicing that until it's mastered. This holds true for learning new skills as well.

Carson was determined to give a TEDx Talk, which is a grassroots initiative created in the spirit of the popular TED Talk concept, an event where people present ideas about technology, entertainment, and design that are worth spreading. My son wrote a ten-minute presentation about something near and dear to his heart: why kids need more than school to succeed. It isn't easy to be accepted as a TEDx speaker. Carson needed to submit his concept, complete several interviews, and then be willing to practice with a coach. It was a yearlong process, one that had the concept of practice as its backbone.

I think Carson gave that speech a thousand times that year in preparation for the big day. He gave it to his family numerous times before he presented it to his church group, school clubs, friends, and the local Toastmasters group. He even gave his speech to our dogs. Then, six months before the event, he participated in his first rehearsal with other speakers. That rehearsal lasted two weeks because the moderators asked each presenter to repeat their speech many times. Eventually, the words flowed over Carson's tongue so smoothly that they were crystal clear. He could also play around with the speed of delivery and the nuances of emotion. By the time he gave the speech, it was flawless. His dedication to repetition made all the difference.

When a child is young, they have time to put in the hours. If they repeat what they wish to learn, they will master it in no time. Carson had a friend who was tired of sitting on the bench for every basketball game. He invited his friend over to practice since we have a hoop. I think the friend was at our house almost every day that summer, shooting hundreds of baskets. By the time the new semester started, he was ready. The coach noticed the huge improvement and made him a starter.

Let your children know that they probably won't always get it right the first time. Set a good example by giving yourself a break when you're learning a new skill. This will show your children how to embrace learning. Then as they battle through the growing pains of a new endeavor, give them words of encouragement.

TEACH YOUR CHILD TO BE A GOOD TEACHER

My sons were born to a pair of entrepreneurs who couldn't help but pass on the knowledge we had gained. They saw Charlie and me not only starting new businesses but also passionately helping various nonprofit groups. I think this might have contributed to their eagerness to teach others what they know. Encouraging your children to spread their knowledge helps others, and it helps your children become better at the pursuits they love.

Carson and Conrad first approached me to start a lemonade stand when they were five and six years old, and my first response was to sit them down to develop a business plan. That probably had something to do with the fact that, at that time, I was helping other entrepreneurs create their business plans. My sons spent a lot of time on their plan. Their focus and attention to detail, even at that young age, contributed to the success of that venture.

Years later, Charlie and I became involved with a national organization called Lemonade Day, which teaches life skills to kids by walking them through the steps of having a successful lemonade stand. In this program, each child finds a mentor and needs to complete a detailed workbook before opening their lemonade stand. Both Conrad and Carson jumped at the opportunity to play a role in helping grow Lemonade Day. They recruited their friends to participate and even gave presentations about their lemonade stand experiences.

In high school, Conrad convinced his school to let him start an after-school program using the national Lemonade Day organization's materials. So many kids signed up that he needed to recruit Carson to help teach. Conrad took the fourth, fifth, and sixth graders, while Carson took the second- and third-grade students. I coached them a little on how to present the material, and they took off running. My sons taught the kids everything they knew about how to set up a successful lemonade stand.

The kids loved the class and really enjoyed having their own profitable business. On the last day, the students all shared their results. It turned out that the children grossed an average of one hundred dollars in lemonade sales! It was clear that my boys changed the lives and futures of these children by sharing their ideas on how to start a business.

How do you know when a child really understands something? When they can turn around and teach that skill to another. As I shared earlier, Conrad and Carson asked to invite their friends to our ranch in West Texas. During the two-week visit, the kids worked in the morning and had fun in the afternoon. Each one learned to cook meals, do laundry, clean bathrooms, chop wood, and perform many other practical life skills. The children learned these skills through a buddy system. For each task, the inexperienced child was paired with an experienced one. The experienced child showed his buddy what he knew. This reinforced his knowledge and skill. I have to say that in the end, I didn't have much to do because the children taught each other.

Remember my friend Laura who taught her daughter, Kimberly, to play chess when she was four years old? By the time she was five, Kimberly was teaching other kids. One day at school, an older child interested in pursuing education as a career spent the day helping out in Kimberly's kindergarten classroom. Kimberly took the opportunity to teach the older child chess. When Laura came to pick up her daughter, the teacher told her that the little girl had lost the game after she'd taught the high schooler. Instead of dissolving into tears, she smiled and said, "I must be a good teacher!" Kimberly was proud of her accomplishment, as she should have been.

Teaching is an excellent learning tool because you can never really teach something you don't know well. When you successfully teach someone else how to do something, you know that you know your stuff.

CHANGE YOUR UNWRITTEN BIOGRAPHY

I have a friend who worked his entire life to get into the United States Naval Academy (USNA). Tom did everything expected of him and was accepted. He made it to his senior year and quit before graduating. He realized he did not want to go into the military and that he had gone to USNA to prove others wrong, not because it was what he wanted to do. That young man is not a failure, not by any means. Today, Tom is an extraordinarily successful entrepreneur. However, when he left the academy, many people called him a failure. Time proved those people wrong.

I believe it is especially important to teach our kids that the story of their lives will change. It will take twists and turns that they can't possibly imagine, and they don't have to follow the destiny laid out for them at the start of life. Our children should know that they are allowed to change their minds at any stage. Each day we wake up, we make choices. The choices you made yesterday aren't always the same choices you will make tomorrow. This means that you can implement changes and work to be a better parent. For your child, this means they can fail out of school one day and still go on to do something brilliant in the future.

One good example of this involves the emphasis put on SAT or ACT scores. We put so much pressure on our kids to score well on these tests. The better the score, the better the school they can attend. The better the college, the better chance they will get a good job when they graduate. That's the logic, but I think it's time to question that age-old wisdom. Too much importance is placed on tests that are essentially meaningless at later stages of life.

I know many people who took this path and then struggled to succeed in their jobs. Recently I learned that a friend had to fire an employee who had a Stanford undergraduate degree and an MIT master's degree because he was incompetent at the job. I'm sure the employee's SAT scores were through the roof and his theoretical assignments in school were exceptional; nevertheless, he had trouble actually applying his knowledge to his job.

> Success results from what you choose to do every single day.

Success results from what you choose to do every single day. It's a way of thinking and a way of life. A successful person has a mindset and a routine. They know how to fail, make mistakes, make bad choices, and get back up because they learned a valuable lesson from those errors. I often quote the adage "Insanity is doing the same thing over and over and expecting different results."

Remember, your child's past does not define their future, and their biography isn't set in stone. That goes for you, too. It's never too late to switch gears and make a change for the better. As parents, we need to lead by example. If you're in a dead-end job that you hate, make a change. Don't let golden handcuffs keep you imprisoned. Don't allow your biography to be written before you've finished living. If you continue to dream and are willing to take a leap of faith, your children might just follow your lead.

Chapter Summary: The Children's Passions

- There's no guarantee that your child will be passionate about any one interest, but if you set the stage for a great first experience, you have a fighting chance to ignite their passion; and if something goes wrong on the first try, persistence just might be the key to spark their interest.

- Get out of your kids' way; they will either learn by making mistakes or learn by success.

- Encourage your children to try new activities at a young age when there's little to lose and they have time to explore areas of interest. That way they can rule out pursuits they don't enjoy and discover which ones they have a passion for.

- People doing what they are passionate about are not working; they are having fun.

- Encourage your child to practice a new skill until it's mastered. Encourage them as they struggle through challenges.

- Give your child the opportunity to teach a skill they have to others. That will cement their confidence that they know their stuff.

- A successful person has a mindset, a routine. They know how to fail, make mistakes, make bad choices, and get back up because they learned a valuable lesson from that error.

Exercises

Answer all the following questions individually, and then share your responses with your partner and kids when appropriate.

1. Make a list of activities you are doing for your kids that they could be doing for themselves. Have your kids make their own lists. Compare lists and actively work on getting out of your child's way of learning for themselves.

2. Ask your child to share with you something they would like to master. Work with them to create a schedule to practice this skill. As your child improves, point it out and praise them.

3. Sit down with your child and write down skills or areas of knowledge that they feel they understand well. Help add subjects your child is knowledgeable about to their list. Find a subject they are passionate about and help them find someone to teach about that subject. After they teach the subject, find out what went well and what could be improved. Did they enjoy teaching?

4. Think about a time you switched gears in life and succeeded. What helped you to succeed? What was your biggest challenge? How could you have done things differently? What was your biggest learning from the change? Share your story with your family, and ask your kids to answer this question and share too.

PART III

FOCUS ON COMMUNICATION

CHAPTER 7

WORDS MATTER

CHOOSE YOUR WORDS WISELY

A few years ago, my husband asked Carson to do a straightforward task. He had to repeat the request several times because our son was ignoring him. Finally, Charlie got his son's attention and asked Carson to acknowledge him and repeat what he was to do. He did so. But then, Carson started doing something totally different than what he was asked to do. Frustrated, my husband stopped and jokingly asked our son if he was deaf, dumb, and blind.

This really hurt Carson's feelings.

While a child can do things that completely irritate you, Charlie learned that day that making offhand comments will almost certainly backfire. Instead of motivating Carson to listen and do the task properly, my son was provoked into responding, "At least I can play pinball!" Yes, the flippant response lightened the tension, but Charlie's comment didn't achieve the desired goal. Charlie apologized and acknowledged Carson's wit. Carson also apologized for ignoring his father. It was

Charlie's apology that ultimately got Carson to do what was asked of him.

> While the world can be cruel, parents never should be.

The words you say, how you say them, and when you say them significantly affect your kids. Inconsiderate words can make children become introverted and form a negative image of themselves. It's your job to help your children develop confidence. I have heard parents call their kids *bad*, *dumb*, *ugly*, and any number of hurtful labels. Some go so far as to claim that name-calling prepares children for the "real world." While the world can be cruel, parents never should be.

Related to this is the use of family nicknames. These can take an embarrassing situation or a bad habit and perpetuate it. Who can move on from such an incident when they are constantly reminded of it? While it might be meant to be cute, these names can leave a lasting scar on your child's self-image. I remember that as a kid I used to call my sister *Messy*. To this day she works hard to keep things neat and clean; however, she struggles with it. More importantly, she does not see herself as a neat person because she was never praised for being neat. She was chided for being messy.

Kids respond well to praise; we all do. Positive words inspire good behavior and just might leave a lifelong impression. The praise doesn't have to be directed at your children—they just need to be in the vicinity. For instance, when the boys were young and Charlie would hold the car door open for me, I'd say, "Thank you for the kind gesture of chivalry!" As a result, Carson and Conrad would hold the door open for me whenever they got the chance, and I'd always praise them for the kind act.

Realizing this was a kind act, they began holding the door for others. Conrad told me that he would race ahead of his classmates so he could hold the door open for everyone. The teacher praised him in front of the class, which I'm sure inspired the other students to do the same for others. Fast-forward twelve years. Carson and I were visiting a college campus. We were waiting for our Uber to come.

He asked, "Mom, how many minutes until the car is here?"

I looked down at my phone to check. "Um, five minutes?"

"Okay. I'll be right back."

He took off jogging down the sidewalk. I'll admit I was a little annoyed that he'd left me standing there, but as I watched, I saw he had a destination: an older couple. Carson carried their bags and helped them to where their Uber was picking them up. They beamed with gratitude.

When he came back, I asked, "What happened?"

"Those people looked like they needed help; they were struggling with their bags," he said. "They aren't from this country and weren't sure where to go, so I directed them."

As a young boy, Carson never missed the opportunity to hold the door open for me when his father or older brother weren't around. That kind gesture blossomed into an urge to help others. I have always been so proud of this.

Early on, Conrad learned that words have the power to encourage and help others; they can provide them with the energy needed to overcome major obstacles. We all possess this power to motivate others. One day Conrad and Charlie were hiking to the top of Pikes Peak with their Boy Scout troop. When they arrived at the meeting place at 4:00 a.m., they discovered that another troop was hiking with them. Unfortunately, this troop didn't appear prepared for the day, and this wasn't a beginner's hike.

The scoutmaster explained the difficulty of the hike and that no one would be left behind. If one person couldn't make it to the top, no one would. Instantly Charlie was concerned. Their troop had been preparing for this hike for months. The other troop, especially some of the dads, seemed out of shape, yet no one backed out.

As they began to walk, Conrad whispered to Charlie, "Dad, you need to think of words that will encourage and motivate this group! That's the only way we'll make it to the top."

Charlie smiled at him. "You couldn't be more right. Spread the word to the others in our troop!"

As the sun rose higher and higher, the elevation rose as well. The kids in my son's troop began saying things to encourage the others.

"We can do it!"

"Just a little farther!"

"This is great!"

"I think there are doughnuts at the top!"

They were almost to the top, and one dad was panting. "I don't think I can make it," he said.

Conrad, a bit winded himself, yelled back, "If you think you can't, you must!"

He told me that the out-of-shape father repeated the phrase, as did many of the other boys. When others in the group thought about quitting, the chant rang out through the group, and everyone kept going. This unlikely group made it to the top. Without those powerful words of encouragement, they wouldn't have even come close.

At the end of the day, it is the words we use, what we say, and what others say to us that form our beliefs. Be positive toward your children, reinforce their strengths, and point out what they are doing that is right, good, helpful, and positive. Give your children attention for the things you want them to do. Use positive words and praise them because *words matter*.

AVOID USING THE WORD *NO*

When my children were young, I'd volunteer at their school. I discovered that for me this was a wonderful proving ground for parenting. One day, I watched a cute little girl with her friends. They played together quietly, but every now and then, she'd scrunch up her face and say, "No!" while pointing her index finger at them or some offending object. She had a lot of fun with it. Although she had the appropriate tone you'd expect from a chiding *no*, her face was filled with cheerful glee.

I'll admit, I was a bit puzzled by this. Then her mother walked in. The little girl ran to her and hugged her tight. The mother bent down, smiled, and planted a loving kiss on her daughter's brow before asking her to get her things together. The child started to do so but got distracted by another lunchbox. The mother frowned and said, "No," pointing at the sparkly pink lunchbox in her daughter's hands. My hand flew to my mouth in a vain attempt to muffle a cry of astonishment.

The little girl was copying her mother's behavior.

The fact was, the girl had been doing that learned behavior all day. However, to the girl it was a game; it wasn't at all serious. Still, that incident drove home to me how important it was to always set a good example and avoid the word *no* whenever possible. After all, there were always other eyes watching me.

I like to emphasize what a child *can* do. For instance, let's say a child is kicking a ball in my living room, knocking things over. I might say, "You can play ball outside in the backyard." Notice that I didn't ask a question. I told them what I wanted. This sets the child up for success and gives them a clear rule to follow. Disney World does something similar. There, the signs say messages such as "Thank you for not smoking" or "Thank you for turning off your phone during the presentation." They are encouraging good behavior by assuming that you'll have good behavior. Their positive assumption about me makes me want to live up to their expectations; it makes me *want* to turn off my phone during the presentation. I am happy to comply.

I used this concept with my children. For instance, when they were young, I would say things like "Thank you for having such good manners. I know you will act appropriately in this restaurant."

As my sons got older and they'd ask me permission to do something

I felt I couldn't approve, I'd handle it differently. For instance, one time Conrad asked to go surfing by himself.

I responded with, "What's the danger involved?"

He thought about it. "I could get caught in a rip current."

"That's right. Anything else?"

"I could get hit by the board, and no one would be around to help me."

"So, what do you think?"

He paused and then said, "I could go with a friend. That would be a better choice."

"Sounds good."

I use this principle of avoiding using the negative word *no* with adults as well. For instance, if someone were to ask me to host a class party, I wouldn't just say no. I would tell them what I was willing to do. "I can donate the plates and cups for the event." If continued to be pressed to host the party, I would ask if there was something other than hosting the party that I could do. "What else still needs to be done?" Then I would tell them what I was willing to do, saying something like "I would be happy to bring the ice and drinks for the event" or "I could help set up for the event."

I recommend avoiding the use of the word *no* whenever possible. Of course, it is impossible to delete the word completely from your vocabulary, but that word places finite barriers and restricts people. It's better to state the positive or what you are willing to contribute versus what you will not do.

SHAPE YOUR CHILDREN'S STORY

Every person's life could be likened to a narrative, and like an author, it is the parent's honor and responsibility to help shape their child's personal story. Each child has a different path, as well as different strengths to draw on. I suggest that every parent have their child take the Clifton StrengthsExplorer assessment.[9] As parents, we need to discover and cultivate our children's innate talents and strengths. It is much easier to be amazing at something you have an innate strength for than something you don't. I found that the Clifton StrengthsExplorer "Top 3 Report" helped me understand which talent themes were strongest in each of my sons. With this knowledge I had the privilege of directing and narrating their paths.

One of the ways you can shape your children's story is through the language you use when you talk about them. You'll notice that when I write about my sons, I avoid negative words. It's important that you're always positive in your attitude and manner when speaking to them or about them to other people. Sure, they'll have weaknesses; everyone does, but if you really consider it, every negative trait you might detect in your child has a positive side to it. Seek these out and use them to your advantage, as well as your child's.

> Every negative trait you might detect in your child has a positive side to it.

As I mentioned before, although Carson is competitive, I deliberately didn't call him a bad loser. Yes, he really hates to lose, and when he was younger, he'd go through a range of strong emotions. Those outbreaks could be disruptive. When Carson plays football, there's no doubt that you want him on your team. He is powerful, a fighter, and will inspire his teammates to believe they can win. This is Carson's personality. He can't turn it off in practice. He will try to do more push-ups, do more pull-ups, and run faster than the other kids on the team. Coaches love his drive and passion.

Early on, I focused on teaching my son to lose gracefully because

---

9   The assessment is available from the Gallup store, at https://store.gallup.com/p/en-us/10093/clifton-strengthsexplorer?c=3.

I thought this was an important life lesson. I soon realized that I was wrong. Do we want our kids to become comfortable losing and feel it is acceptable to lose? No! We want our kids to be winners, so why was I trying to get Carson to embrace losing? When I had that realization, I changed my strategy and encouraged him to not give up until he won. In life, the games we play aren't over unless we say they're over. It's better to keep fighting each match, each battle, until you can score a win rather than concede quickly and "lose gracefully." As a result of my viewpoint shift, Carson stopped his outbursts of frustration when his team lost, but he didn't become less competitive. Today, he's still intense in his drive to win, and I applaud this attitude. That's a strength that will carry him forward in life, forging the way for him to succeed in all his endeavors.

Of course, there should be consequences for bad behavior. For instance, I'd remove him from the situation when he was acting up. He had to apologize many times for ugly words, inappropriate behavior, and poor sportsmanship as he worked to focus his anger on getting better instead of complaining or blaming others. Over time Carson grew to believe in the long-term game rather than focusing on the short-term loss. And he knew his mother believed in him and admired his passionate, driven nature.

When I speak of my son to others, I often use the term *driven*. It's a good, positive word that describes him well. What's interesting to note is that others have picked up on this word and will use it to describe my son too. Carson is now perceived as *driven*. He's often picked first for his sports teams because his teammates know that he'll never let them down. He has that reputation, and I had the opportunity to shape it. I'm proud to say that it has become a branding point for this young man. You have this opportunity with your children too. I could have branded him as a bad loser by calling him that. I refused to do so. Instead, I admired his drive and passion and focused my attention and words on these points.

As parents, we don't mean to give our children bad publicity, poor stereotypes, and insecurities; but if we're not careful, we can reinforce negative traits in our children, marring their reputation irreparably. It's never our intention, so we must watch our language and use our words as opportunities to shape their stories.

BELIEVE IT AND YOU CAN DO IT

One way we can use our words to shape our children's stories is through encouragement to believe in themselves. I once asked one of my son's friends to tell me three things he knew he could do without a shadow of a doubt. Jason shared the skills he had. I nodded and told him that he sounded confident about his abilities. Then I asked him to tell me something he would like to do but wasn't sure about.

Jason thought about it and said, "I'd love to run cross country at my school."

"Why do you doubt you can do it?" I asked.

"I've never done it before," was his quick reply.

I explained that just because he had never done it, didn't mean he'd be bad at it. "It just makes you less experienced."

Then I asked Jason if he was willing to work hard with the cross-country coach and gain experience. The boy nodded vehemently. Later I discovered it took him all of one cross-country practice to discover that he was a good runner. He just needed a little training and practice.

Every time I saw Jason after he joined the team, I would ask, "Are you a cross-country runner?"

He'd look me in the eye and say, "Yes!"

After several weeks of this routine, Jason asked me why I kept asking him the same question.

I smiled and said, "Do you believe you are a cross-country runner?"

He returned my smile, as he understood. "I believe. If I believe I can or if I believe I can't, I am right."

When you are encouraging and positive and truly believe in your child, there is no limit to what your child can accomplish. On the flip side, if you tell your child they can't do something, you crush that spark of hope before it can ignite. The world might chant the reality of the mundane and "realistic" goals, but we don't need more mundane adults. We need the next generation to have an imagination that can see beyond what is now so they can create a better future. Even if you have trouble believing in the impossible, keep it to yourself and encourage others around your children to silence those impulses to share how impractical their goals might be.

During Charlie's and my first year of marriage, we traveled the country in an RV interviewing successful entrepreneurs. We learned that these people tend to be surrounded by others who are supportive. These entrepreneurs had others in their corner who gave them encouragement and believed they could do what had not been done before. As parents, it's our job to open the world of possibilities for our children. It is our job to believe in their dreams and give encouraging words. Our kids have so much potential!

As I write the preceding words, I think about all the failures, mistakes, and wrong paths I took in my life. The fact that my husband believed in me gave me the strength to get back up, continue, and learn from the past. We have been successful together because we believe in each other. Charlie learned to be supportive from his parents, who gave their time and financial help when they had little to give. Today they continue to believe in him. While many times Charlie's father does not understand when he hears what his son is working on, his words are always encouraging.

Chapter Summary: Words Matter

- The words you say, how you say them, and when you say them affect your kids.

- Words have the power to encourage and can provide your child with the energy needed to overcome obstacles.

- Be positive toward your children, reinforce their strengths, and point out what they are doing right, good, helpful, and positive.

- Work to eliminate the word *no* from your vocabulary. Instead, focus on what your child can do and encourage them in that direction.

- Encourage your kids' good behavior by thanking them in advance for that behavior.

- Reframe your child's negative traits into positive strengths. This will help shape their story into something beautiful.

- As parents, it's our job to open the world of possibilities for our children. It is our job to believe in their dreams and give encouraging words.

Exercises

Answer all the following questions individually, and then share your responses with your partner and kids when appropriate.

1. As a family during dinner or a family meeting, talk about the words everyone is using. Are they positive and encouraging or are they negative and hurtful? Do your words build people up or tear people down? Decide to use positive and encouraging

words. As a family, help each other be accountable. Invite your children to correct you, and you correct your children. Slip-ups will happen; own it. If you feel it's appropriate, set a consequence that fits the offense and hold everyone to that consequence.

2. Think about the Disney way, thanking someone for a desired behavior instead of asking for a desired behavior. Example: Thank you for not smoking. Thank you for using the trash cans. Write down phrases you can say to your children and partner that are positive, encouraging, and get your desired outcome.

3. Write about your child, describing them to someone who has never met them. Be detailed, positive, articulate, and give elaborate examples. Focus on your child's strengths, giving examples of their successes. Challenge yourself to reframe any trait you believe to be negative. When could that trait serve them and others around them? Share what you have written with them and the family.

CHAPTER 8

OPEN DIALOGUE MATTERS

There are many tips and tricks for how to parent, but not all will be successful for you. The way to truly help your children and know what's best for them is to fully understand the world in which they live. To catch a glimpse of what your kids are thinking and feeling, you must communicate, listen, and observe. Communication, the exchanging of information, is a necessary way to understand your child's world. Listening and accurately receiving the information in the exchange is central to communicating effectively. Last, observing attentively over a period of time gives you valuable insight. Dialogue, active listening, and observation form three parts of an effective strategy for learning about your children and their world.

GET TO KNOW YOUR CHILD BETTER

One of the best ways to get to know your child when they are young is by asking if you can play with them. Join them in their favorite activities.

Do what they want to do, how they want to do it. You will get an insight into your child and their personality.

When Carson was little, he'd ask me to play with his action figures with him. He'd make up colorful stories and ask me to play the part of various characters. I'd move the characters the way he instructed and marvel at his creativity. His plays were always complex, and I found myself engrossed in the plot. Through these stories, I could see how his mind and imagination worked.

Conrad was quite different. He loved spending time building intricate train tracks. Those moments with him were filled with silence, but he'd direct me to put a piece he needed in a particular location. Then he'd push the train around the track saying, "Choo-choo." He knew the name of each train and corrected me if I got one wrong. Through these experiences, I learned how well he could build something he could see in his mind's eye and that he valued precision.

As my sons grew up, I continued to play with them and learned about what was going on in their lives. They confided in me what caused them angst and what brought them joy, as well as what their latest interests were. Through sharing these activities (of their choosing) I learned what influenced them and what their thoughts were on a variety of subjects.

I extended this philosophy to my sons' friends, wanting to get to know them and create a safe place for them to hang out. I filled my home with snacks the children would enjoy and then gave them all keys to the back gate and the code to our home. Since our home was so close to the school, some chose to eat lunch at our place. Sometimes Conrad would bring someone home. They'd play pool and eat; it was a good break from the routine.

When the kids got older, they'd sometimes park at our home and walk to school. My open-door policy was extremely popular, so much so that one day when Conrad's friend came looking for him and discovered he wasn't home, he sat down and chatted with me. We had a delightful conversation. The next time he came by the house, other children were there, and we all had a wonderful chat in the kitchen.

I kept my distance most of the time, as I knew my sons didn't particularly want their mother always joining their basketball game, but I enjoyed playing host and would offer water and snacks during their breaks. If anyone needed to talk, I was always available for them. When those children grew up and left for college, a few stopped by to say good-bye. That gesture was meaningful to me. I let them know that they would always be welcome—they could keep their keys and come back anytime.

LEARN WHAT YOUR CHILD IS THINKING

One year our family chose to visit Ecuador because this lovely country had an impressive historical and cultural heritage, as well as a variety of multicultural people we could meet. We were especially drawn to the indigenous market, which caught the attention of both my children with its bright colors and variety of merchandise.

One stall in particular caught Carson's attention and he asked to stop. The vendor displayed a wide variety of knives. Carson turned to me and asked, "Mom, can I buy that one?" My son was in kindergarten at the time, and I wondered what on earth he'd want with a knife. The word *no* was on my lips, but then I paused and asked, "Carson, why do you want the knife?"

"I want to have a knife collection to remember the wonderful places I have visited."

Surprised and pleased at the idea, I let him buy the knife. Today Carson has an amazing collection of knives from places he has visited. By controlling my automatic urge to say no, I was able to get to know my son better and help him develop a tradition. Too often, I can go on automatic pilot with my kids. I don't listen; instead, I react. I think I know what they're thinking. Sometimes I'm right, but many times I get it wrong if I don't ask. By understanding my sons' thoughts, I could appreciate their struggles and help.

Some children will not communicate their thoughts but just go about their life making decisions they feel are best for the situation. While Carson always made sure you heard him, Conrad didn't always speak up. I learned to ask the right questions and really listen to his answers.

One day Conrad asked me for a candy bar with nuts. Now, since I know he knows that he has a nut allergy, I was puzzled and asked questions to learn more.

"Why do you want this candy bar?" I asked.

"I'm going to give it to a friend."

"Which one?"

"George."

I was immediately confused because he'd told me the day before that George was mean to him. After more questions, I discovered that Conrad's solution was to give George a candy bar, hoping that would stop the bullying. Since I'm a big believer in allowing my children to solve their own problems in their own way, I let the situation play out. However, I wanted to be involved, so I encouraged him to give the candy to George in front of the boy's mother and me.

George's mother smiled and said, "That's George's favorite!"

I gave Conrad an encouraging nod, and he explained why he was giving her son the candy. The mom was horrified. She turned to George. "Is this true?" When George nodded, his mom immediately gave the candy bar back to my son. Then she turned to George and asked, "Why aren't you nice to him?"

Calmly George said, "Conrad needs to give me something if he wants me to be nice to him. That's how it works."

The mom asked more questions and discovered that George's older brother had demanded something from George in exchange for being nice, so George figured that was the way things worked. It was an eye-opening conversation for George's mom.

Conrad gave the candy to George and said, "You know I'm allergic. You take it. Please just leave me alone. Okay?"

George's mom nodded. She still looked a little shell-shocked by revelations about her children, but she seemed to understand Conrad's dilemma. She told George to stop picking on Conrad and encouraged Conrad to come to her if there continued to be a problem. I could tell that she and George would have a more in-depth conversation when they got home. She'd missed the signs, but it's never too late to turn things around.

I didn't know how things would work out when I suggested that Conrad give George the candy in front of his mom. I was pleasantly surprised by the civility of the encounter and admired her handling of the situation. She discovered how her son thought and could then take steps to help George. It's what I would hope I would do if I were in her position. In addition, I was able to empower my son to feel that he could do something about his own situation. He had a solution. I didn't rescue him. Through listening to him and supporting him, the situation was resolved.

USE QUESTIONS TO IDENTIFY AND UNDERSTAND EMOTIONS

Questioning can be an effective way to gauge the emotional welfare of your children. For instance, when a toddler is upset or angry for no good reason, it could be that they are tired or hungry. However, people tend to forget that these two factors still come into play as a child grows up. After all, how do you feel on those days when you have a full workday and forget to eat? Don't you get cranky? I know I do.

If you can help your child identify their feelings as they are happening, they will understand the effect their body has on their mind and emotions. Never *tell* them what they are feeling, though, as that won't be effective and can work against you. A child needs to be able to correlate their negative emotions with what is going on with their body without your input. If you do this correctly, the moment your child feels irrationally angry, they'll reach for an apple rather than a bat. Or if they recognize they are tired, they'll take a nap of their own accord.

If you don't teach them this connection when they are young, they are liable to throw temper tantrums as adults. Think about those poor servers who must constantly wait on hungry people. We've all seen those people who lose it because they didn't get the lemons they asked for or their food is taking a little too long. Perhaps they would act differently if their parents had helped them identify and control their emotions when they were young.

The first step is to help your child to put their feelings into words. When they want to eat, ask, "Are you hungry?" When they say yes, ask, "Do you feel other things with your hunger?" They might identify that they feel tired, but hopefully they'll identify that they feel angry or sad or something else. The next step is to ask your child, "Why do you think you feel that way?" This might take a few tries since they might not be able to link the pieces together. Be patient. Let them connect the dots and see the correlation. You might be tempted to answer your own questions, but don't. That will rob your child of the learning process and their own discovery that their body needs fuel on a regular basis. It will be far more effective in the long run if they see that they might have negative emotions when they are hungry.

Another important point is to never correct a child regarding their emotions. You can't possibly do so because they are *your child's* emotions. They own them, so only they can identify them. Accept any answer they give you. If it seems off to you, ask questions. The questions will help your child to eventually get to know what they are feeling. It's important that you include a discussion on how a person can change what they are feeling. For instance, if your child is angry because they are hungry, ask them how they might handle that. Guide them toward the answer that eating might alleviate the negative emotions.

I've also taught my children another tool that can help them control their emotions. I use it myself to help me feel happy. I tell my sons to put a smile on their faces. This will give them a sense of well-being. It doesn't always work right away, but it never fails to do the trick eventually.

As you work to help your children identify their emotions in a safe space, you can help your children learn to understand their emotions so they can ultimately accept what they are feeling. These skills will help them throughout life. Too many adults haven't properly learned to control their emotions, and that lack of control ends up harming them and others.

I don't always choose my feelings, and I can get overwhelmed by other people's emotions. When this happens, I'm aware of it and can change my feelings as quickly or as slowly as I want. I am in control. Teach your children that they can choose how to react to their emo-

> **Teach your children that they can choose how to react to their emotions.**

tions. The first step is for you to understand your children's emotions. Look and carefully observe. Why are they crying? What has happened to make them angry? What is the cause of their frustration?

If your child is very young, they won't be able to tell you what they are feeling. So you will need to observe closely to identify your child's emotions. That way you can understand better how they are expressing themselves. Avoid providing words to describe what you think they are feeling; don't correct them when you think you have a better word for their feelings. If your child says they feel a certain way, that's what's true for them and that's all that matters. I once had a friend's son tell me he was happy in a monotone voice and with a blank look on his face. For that child, that is what *happy* looked like.

If you see your child upset, it's best to take them to a safe, quiet space where they can calm down. Next, ask them what happened. Guide them to see the connection between what happened and their reaction. Ask your child to name the feeling they had at the time of the reaction, giving it a name. It's important to note that unpleasant reactions and emotions can be based on an unmet need, one that could possibly be fulfilled. Understanding what need is not being met can help you understand the emotion your child is experiencing. With that knowledge, you can then teach your child to name and eventually control the emotion by understanding the underlying reasons behind it.

We all know being *hangry* is a real thing. As a baby, Conrad cried only when he was hungry. Being hungry created strong emotions and the unpleasant reaction of anger. Because he was a baby, he could not talk and tell me he was hungry. I had to learn through trial and error. When he learned to talk, Conrad still had a strong, unpleasant reaction to being hungry. He didn't know why he was being unpleasant; he didn't know how to connect his reaction to a cause, and especially to a feeling. He would calm down after I fed him, and then I could talk to him about what had happened. I let him put words to his needs and label his emotions. I taught him to understand why he was feeling the way he was. I knew Conrad understood what I was saying when he explained, "Mom, I don't want to work when I'm very hungry, just like my toys stop working when they need new batteries." As Conrad got older, he learned to name the emotions he felt and knew the action to take to prevent an unpleasant emotional outburst.

Find the opportunity to have your child reflect on their feelings and ultimately know why they felt the way they did. Guide them to see how what they are feeling ties in with what they are experiencing. Understanding why they are feeling that way will help them be able to communicate and control their feelings. Finding an emotions chart online and having a printed copy handy might be one way to help your children identify what they are feeling at the moment. Have them point to what they are feeling and try to name it.

While you don't want to correct a child when they are giving you words to describe their emotion, you also want to encourage them to really explore the feeling. I've noticed some people will avoid answering the question by saying, "Good." This can mean *great, okay,* or even *not so good*. When my sons answer that way, I acknowledge them and ask for a second emotion.

What we are feeling at any given time is the emotion we are focusing on. Change your focus, and you can change what you are feeling. As a parent, you can help your child learn to change their emotional state. This is particularly helpful if you want to help your child move beyond any negative or strong feelings back to their normal state.

This is the process I have used successfully with my sons:

1. *What are you feeling now?* Have your child identify what they are feeling at that moment. Why are they feeling this emotion? Is there a need not being met? What does your child want to feel?

2. Invite your child to tell you about a time when they were feeling a positive emotion.

3. Ask your child to describe what was going on when they were feeling this positive emotion. To help, ask them to close their eyes and imagine themselves back in that place, feeling that emotion. Have them in their own words name the positive emotion.

4. Invite them to open their eyes and tell you what emotion they are feeling now.

5. If your child is feeling positive, or the emotion they told you, then they have been successful in changing their emotional state. If not, repeat the steps. The second time through, have them keep their eyes closed longer and concentrate on what they were doing and feeling during the positive emotion. The longer they can relive the event, the easier it will be to feel the emotion.

One thing that I've noticed is that when my children start to share a lot of details about what was happening in the memory, that's a sign that they are reliving that moment as if they were actually there. Often, I can tell that they're actually feeling the same emotions again. This is a simple but powerful exercise. I have used the preceding process only on older children. Yet changing the focus of a younger child can be easy. Even though the younger child does not have the words to express their feelings, you can redirect their focus, thereby changing their emotional state. Take a baby outside or give a toddler a toy.

Kids need to learn to name their feelings. This is important to understanding their own emotions and ultimately being able to process them. Start early with teaching your kids to connect words to their feelings. Ask them frequently to name what they are feeling. This process might not happen the first time you try it. Give it time. You may find that as your child gets older, they will improve. Even a slight shift in their ability to control their emotions is highly beneficial. At the very least, getting your child to name their feelings will help your child understand their emotions.

CREATE A SAFE PLACE TO TALK

Having the space and freedom for children to understand their emotions and solve their problems requires a feeling of safety. Who is at their best to solve problems when they feel unsafe and unheard? One day my friend Lizabeth came over. I could tell that something was weighing on her mind, so I poured her a cup of coffee, laid out some cookies, and encouraged her to talk.

"Promise you won't tell anyone?" she asked hesitantly.

"Of course," I answered with a quick nod.

Lizabeth has two girls: Sienna, age eleven, and Carry, age thirteen. These girls had been spending a lot of time with another girl, Wilma. Wilma was only ten but had discovered a new hobby: online pornography.

"I had no idea that someone that young could be interested in *that*," Lizabeth said with a shudder.

I was surprised too. "How did you find out?"

Lizabeth let out a ragged sigh. "Carry finally confided in me. She was having headaches, and I couldn't figure out why. We went to the doctor, and everything checked out."

"What do you think was causing the headaches?"

Lizabeth paused and then looked me in the eye. "Keeping secrets from me."

I knew my friend, and she prided herself on having an open relationship with her girls. Like me, she did everything she could to create a safe space for them to come to her.

"How did you respond when she told you?" I asked.

"I did my best to keep my cool, but I can tell you, my insides were churning."

"Did you get angry at them?"

"Of course not," she responded. "I know that's not going to help anything."

I nodded. "So how did you leave it?"

"I thanked her for telling me, and we talked about other things."

I bit my lip and paused, giving her a tentative look. "Would you like to hear my thoughts?"

"Sure," she said with a relieved look. "I could use a sounding board."

"Well," I began, "I think Carry might have more to tell you. Did her headaches go away?"

"Not completely."

"It's just that there's a lot of nasty stuff out there. It might help if you talked to *both* of your daughters and continued to make it safe for them to share everything with you. And I mean everything. You must be willing to hear it, though. It will probably shock and disgust you, but you can't let them know that it does."

Lizabeth nodded but looked like she might be sick. "I can't believe my little girls were exposed to this stuff. I'm so careful!"

"It's out there," I said, feeling heartbroken for my friend.

A few days later, Lizabeth asked if she could come over again to update me. I readily agreed, put on a fresh pot of coffee, and waited. She arrived within twenty minutes.

After a few niceties, I asked how the conversations had gone. Lizabeth looked to be on the brink of tears. "Oh, Kate, you have no idea!"

I cringed as I watched my friend struggle.

"Tell me," I said quietly.

Once she started speaking, the floodgates opened. Apparently, Wilma had been watching porn for a few years, meaning she'd started around age eight. She'd discovered every kind of deviant video that was available and had shared them with Lizabeth's girls. My friend said Wilma was acting out some of the porn scenes with the girls, forcing them to do sexual things to her. I sympathized with my friend as she emotionally recounted this story. I nodded silently, letting my friend get out all the horrible details before I said anything. We cried together for their loss of innocence.

"Did you tell Wilma's mother and father?" I asked.

Lizabeth nodded. "Yes, I sat down with them. It was hard, but I knew they needed to know. They were in disbelief and stunned at first, yet they knew something had been troubling their daughter. We talked and we cried. In the end, they said they were going to get their daughter help."

"That's all you can do," I said. "Are you going to get your daughters help?"

"Yes, and each of my girls is quite different. Consequently, the help each of them needs will be very different, too. It's most important for me to listen to them and cater to their needs. I know I'm moving in the right direction because my daughters are feeling better. We've had many conversations since you and I talked. Each time they share additional details. The more they talk about it, the better they feel, and they seem more like themselves."

"Keep inviting more discussion."

"For how long?"

I smiled. "As long as it takes. There's no time limit. Let them continue to tell you about it until they're done."

Lizabeth nodded. "You're right."

By creating a safe place for her girls to come to her with their problems, Lizabeth was able to help them. She sought to understand their world. It must have been hard for Carry and Sienna to share such horrible events with their mom and extremely hard for Lizabeth to listen to what her daughters were saying. Yet through love, compassion, and understanding, this mother was able to get her children help and relieve some of the trauma they experienced.

Life is complicated, and you can't expect your child to tell you much of anything if you make them feel wrong or punish them the moment they tell you something you don't want to hear. If you do this, they will stop talking to you, robbing you of the chance to talk to them about the choices they made and what they were thinking when they made those choices. By taking punishment off the table, you will help them reflect on what happened and learn from their mistakes so they won't repeat them.

The goal is that your kids will come to you for help and advice. They will only do so if they know that no matter what they tell you, you will not freak out, get angry, or judge them. They need to trust that what they tell you is confidential. Confidential until the day you die. I call this *a safe place to talk*, and it is one of the best gifts you can give your child.

It can be difficult to do this. You might want to jump in and do something with the information they share. You might be tempted to use what they tell you later to prove a point when you are trying to guide them. Don't. It will harm your ability to build trust.

A safe place to talk means that your kids can tell you anything without the fear of being disciplined or having their words thrown back at them later. Keep your goal in mind—to help your children learn from their mistakes. Children will begin to recognize their bad behavior and what they could have done differently to change that behavior. If you do it right, they will start recognizing how these talks help them make better choices.

FOSTER CHANGE BY SAYING
WHAT IS UNSPOKEN

Naming unspoken emotions is one part of the process of learning to speak the truth of our experiences. As I've mentioned before, making mistakes is part of life. It is how we learn. Naturally, nobody likes to admit they made a mistake. However, you can't learn from your mistakes if you hide them. You will not grow or change for the better until you speak the truth, until you say the unspoken. This is true for children of all ages; however, it really comes into play with teens, who generally don't like to share things with their parents.

To get your kids to talk frankly, openly, and honestly with you, start by talking to them in the same way. Set the example. Don't worry that what you share will be too much for them. Most likely your teens aren't as sheltered as you think and have been exposed to more than you realize. The more honestly and openly you can talk to your child, the more trust and respect you will build with them. I tell my sons about what I did in high school and what I learned from my experiences. I tell them about the things I would never have told my parents at the time I told my kids. These stories serve as excellent cautionary tales. I want them to learn from my mistakes and not have the idea that I was perfect. No one will want to confide in a perfect angel.

In the spirit of open and honest communication, I've made the agreement that they also share with me what's going on in their lives. Everything. This has not been an overnight process. Like most kids, they tried to hide their mistakes in the beginning, but over time they have learned the truth is a better route to take. They understand that they will always get caught; it is just a matter of when.

In the case of Lizabeth's girls, she discovered she really needed to pry. Often you need to dig and push to get the answers. In her case, dealing with such a sensitive subject, the truth needed to be revealed in layers. It's a bit like peeling an onion. It was too much to expect her girls to confide all the gory details in one sitting. It took Lizabeth a few months for her girls to disclose everything. She worked to provide a safe space, understood the needs of each girl, provided the needed help, and allowed them to tell her anything.

It is helpful to remind ourselves that since every child is different, some are more likely to talk than others. For instance, Conrad never seems to think his problems are worth *bothering* anyone about, and many times he prefers to open up to Charlie. I never let my ego get in the way, because the most important thing is that Conrad has a trusted advisor. His father always takes the time to sit down with him and offer a safe space to take a bit of the weight off Conrad's shoulders.

My sons know that I have a good idea about what's going on in our environment because the moms in our group share information about their kids. So I know things like who is having a party, whose parents are going out of town, who got into a fender bender, who stayed out too late, and so on. I tell my kids what I heard in the chats, and this opens the door for them to share the rest of the story. I stress to my sons that the consequences will be less severe if they tell me what happened as opposed to trying to hide it. I remind them that I will probably find out later anyway. In addition, I promise to work with them to figure out how to make the situation better. That way they get the benefit of my experience, if they want to listen to it.

My boys and I have an agreement that we do not share with others what we talk about. I do not even share things they have told me with Charlie unless I get their permission. If they do not want me to share and my husband asks me a question about a situation they confided in me, I tell him that it's not my story to tell and that he should go talk to Carson or Conrad about it. This agreement gives my children the confidence that they can safely share their stories. Every story that has appeared in this book is here only because my family gave me their blessing.

CLARIFY AND VERIFY

Early on I established a *no-secrets* policy in our home. That means I can look at my sons' phone history anytime I wish. I also can walk into their room when they aren't there because I need to put clothes away or store a few things in their closets. I also give them the same privileges. They can look in my purse, on my phone, and walk into my room whenever they wish. We all knock first if we are home. If we have no secrets, there shouldn't be a burning desire for privacy. My purpose is strictly to protect my sons. I'm not interested in snooping, but I need to know what's going on in their lives.

The idea that if we have no secrets, there shouldn't be a burning desire for privacy became clear to me when my sister came to live with my family after she finished an inpatient drug rehabilitation program. I was given lengthy instructions and advice on how to help my sister reenter everyday life. I thought I was following the instructions. I told her the house rules and what I expected. She also asked questions and made sure we had the same understanding. She added to the rules that I was to respect her privacy just as she would respect my privacy. No one would go into anyone's room without explicit permission.

Then one night I happened to wake up several times, and she was awake each time too. Another day I happened to be driving by the NA meeting she told me she was going to and did not see her car. She stopped eating dinner with the family, and she started to avoid me. I suspected something was off. I stayed up until she came home that night at 2:00 a.m. I told her we would have a conversation in the morning. The next morning I canceled everything I had planned for the day and waited for her to come out of her room. I sat down with her and asked what was going on. I asked if she was using drugs again. She said no. I went over the house rules with her, and this time she told me she would not live by my rules. She chose to leave. The next day I went into her room to clean and found drug paraphernalia. I trusted but I did not verify. I gave privacy to a person who needed supervision. I failed.

Kids need supervision. Kids experience more challenges today than they did when we were young. Not all of them have the skills to navigate the mental, physical, emotional, or environmental stresses they encounter. Yet often children don't know who to ask for help to get through these challenges, and some aren't even aware that they need help. The result can be tragic.

For example, my friend Penelope had a son who began withdrawing from friends and family. Penelope noticed that he was less talkative and asked him about it. He only told her that he was having a hard time at school. My friend offered to step in and help, but he begged her not to do anything, as that would just make the situation worse. She respected his request, assuming it was the normal high school stuff. One week later the child committed suicide. It turned out that Penelope's son was being bullied. The kids that knew about the bullying didn't say or do anything, and since her son didn't open up to her, Penelope had no idea how bad it had gotten for him.

Of course, we can't stop all bad things from happening to our children. But this experience taught me that ignorance of what was going on could put my sons' lives on the line. That is a risk I am unwilling to take. It is our duty as parents to decipher what is going on in our children's lives. Sometimes they don't know how to communicate. They are still learning to identify and understand their own emotions. Parents need to use their communication skills and emotional intelligence to uncover what is not being said and get their children to talk. If you feel you don't have the skills and emotional IQ you need, then seek help—for yourself and your children. As much as we think we know what is going on in their world, we must constantly strive to understand even more.

To keep up to date with my kids' lives, I do what I call *clarify and verify* to figure out what is going on. If I don't know, I'm helpless; when I know, I have a fighting chance to help my children.

To *clarify and verify* means to play detective to get the full picture of what's happening with our children. We often think we understand, but we have limited data; we can't possibly know what is going on, and we can't expect our kids to tell us everything. They might tell us what they think is important, but children sometimes don't know what they don't know. It can be hard to teach if we aren't aware of the problems. *Clarify and verify* does not mean criticizing or second-guessing every choice your child makes. It means to make sure they aren't in danger and to provide advice, whether they take that advice or not. *Clarify and verify* is not to save your child from the consequences of their actions or to give more consequences because you do not agree with their actions. You do it not because you do not trust them but because they are learning. You want to teach the most pertinent and relevant topics before they need the wisdom. You want to provide wisdom and knowledge to your child before they make their own life choices.

The key is to start talking to your children, their friends, their friends' parents, their teachers, their coaches, and everyone in their lives. Here are some activities you can do to set up a good foundation for open communication and learning:

1. Make family dinner a priority so that the family can get together and share the events of the day. I changed my schedule to match up with my kids' schedule. Sometimes that meant I was eating dinner at 8:30 or 9:00 p.m.

2. Go to your children's activities and talk to the other parents. You'll learn about the drama happening at school. Then ask your children to fill in the gaps. It's not gossiping but clarifying and verifying what's going on in your child's life.

3. Ask questions about your children's education, school, and grades. Make it a point to pick up your kids or go to school for any reason. Find ways to bump into teachers. Don't do this to simply check up on grades, as grades aren't everything. However, monitor any drastic change in grades and find out why there is a change. Find out if your children are happy at school, with the work they are doing, and if they are doing their best.

4. Get your children talking about their friends, and spend time with your kids and their friends. Have your children describe their buddies and tell you about their hobbies. Invite their friends to your house or on a fun outing and go with them. Take a group of your children's friends out to dinner after a sporting event or buy them ice cream after school.

You clarify the information you get from your children by asking questions. Hard questions. Questions that will give you a clear picture of what's going on. Since you may only have a short amount of time to decide whether your child can participate in an activity, you'll want to ask the most revealing questions about who they are going to be with and what they are going to do. Here's an exchange I had with Conrad:

> Conrad: May I go out with my friend John?
>
> Me: Where are you going and who are you going to be with?
>
> Conrad: John and I are going to the park. He wants to play some pick-up b-ball.
>
> Me: How are you getting there?
>
> Conrad: We're walking.

Me: Together?

Conrad: First, I'm walking to his house. Then we're going to the park together.

Me: This is a new activity?

Conrad: Yeah. He asked me because I'm tall and he doesn't want to go alone.

Me: Remind me, who is John? Where does he live?

Conrad: He lives across from school. He's the kid who teaches basketball to your friend Jill's daughters. He's also dating Jen.

Me: Is he nice or a "cool" kid? How would you describe him?

Conrad: He's nice to everyone, but some of his friends are the "cool" kids. They don't play basketball with him at the park.

Me: How long has he been dating Jen?

Conrad: I don't know. . . . Four or five months.

Me: Are they having sex?

Conrad: Mom, I don't know.

Me: Do I know John's mom?

Conrad: Yes, she's Beth.

Conrad: Mom, I'm going now.

Me: Okay. Have fun.

In the preceding exchange, Conrad wanted to go play basketball at a park with John, a teen he didn't regularly hang out with. He wasn't really *asking* me if he could go, because he knows he can go to the park and play basketball with his friends. However, he wanted to keep me informed. I let my kids plan their lives within limits. One limit is that they must always tell me where they are going, and they must always tell me goodbye when they leave and hello when they get home. Conrad was doing that. In this situation, things seemed a little out of the norm, so I asked questions. I only had a short amount of time to *clarify and verify* what was really happening.

Having no reason to suspect anything, I was looking to get the rest of the story and enough information to make an educated decision about the situation. I clarified how he was getting to the park and if he was walking alone or with John. I also asked for references on John by asking the rest of the questions. Learning what my son thought of the teen told me a lot. It also helped that I'd seen John give Jill's daughters basketball lessons.

While this was a pretty straightforward situation, I will also ask the questions no one wants to ask. Like the prying one about John's girlfriend. You never know what the answer is going to be. The point is to start asking taboo questions so that your kids will think that any question is normal and expected. I let Conrad go to the park with John. Even if I had gotten no good verification about the nature of John, I would still have let Conrad go. Then I would have done a verification drive-by of the park. Sometimes even when I do not suspect anything, I do a verification drive-by, drop in, or cross-reference phone call.

Clarify and verify means that you let your child make decisions for themself, yet you clarify what the decision is, and you verify that your child made a safe decision. They are learning, and they need to be able to explore and try new things. They will sometimes make bad choices. You just need to keep them safe. There is a fine line that parents must walk: letting kids have the freedom to choose their own path and learn while keeping them safe from things they might not understand. Most of the time, my sons never saw me verifying, yet they always knew I was.

There are a lot of ways to check up on your kids without letting them know what you're doing. Talk to other parents. Find out how your kids are doing when they are at their friends' homes. Show up at their sporting practice unexpectedly. Go to the games. Observe your children. Talk to the other parents and to the coach. Ask questions that relate to your kids. You never know what you will find out. *Clarify and verify* also means you know the stories of the kids your child is hanging out with. They are a part of your child's life, so you need to know about them as well. Make sure these friends are telling you the truth.

It's a good idea to apply this concept to your children's medical issues as well. Most parents take their children to the doctor for an annual checkup, but you still need to ask your children questions and make sure your kids are facing whatever is going on. When my boys were young, they had a lot of questions about their bodies. Some things I could answer, and others we'd bring up to the doctor during their wellness visits. By arming them with questions and making sure they knew what to expect at the doctor's visit, I made sure they could take an active role in their well-being. I also made sure to always be an advocate for my boys if I felt the doctor wasn't giving them the time they needed or wasn't listening to their questions.

I feel it is important that my sons know our family medical history, as that can play a part in their health. Whenever possible, I allow them to be a part of the decision-making process. When Conrad had serious acne, I gave him three choices: to buy over-the-counter medication, to get regular facials, or to see a dermatologist. Conrad chose the last option and was pleased with the outcome.

When clarifying and verifying, the questions you ask shouldn't be like an interrogation—it's a two-way street. Use the questions to engage your children in conversations. Don't just accept *good* as the answer when you ask them how their day was. That's when you ask, "What does *good* mean?" You want to find out what they are really thinking and feeling. Only then will you have enough information to help and guide them if they need it.

Chapter Summary: Open Dialogue Matters

- Learn to ask the right questions and listen to the answers. By understanding your children's thoughts, you can appreciate their struggles and help them.

- Create a safe place for your child to share anything. A safe place to talk means that your kid can tell you anything without the fear of being disciplined or having their words thrown back at them later.

- Help your child learn to correlate their negative emotions with what is going on with their body by asking questions. Guide them to see how what they are feeling ties in with what they are experiencing.

- You can help your child learn to change their emotional state.

- Change your focus and you can change what you are feeling.

- Grow for the better by speaking the truth—saying the unspoken.

- To get your kids to talk frankly, openly, and honestly with you, start by talking to them in the same way. Set the example.

- It is our job as parents to decipher what is going on in our children's lives, and if your child has no secrets, there shouldn't be a burning desire for privacy.

- *Clarify and verify* to figure out what is going on. Find ways to make sure your kids are doing what they tell you they are doing. If you don't know, you are helpless; when you know, you have a fighting chance to help your child.

Exercises

....

Answer all the following questions individually, and then share your responses with your partner and kids when appropriate.

1. Set a recurring time to spend quality one-on-one time with your child. Allow them to pick the activity and permit them to direct it. After each activity write down your insights and observations. What surprised you? What did you expect versus what you experienced? Note: During these quality times with your child, really listen to your child. Refrain from doing most of the talking. Instead, encourage your child to tell you more. When they pause, try pausing as well.

2. Think about times you have used the word no. What could you have said instead? Consider whether you could have allowed your child to do the action. Write down various scenarios, including the positive words you could use and what activities you could permit. What will you do the next time you want to say no?

3. Write a letter to your child. Express how much you love them. Next, add why they can come to you for advice or just an ear to listen. Make it clear that you are going to keep what they say confidential and that you will not judge or punish them. Tell your child that what they say to you will not ever be used against them in the future.

4. Talk to your kids about your unspoken stories. Write out a few personal stories and anecdotes about mistakes you made in your past that might serve as cautionary tales for your child. If you can, include parts you never told anyone about and

how you handled the problem. Include what you learned and things you'd like your child to learn from your mistakes. Share those stories with your children. Ask your child to share a story with you.

5. Write down your foundation for open communications with your kids, a no-secrets policy. Determine, with your partner, what your family's no-secrets policy entails.

6. Write down some activities you can do with your child that will foster communication. Implement what is possible. Here are ideas from the book:

    a. Make family dinner a priority.

    b. Take your child to school and/or pick up your child from school.

    c. Take your child out to a restaurant.

    d. Attend your child's activities with them.

    e. Create new family activities.

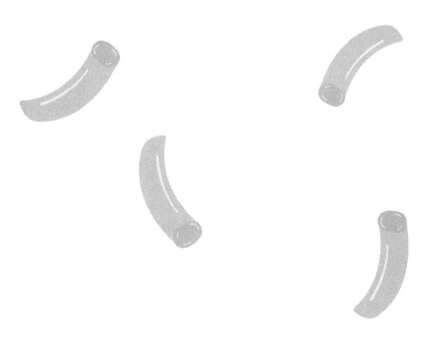

PART IV

FOCUS ON CREATING ORDER

CHAPTER 9

BEING A BENEVOLENT RULER

EMBRACE YOUR INNER RULER

My friend Anne is what I'd call a *fun mom*. She always says yes to her kids, and they love it. I asked her why she did this and she said, "Why not?" Her kids were always ordering milkshakes at restaurants and had the run of the house. No boundaries.

One day she called me from inside her locked bathroom.

"Kate, I can't take it anymore."

"What's happening?"

"My kids want to go to the park, but I can't. The plumber is coming in the next few hours."

Anne had lost control because she never had control. Since she always said yes to everything her kids asked, she now had a couple of rebels on her hands.

"Anne, bring them over here. I'll take care of them while you take care of the plumber."

She was grateful, and her kids were excited to have a playdate with my sons. The first thing I did was sit down with all the kids and lay out some rules and boundaries. I explained that I must be told when they were going into the backyard before they walked out the door. I stressed that this was a safety rule and that there were no exceptions. Then I let the kids know that if my rules weren't followed, they wouldn't be allowed to play in the backyard. I had all the kids repeat, "I must tell you before I go outside." Then I left them to play hide and seek. I began to bake cookies.

It wasn't long before I heard the back door open. I went to investigate and found that Jack, one of Anne's sons, had gone outside to hide on the patio. Just then, he came running back inside to go to home base. I gave Jack a stern look and then walked over to him.

"Come with me," I said.

Jack followed me to the kitchen and I sat him down. I sent the other kids to play in the backyard and put the cookies in the oven.

Turning back to Jack, I asked, "Did you go outside?"

"Yes."

"What was the rule about that?"

"That we should tell you first."

"I didn't hear you ask me to go outside, but I saw you go."

"I was just on the other side of the door. I didn't think that counted."

I shook my head. "It does. When you walked out that door, you were outside."

"But I'm inside now."

"That's true. But, Jack, you broke a rule, and now there is a consequence."

"Okay. But can I go play with the other kids outside?"

"No. You broke the rule, and the consequence for that is that you can't play with the others in the backyard."

I never raised my voice, but he looked startled.

"You'll need to sit in that chair until you can tell me why you aren't allowed to play outside with the others."

I stood up from the table and went over to clean off a counter, giving Jack a little time to think things over.

He began to cry. "I want my mommy."

"I'm sorry, but she's busy. When she's done, she'll pick you up."

I then sat next to Jack and asked him if he wanted to talk to me. He said no. I asked him if he wanted me to stay with him or walk away. He said nothing. I looked at him again, smiled, and made a joke. He laughed and stopped crying.

Once he was calm, I explained that I was teaching him about consequences, and he was learning about life. He seemed to understand. We talked; I asked questions and he answered, he asked questions and I answered. In the end, Jack knew that in my house he was going to be heard and held to his promises. He learned that rules had to be followed or consequences would happen. The other boys came in, and I gave Jack a chance to let everyone know what he'd learned, including that when I say something, I mean it. He said, "I broke a rule, and rules have consequences." I told Jack that he learned a lot very fast and that I was proud of him. Then I announced to all the kids that the cookies were ready.

A parent must learn to be comfortable being the ruler, the boss, and even the dictator of their domain. This may not come naturally to all parents, and if that's the case with you, I recommend that you practice until it is grooved in. It is a vital concept to master. Setting this standard is important because children require boundaries, for their physical and emotional safety. They need to learn what is acceptable and what isn't. Parents who are wishy-washy relinquish their authority. Being a strong leader doesn't mean that you should never listen to your children or that you should exclude them from parts of the decision-making process.

Listening and inviting their input is an important part of parenting. However, there is an appropriate time and place for back-and-forth communication. When my sons were in elementary school, they had a fourth-grade teacher who would hold up a remote control and pretend to push a button on it while saying, "Volume off." Every child in her class would immediately be quiet. She had successfully taught these students that she was in control.

This teacher made a point of inviting each of her sixteen students to lunch with her, one-on-one, at least once during the school year. During that time, she would give them the chance to talk about anything they wished to discuss, and she would listen attentively. I believe this custom had a lot to do with why she was such a successful ruler of her classroom. By connecting with each child, she built leverage to motivate and inspire them. She genuinely appreciated their world, and they were willing to talk to her openly. This teacher gained the respect of all her students, their parents, and the school administrator.

Our children need to learn when it is appropriate to ask questions and speak up, and when they just need to follow orders without question. It is tempting to yell back when our children are yelling, to be sarcastic, to use foul language, or to act like they do. However, this does not demonstrate our maturity, and we will lose our authority. Our children need to know, without any doubt, that we, the parents, are in charge.

Along those lines, it's wise to curb the impulse you might have to *ask* your child to do things. That gives them an option *not* to do what you need them to do. Instead, embrace your inner dictator and *tell* your children what to do. When I was little, I taught my mother this axiom well. Early on, she asked me, "Would you please wash the dishes?"

"No, thank you!" I replied.

This response got many laughs from my family but not the desired action. My mother learned to say, "Go wash the dishes." And then she amended that to say, "Thank you for going to wash the dishes." No option. No discussion.

If your directions are met with continual why responses, consider how you approach your directions. I think our parents had it right when they replied, "Because I said so." It tells the child that right in the throes of a situation isn't the time or place to debate an order. There is a time for your kids' input, and there is a time when they need to just do what you say. My sons know when I respond with, "Because I said so" that they need to do what I said and now is not the time to ask questions. Nevertheless, they know also that they can wait until an appropriate time to ask why and I am happy to explain. This isn't to say that you can never phrase your order as a question out of a sense of politeness if that is more your style. That can work, as long as your child knows it is really an order and not a request that can be declined.

CREATE GOOD RULES FOR YOUR CHILDREN

Rules should never be made on a whim. If you make a rule, stick to that rule while your child is following it. Only change it on your terms when the rule is outdated or not working. If you change your mind midstride, your orders will lose their effectiveness and you will lose control; your child's new expectation will be, "Mom will change her mind if I push hard enough." Your kids will only follow the rules they want to follow when they want, which is detrimental to your ability to lead them into the future.

I do my best to think of all the possible circumstances that could come up ahead of time. Charlie and I will often discuss a new potential rule around the dinner table, inviting input from the children since it will be a rule they will need to observe. Regardless, at the end of the day what Charlie and I decide is what goes, and they know that. For example, I have fixed bedtimes for my sons. When I set up this rule, I created exceptions for weekends and travel days. Now, one evening

Carson came to me and complained he couldn't fall asleep at his 8:00 p.m. bedtime. He proposed that he be allowed to read for an additional thirty minutes, as that would help him go to sleep. Since this was a logical solution, I told him I would consider it, but I held firm on that night's bedtime. He didn't question me on this because he knew to expect that response from me. I had always been consistent with rule changes in the past.

The next morning, I sat down with Carson and spoke to him about his idea. I proposed that if he got to bed at 7:45 p.m., I would allow him to read until 8:15 p.m. He would be in bed earlier but could stay up a little later. That way any problems with the rule would become blatantly obvious, making it easier to adopt better policies. He agreed. One night a few days after the 7:45 p.m. bedtime had been implemented, our whole family was playing a game, having a great time. Now, I wanted to continue to play the game, as did the rest of the family, so we raced the clock. In the end, we didn't finish, but we made a game out of it so Carson could still get to bed on time and not lose the privilege of staying up later.

My children knew I was the dictator and would not bend, so no one was disappointed. Over the years, my sons have learned that rules are important to follow, even when you make them for yourself. They saw me make rules, and then they watched me follow those rules precisely. I had to stop playing the family game, just as they did, because I was following the rules just as they were. The price for breaking the rule was too great. After a week or so, it became clear that 7:45 p.m. wasn't a workable bedtime, but I could see that reading before bed was a good idea. So I adjusted the rule so that Carson could go to bed at 8:00 p.m. and read for fifteen minutes. That's all he needed: fifteen minutes of reading and he'd fall right to sleep.

I have found that when I am consistent as a leader and get input from my sons on rules before I put them in play, Carson and Conrad don't fight me. Having said that, if I start to get a lot of pushback, I know it's time to reexamine the rule. That happened periodically as my kids got older. However, with our family rules in place, my sons knew what to expect and were able to rely on me to make good decisions. This helped them to follow my orders without always asking the dreaded question, "Why?"

BE A SHINING EXAMPLE

Creating good rules means living by them yourself, which means we must set an example in all things we expect of our children. Children are incredibly perceptive. They can spot when we say one thing and do another. Parents sometimes say, "Do what I say, not what I do," but that doesn't mitigate the problem the parent created. It creates new ones by sending the wrong message: our words can't be trusted. The bottom line is that whatever you say to your child you must mean; otherwise don't say it.

> We must set an example in all things we expect of our children.

Doing what you say and saying what you do is a golden rule of parenting. Raising kids becomes a lot easier when you achieve this consistency. I take it one step further and ask my children to hold me accountable. For example, if I use my fingers to eat food off my plate, they will correct me. I'm okay with that because I want to be held to a high standard of table manners. We all have our problem areas, but since you have little eyes watching you, you need to keep the example you always set firmly in mind. Personally, I have a bad habit of entering the house, taking off my shoes, and leaving them wherever I happen to be at that moment. This means they are left in random places, sometimes in the middle of the hall on the way to my room. Not a great example for my kids. If every member of the family did that, we'd have eight shoes scattered all over the house, like little land mines to trip over. The first step I took to correct this was to admit my error. Only then could I fix it.

If you're going to set a good example, you must own up to your mistakes. Admitting mistakes doesn't weaken your position; it can strengthen it because that honesty shows you can be trusted. Even a quick "I'm sorry" or "I messed up" goes a long way, and kids are quick to forgive. It's my experience that children don't hold grudges like adults, but they do learn ethics from their parents. That's a lot of responsibility. It's important to remember that ethics really are *what you do when no one is looking*. Why? Because that shows what's in your heart. No one can get away with something forever. Eventually, it will catch up to you, and your children will observe what you really do.

I have a friend who did her best to limit the amount of sugar in her family's diet. She had researched the problems it could cause for kids (and adults) and wanted to protect her children. However, at night, when the kids were in bed, she would sneak a pint of Ben and Jerry's hidden at the back of the freezer and eat it in secret. It was a bad habit, and she knew it was wrong, but she couldn't help herself. She thought she had successfully hidden it from her three children, so no harm had been done. One night, her six-year-old daughter woke up and caught her. It was embarrassing for my friend, and it cut her credibility on the subject. It took her awhile, but she realized that she didn't need the ice cream that badly. Her integrity was more important, and she didn't want to set a bad example. She kept in line with the family rules and didn't indulge in late-night binges anymore.

In this case, the children got on board with fighting the sugar monster for the sake of health, not because there was a rule against it. Today, when she shows weakness at the supermarket, her children playfully push her away from the sugar. As a result, she resists the urge to buy something she knows she shouldn't eat. And the children feel good about helping their mother live a longer, healthier life. It's all honest and out in the open. After all, a family can conquer any foe when parents set the right example and everyone works as a team.

TOLERATE ONLY WHAT YOU WANT TO GET

Teams work when every teammate can be trusted to fulfill their role on the team all the time. Pushback from children stems from the parents not following through on their rules one hundred percent of the time. I learned this the hard way. When my sons were young, I'd frequently take them to the park. After a while, I'd let them know it was time to go. Conrad and Carson would always say that they needed five more minutes. This made sense to me because they needed to say goodbye to their friends. Of course, saying goodbye turned into going down the slide and one more time on the swing. When I'd ask them again to come, my sons inevitably became immersed in a game of tag, and so on and so forth. As I tolerated their delay tactics, which seemed reasonable at the time, my kids would come up with more activities that just had to be done. It would be twenty to thirty minutes before we'd leave the park. One day, I realized that I'd lost control, so I put my foot down. I told Conrad and Carson they had a five-minute transition time and after that, I was leaving. I waited the five minutes, giving a warning as the time ticked away. Then time was up.

I said, "We have to leave now, and I need you to get in the car."

"Aw, Mom!"

I looked them both firmly in the eye and said, "If you choose not to come now, I will leave you."

I then asked my sons to repeat it back to me to be sure they understood. They repeated, "If I do not go to the car now, Mom will leave me." Right after, the boys went back to playing. I watched them for a moment and then began to walk slowly to my car. I turned and located them before getting into my car. I put on my seat belt and adjusted my rearview mirror. Both Conrad and Carson saw me, but they weren't moving toward me, so I began to pull out of the parking space— slowly. It was only when I started to drive toward the exit of the park that they started to run. By the time I got to the stop sign at the exit of the park, the two were running and crying. I waited for them and they got into the car.

Carson was angry. "Why did you do that?"

Remaining calm I said, "I'm not going to tolerate being taken advantage of anymore. I am going to do what I say. And I expect you to do the same."

I was mindful of my tone and my words. Although I was frustrated, I didn't want to show that emotion to my children, as I was more frustrated with myself than I was with them. I showed them a matter-of-fact attitude. I simply wasn't going to tolerate that behavior, and they got the message. That day I learned a lesson that I would continue to learn over the years. You really do get the actions that you tolerate. If you stand up and refuse to accept certain behaviors from your children, they learn fast. In fact, this learning begins from the moment they're born: that's when you start setting the tone for what you will tolerate from them.

When Carson came home from the hospital after being in the NICU for ten days, I was dying to hold him. I had missed those precious moments and was eager to have him in my arms. He loved to be held, so at first it was perfect and continued to be wonderful for a while. Unfortunately, I soon realized that every time I went to put him down, he screamed until I picked him up again. It got to the point that I couldn't even take a shower without Carson screaming to be picked up, which made my heart race out of control.

I think many mothers are programmed that way. Baby cries and mom thinks, "Oh, no! Something is wrong." Cue the dramatic music. After I rushed over to Carson the first thousand times only to realize that my baby was fine, I caught on that his crying was a biological function not related to danger. To change this response mechanism within me, it took a good friend who is a nurse to sit me down and explain a simple fact. "If they're crying, they're not dying." That piece of advice changed my outlook. I realized that my child's cries were his way of communicating, and that was a good thing. On the flip side, if he wasn't crying, he wasn't communicating, and that might mean he was in trouble.

If you think about it, both children and adults truly in distress can't talk, let alone scream for help. That's because their airways are blocked or they are bleeding to unconsciousness. So, if a child is crying, you can be sure he isn't actually dying. It's when they are hurt and not crying that you really have to worry. This doesn't mean children are not telling you something when they cry. My mother has told me that when I was an infant, I would cry bloody murder when my diaper was wet. That was my way to get the wet diaper off because if Mom didn't change me quickly, I'd get bad rashes. Children know what they need, so you should attend to the needs of your child.

However, crying is simply a baby's way to get attention; they are letting you know that they need something. Knowing that, understand that you don't need to immediately run to your baby. They can usually wait. A calm response from a well-rested parent is the best kind of response. A parent who is nervous and concerned about every cry becomes sleep-deprived and stressed out. Babies sometimes cry because they *desire* something rather than urgently need something.

You need to distinguish a *need* from a *desire*, and it starts at birth. Most newborns cry because they need something, but as they grow, they can learn to cry because they want things. After all, a need as a baby may not be a need as a toddler. For instance, an infant can't feed themself, but a toddler can. Yet a toddler might prefer to be fed by their mom. So now the question becomes, do you let the toddler cry when they simply want mama to feed them? Give in to that and they'll continue to demand that you do it for them. If you let them sort it out themselves, most kids will opt to self-feed. Parenting is always a balancing act.

I have a cousin whose wife died two weeks after childbirth, one day after their child was sent home from the hospital's NICU. My cousin pulled through and instantly became an amazing father. Do you know that I never heard the baby cry? It really surprised me. I later discovered the reason for this was that my cousin was a very sound sleeper. As a result, the baby learned that crying didn't do much. Many assumed that the baby slept through the night, but the truth was that the baby would just play in his crib until his father woke up. He adjusted, and the baby was a happy baby because of it.

Letting my child cry, even for a few minutes, was difficult at first. I had to remind myself that if he was making noise, he was relatively okay. Repeating the phrase *If they're crying, they're not dying* really helped me to calm down. I'd whisper it to myself every time my son cried and, before I knew it, the emotions, the adrenaline, the irrational fears stopped, and I knew I was free of the trigger.

TAKING CARE OF THE PARENTS, TOO

To keep our household a happy one, we created a schedule that everyone could live with. My sons knew they were going to get fed and go to sleep at a set time, so their bodies adjusted. In our house, a schedule helped my children to cry less often. And I'd joke that it kept my husband from crying as well. As a new mother, my focus was on the children to the point where I didn't even recognize anyone else. Charlie would ask me when we could just hang out or if he could take me on a date. My reply was always, "Sure, when the kids go off to college!" After a while, that joke began to wear thin for both of us. I missed spending time with Charlie, and he missed me as well. I needed rest and to prioritize my relationship with my partner.

New mothers should keep in mind that a well-rested mom is happier and better equipped to handle the complex job of parenting. When you are happy and calm, your baby will be happy and calm. This will lead to a more self-confident and self-reliant toddler, and ultimately a well-adjusted young adult. If you are the kind of mom who allows her toddler to interrupt every conversation she tries to have with another adult, now is the time to stop. I know how easy it can be to be pulled into watching your child's every movement, forgetting there are others in the room. The problem is that your world then has one center, and the child knows it.

When my kids were very young, I had them practice how to get our attention when we were in the middle of a conversation. Instead of saying, "Don't interrupt," we taught them something a little more positive.

"When you have something to say," I told them, "you can use the words *excuse me*. Then wait for us to respond."

We presented it as a game, so they thought it was fun. Charlie and I would start to talk, and then Conrad jumped in with, "Excuse me." Then it was Carson's turn. My sons enjoyed the game. We did it only a few times and then moved on to something else. We played it a bit more at a later date, and then I reminded them about it right before a group activity with other parents and kids. I was pleased when I was talking with a friend and Conrad came running up to say, "Excuse me!" Wanting to reward him, I immediately said, "Excuse me" to my friend and gave Conrad my full attention. He asked for water, and I gave it to him. I was so proud of him, and the other mother praised his politeness.

I also made a major change involving food in our household. I'd been tailoring the food in our refrigerator around my sons. I thought I was being a wonderful mom, catering to the needs of my kids, but the fact was that I was missing out on teaching my sons about other culinary delights because I wasn't providing options and variety. And, on top of that, I was sending a poor message: that they were the center of the universe. This can easily lead to entitlement and selfishness, and that ultimately leads to failure and hurt for your kids. One day those coddled toddlers will grow up and figure out that they aren't the most important person in the room just by virtue of being there. Learning this late in life can be dismal. Why not help your children learn this lesson early? There's no reason any parent should have to endure the *terrible twos*. The secret is to not create the monster in the first place.

When I was young, I remember my mother putting me in a playpen. It was a safe space where I couldn't get into trouble. This gave my mother the time to do the things she needed to do. I've noticed that today these playpens aren't as prevalent and that there seems to be a stigma attached to them. Of course, too much of anything is never good, but playpens can teach children to entertain themselves. Allowing your child to learn to play by themself is a good first step in teaching them independence and self-reliance. Help your child discover the joy in learning that they can do without you for a while.

Chapter Summary: Being a Benevolent Ruler

- Embrace your inner dictator and *tell* your children what to do.

- *Do what you say and say what you do.*

- If you make a rule, stick to that rule while your child is following it. Only change it on your terms and when the rule is not working.

- Admit your mistakes without hesitation. It shows you can be trusted.

- Children learn ethics from their family.

- You get the actions that you tolerate.

- *If they're crying, they're not dying.* A calm response is more important than speed.

- Making your kids the center of the universe leads to entitlement and selfishness, and that ultimately leads to failure and hurt.

- Allowing your child to learn to play by themself is a good first step in teaching them independence and self-reliance.

Exercises

Answer all the following questions individually, and then share your responses with your partner and kids when appropriate.

1. With your partner, create a rule-making process for the family. At a family meeting, go over with your child how rules are made (or changed) in your family. When adding a new rule or changing a rule, consider the following:

    *   The purpose of the rule

    *   A possible trial phase for the new rule

    *   Possible unintended consequences of this new rule

    *   How your child feels about this rule

        Note: If your rule-making process isn't working for your family, adjust it until it does, or scrap it and start over.

2. Make a list of all the areas where you and your partner are setting a good example. Make a list of areas where you and your partner are *not* setting the kind of example you wish to set. Note specifically what you are doing and how these instances affect your child. What can you do to change, and who will hold you accountable?

3. Write a list of habits and actions you are no longer willing to tolerate in other people, including your child. Be specific and detailed. Include why you are no longer willing to tolerate those actions and habits and how they make you feel. Consider in detail what you will do, as well as what you will say to the person to let them know you will no longer tolerate their actions.

4. Write down any areas where your child is dictating your life.

Consider how you might have made the child the center of your attention. How has your child affected your other relationships? What will you do differently?

CHAPTER 10

CREATING BENEVOLENT GUIDELINES

SET BOUNDARIES

In contemporary society, parents sometimes make the mistake of running their family by majority rule, where a young child gets an equal vote. There is no family constitution with an executive branch. The logic seems to be that children deserve the inalienable right of democracy. While equality can work well for adults, it fails miserably in the home with children who are learning. Of course, I'm not implying that children are just miniature slaves without the ability to think; they're more like indentured servants or apprentice adults. I don't subscribe to the *children should be seen, not heard* philosophy. My stance is simply that it's the parents' job to set boundaries so that children can learn in a safe environment. In the book *Boundaries with Kids: How Healthy Choices*

Grow Healthy Children, Henry Cloud and John Townsend reinforce this idea that parents should establish and enforce the rules of the house. We want children to grow into adults who understand and operate within acceptable societal guidelines.

If you are part of an organization, you'll have a boss. The rules are set by the executives, and those rules are ingrained within the corporate climate. Without an organizational chart there is confusion. The home is similar. There needs to be a hierarchy so that your children know there are people in charge they can look to for guidance. An environment where everyone knows who makes the rules creates order and stops chaos.

Routines and rules give your children discipline and predictability in a life that can feel out of control. With predictability comes a sense of security that youngsters crave. When my sons were young and I saw they were not doing what I asked, I used to tell them they had until the count of two to get started. I never counted to three. Why give them another chance to pause and think about doing what I asked? I remember one time before I took up this technique when I asked Conrad and Carson to clean the toy room and they walked away from me. Just like that. Not good. So I gave the boys a warning and told them that if they didn't pick up their toys, their toys would become mine. I gave them a few minutes, and when they didn't start cleaning up, I told them that they had until the count of two to take action. *One, two.* When Conrad and Carson didn't move, I calmly told them to go to their room, and then I put everything in trash bags, tied the tops, and left the bags in the toy room.

I had the boys come out of their room and told them that I now owned the toys. I said that they could do jobs around the house to buy back their playthings. Then I explained that any toys they didn't earn back within two weeks would go to children who understood the importance of taking care of their toys (children who didn't have toys).

There were many tears that day. I could tell that I'd made an impression. Conrad and Carson learned that there were consequences. In the end, my sons worked hard to earn back their toys and learned that they needed to listen when I asked them to do something. After that instance, when I started counting *one*, they were on their feet, moving.

As the boys got older, I stopped counting and started using the word *trust*. This word put on them the responsibility that I knew they deserved. I would say something like, "I trust you will take out the trash in the next fifteen minutes." I respected that they might be in the middle of doing something, but that I could ask and they would do it. A simple word tells your kids you believe in them to make a good choice. Ultimately, setting rules and boundaries paves the road for independence and self-discipline later in life.

Setting good boundaries has the bonus of teaching children social manners. I can attest that this isn't fun to discover by accident later in life. When I first entered college, I made a huge social blunder that cost me a friendship. A new friend, Jane, loaned me a pair of black jeans one day because I didn't have a pair. I loved those jeans and took exceptionally good care of them, returning them washed and folded. A few weeks later, I went to her room to borrow them again. Jane wasn't there, but her sister was visiting. I told the sister I was borrowing the jeans and that Jane would be fine with it. The sister looked uncomfortable, but I was in a hurry, so I took the jeans and left.

When I went to return the jeans, I realized I'd crossed an important boundary. Jane was furious with me, as well as with her sister for allowing me to take the pants. Jane felt it was unacceptable that I went into her room and took the pants without her express permission. Before that moment, it never occurred to me that it was wrong to make that assumption. I apologized, but that friendship never recovered.

I traced this incident back to my childhood, where the boundaries of personal possessions did not exist. My sister would constantly borrow my clothes without asking. My parents drilled into me the concept that it was my duty to share my things with my sister. It would frustrate me, but I grew up thinking that was the way the world worked. So, logically, I assumed that if I borrowed something once, I could automatically borrow it in the future. Looking back, I see how silly that logic was, but at the time it seemed sound. It was a hard lesson to learn so late in life.

I think my parents could have kept their philosophy while giving us children each the right of refusal. After all, the clothes were our responsibility. They could teach us the virtues of sharing without forcing us to do so. I taught my boys that sharing can never be forced. If, for instance, you are obliged to allow another person to use your clothes, you aren't truly *sharing*. With boundaries, you can sometimes curb a steep downward trend so you don't wind up out of control on a perilous road. It's better to set rules up front that everyone can follow.

My sons chose to share a room, but having learned lessons from my sister, I set boundaries regarding several areas. For instance, Conrad and Carson liked to share their stuffed animals. However, this led to countless arguments, as each child inevitably wanted the same animal at the same time, or neither wanted to clean up the toy, saying that the other person was the last to play with it. One day, I sat them down and we painstakingly divided all the animals, one by one, making clear who was the owner. "Each animal needs a parent," I said. "And the parent needs to take proper care of them. You're responsible for your animals."

One day Conrad gave permission for Carson to play with a particular stuffed animal. When it was time to clean up, Conrad noticed that Carson hadn't put away that toy, so he pointed it out. Carson became irate and complained to me that "Conrad is bossing me around!" I pointed out that Conrad was in fact being responsible for the welfare of his animal. I also instructed Conrad that he could be gentler in tone and give his brother a chance to clean up. These are all appropriate boundaries for kids to learn.

CREATE AGREEMENTS WITH YOUR CHILDREN

As my sons got older and entered middle school, I began to create agreements with them. I was clear from the start that our agreements were like contracts. Looking back, I realize that it would have been wise to put these agreements in writing. That way I could have simply directed them to the document instead of getting into emotional arguments where I needed to resort to a dictatorial ruling. I quickly learned that the simplest agreements were the easiest to follow. The more complicated they were, the more problems developed. That made keeping the agreements harder.

Since Carson loved football, I worked out with him that I would only take him to football practice if he got his schoolwork done before we left. Additionally, there would be no arguments if he didn't get the work done. He'd simply miss practice. He agreed. For Carson, that was a huge motivation. Every night there was football, he'd come home and get to work. Soon, I discovered that on the nights when there was no football practice, Carson would take forever to complete his assignments. So I adjusted the contract and implemented the *football rule* every night. That meant Carson had to get his homework done within a reasonable time or he would not be able to go to football the following night. Carson soon learned there were many advantages to getting his homework done early. A whole new world opened to him and he had more time for things he enjoyed doing. Today he is more likely to complete his homework on a Friday night rather than wait until Sunday night.

As my two sons entered high school, I permitted them to negotiate more. I allowed them to push back a little in our safe, controlled home setting. This is good preparation for life, as teens enter adulthood where every decision isn't dictated to them. Eventually, you must trust that you've taught your children to think and reason. Take the time to test their decision-making skills. And hopefully you can retain the coveted role of the first consultant of choice in their lives.

I found it was helpful to consult my teenage boys on bedtime, asking them for thoughts on a reasonable time. Teens are much more likely to comply if they are part of the decision-making process. I made sure they did their research so they knew what health experts suggested based on their ages. Regardless of their findings, my sons' personalities came out. My younger son, Carson, wanted an 11:00 p.m. bedtime, whereas Conrad said 10:00 p.m. made sense to him. Carson liked to stay up late and sleep in, whereas Conrad went to bed early and woke up early.

I agreed with Carson that he could set an 11:00 p.m. bedtime, but he'd need to get up at 6:30 a.m. without fail and get to school on time. Since I have been giving my boys the responsibility to wake themselves up since first grade, he knew my expectations. Carson got himself to school on time because he didn't want to lose his power of choice. The first week went fine, but by the second week he was dragging. When I asked him for his thoughts regarding a solution, he realized he needed more sleep. The next night Carson was in bed by 10:00 p.m. He'd made the change on his own and didn't argue with me about it. We always need to guide our children to boundaries that make sense to them. Know your kids and help them make choices.

Again, I would not do this with a young child. They need more precise boundaries set by the parents. However, when my sons became young adults, the boundaries I set were more in line with teaching them to be responsible for their actions (and accepting the consequences of those actions). I let Carson fail early and easily while the consequences were low. I knew he would choose to stay up late. However, he learned that it wasn't sustainable on his own terms.

SAY NO FOR NOW, NOT FOREVER

Regardless of age or the stage of life, a parent must take their children's abilities and personalities into account when making crucial decisions. Simply giving kids the right to do certain things just because they are a particular age isn't a good idea. For instance, some children aren't ready to drive at age sixteen. That is why I came up with the concept *no for now, not forever.*

No for now, not forever means that I might not allow my child to do something at this very moment, but that doesn't mean that I won't change my mind later when I feel they are ready. I encourage my kids to write down what they want to do, how they will do it, and when they think they can do it. If I feel they aren't ready, it's up to them to show their dedication to get to do what they want to do.

My sons really like to go snow skiing, but we live in Puerto Rico, so snow skiing is not in our backyard. Two years in a row, we had the opportunity to travel to ski, and the boys were happy. The following year, we talked a lot about going but decided against it. The boys were devastated. They felt my decision was unfair and arbitrary. I sat down with them and explained that my no was not forever. I wasn't saying we'd never go skiing. It was just for now. If they came up with a plan, I would consider it. I also discussed the obstacles I felt held us back from going (the biggest being the lack of snow). This conversation empowered Conrad and Carson to overcome the problems. In the end, they realized that the lack of snow was a good reason not to go. They stopped fighting the decision because they did their own research and agreed.

Stepping back a bit, this conversation had broader ramifications for my children. It taught them that *no* isn't a death sentence for their ideas. It didn't mean they could never achieve their goals. They learned the best response was "What can I do to get a yes?" It's better to strive to get a yes than be stunted by the world's collective no. There were times when I purposefully said no to Conrad and Carson to get them to turn my answer around to a yes. They knew I was doing this and that it was an exercise. It was meant to teach them that nagging doesn't count and isn't rewarded, but a well-thought-out argument and polite persistence will win me over. I got this concept from Charlie. He's so good at turning a no into a yes! He never gets upset with the person and doesn't tell them that they are wrong, but he politely works with them to change their minds. I think it's a combination of his huge heart, hard work, and perseverance. I no longer say no to my boys. I say, "Not now" or give them the reasons I have for the answer and see if they can solve the problem.

ENFORCE CONSEQUENCES

> Setting or negotiating boundaries requires consequences when those boundaries are violated.

Setting or negotiating boundaries requires consequences when those boundaries are violated. Otherwise, why have boundaries? One day Carson was getting ready for kindergarten and put on a pair of pants that had well-worn knees. When I saw them, I said, "You might not want to wear those pants. You might get a hole in the knees if you play on the floor."

"I don't care. I want to wear these pants," he replied.

Knowing it was important to allow him to make his own decisions, I let him go to school with those pants. Later that day I got a call asking me to bring in a new pair of pants. When I got to school, I saw that Carson's pants were ripped from the knee to the front pocket. The teacher let me know that the other kids in the class had laughed at him because they could see his underwear. Carson was upset and frustrated.

I consoled him and began to ask questions. "What happened?"

"Am I in trouble?" were the first words out of Carson's mouth.

I knew instantly that if I told my son he was in trouble, he would not talk to me. I knew he would get angry and become defensive. My job was to get Carson to consider the choices he'd made to get to this point.

I told him he'd received the consequences already. There is never a need to pile on punishments when natural consequences occur. With that, Carson relaxed and told me his story from his perspective. My son told me that during recess a hole appeared in the knee, but he had no idea how it happened. Then at nap time, he was bored, so he began to play with the hole. Interested, Carson kept ripping at it and the hole got bigger. When he stood up after naptime, everyone could see his underwear. The kids laughed and pointed.

I listened to Carson's story without interrupting him. Then I asked him questions: Did you make a good choice in choosing those pants to wear today? What do you normally do at naptime when you are bored? Could this situation have been prevented? What would you have done differently? By asking these questions and others, I was able to help my son see the series of bad choices that got him to this spot where his friends laughed at him.

Natural consequences will happen whether you wish them to or not. Parents sometimes attempt to shield their children from these, but that's usually a mistake, as it just puts off the inevitable. Instead, I suggest teaching children about the cause-effect nature of actions. The plain and simple fact is that all actions have consequences—some positive and some negative. It's a bit like Newton's third law: Every action has an equal and opposite reaction. You kick the ball; it flies. Say your friend walks in front of the path of the ball after you kick it. The ball will hit your friend and your friend will be in pain. There's no getting around the fact that your action of kicking the ball led to the ball hurting your friend.

While it's true that their action of walking into the path of the ball also caused the ball to hurt them, you can only take responsibility for your own actions. There are several potential consequences resulting from your actions: you could feel bad, your friend could be angry at you, your friend could no longer want to play the game, and the enjoyment of the game may be curtailed. You will find that children learn from both good and bad consequences. If they do a good deed and no one notices or comments, will they do it again? Maybe. Maybe not. However, if you praise their actions, they are more likely to repeat them. It's safe to say that we all want and need affirmation for our good work.

If your children do the wrong thing and you don't point it out, they might keep doing it. However, if you allow the natural consequence of their action to unfold, refusing to shield them from any pain or discomfort they might experience, they will learn and probably won't repeat the behavior. Natural consequences are really the best for learning. For example, the outcome of the story I shared from my college days when I borrowed my friend's jeans without asking was enormously powerful for me. I learned a valuable boundaries lesson that I carried forward through my life.

As parents, we can also create incentives to encourage certain kinds of behavior (and consequences for the reverse). As Carson was growing up, I tried to communicate to him how important it was to get his homework done early. Despite this encouragement, I'd often find him cramming at the last moment on Sunday. For this reason, I'd sometimes schedule fun activities for Sunday evening, letting Carson know ahead of time, so he could plan. If he didn't get the work done, he wouldn't be able to join in with us. This gave him a strong incentive to complete his homework. One time I hired Carson and Conrad to paint an outside wall for me. I offered them good pay if they got it done by a certain deadline a few days away. It was Saturday and sunny, so I suggested they get started. They both decided to put it off. I allowed them to do so but reminded them about the firm deadline.

The following day it rained, so it wasn't possible to paint the wall. I didn't say anything, but when it rained for the next three days, I pointed out that they had missed their deadline. I painted the wall myself and realized it was a lot easier than I'd thought and that I would have overpaid them. My boys were sullen about the whole situation and felt I wasn't being fair. It was a perfect lesson for them to learn when the consequences weren't high. I couldn't have planned it that way, as the weather report hadn't predicted four days of rain, but I did take advantage of the teaching moment. "If you miss a window of opportunity, you might never get it back," I explained.

It isn't always easy to find the perfect consequence for a misstep. When you are forced to create a consequence, it is best to come up with something that relates to the offense. For instance, if a child littered, I wouldn't take his tablet away for a week. There's no correlation. What does one thing have to do with the other? If I saw my child litter, I'd stop and make them pick up their trash. Then I would have them pick up all the litter they saw around them. If there was no trash in that area, I'd take them to a place with litter and make them clean it up. In situations like this, immediacy is important. It can disrupt whatever is going on, but it teaches a better lesson. Not making the right choice in life disrupts life.

One time, when they were in eighth and ninth grade, I took my sons to a party with only adults. They were well behaved for the first hour, engaging in conversations with various people. When they became bored, the host kindly offered to let them play in their side yard. So, being the creative children that they were, Conrad and Carson took an empty water bottle and two rakes and began playing "hockey." The metal rake survived, but the plastic one was ruined; it more resembled a stick than a rake.

I was mortified. But more than that, I was disappointed in my children. They knew better. The host was gracious and told me not to worry about it. However, I realized this was a good chance to teach my sons an important lesson. The next week, I took Conrad and Carson to the garden supply store so that they could replace the rake with their own money. They reached for the cheapest one, but I steadied their hands. "No," I told them. "The rake you broke may have been cheap, but you should replace it with a better one." If I had thought of it, I would have also suggested that they rake up all the leaves from the host's yard. It would have been fitting and would have left the host with a good feeling. It's always best to leave an area better than you found it.

AVOID BLAMING OTHERS

When you seek to enforce natural consequences, you quickly find that a child's natural inclination is to blame someone else so that the consequences don't fall on them. If not taught when young, adults will continue this behavior. My mom told me, "Sticks and stones will break my bones, but words will never hurt me" when I complained to her that my brother called me hurtful names. I tried it and, lo and behold, I felt like I had a little bit of power to choose not to get hurt by his words. That kernel of power blossomed, and I learned not to give his words the meaning he wanted me to give them. They were simply words that were not true for me. These words, any words, could only hurt me if I *chose* to let them do so. That day, I decided to not believe the words that my brother was saying, and more importantly, decided to not *blame* my brother for my feelings. I took control of my feelings and of my choices.

Too many take the easy out of blaming others for their situation in life. I'm sure you know someone who does that. One friend had been waging a losing battle with drugs and alcohol for years. When Maggie lost full custody of her child, she didn't see the correlation at all. Although it was clear to me that her actions were the cause of her downfall, Maggie simply blamed others for her misfortunes. Because others were at fault for her situation and she couldn't see her contribution to the problem, Maggie had no ability to change. Happy people are the ones who learn that they played a role in their problems and that *they* are the ones who can work to remedy their situation.

I made it a point to teach Conrad and Carson how much control over their life they give away when they blame others. Our home is a blame-free zone. It's such a slippery slope to start holding others accountable for your lot in life. Some situations are difficult, as it can seem like an obvious choice to blame someone else. Conrad took an advanced film class with a new teacher at his high school. She'd transferred from a community college and was eager to work with younger students. When I read the syllabus, I was concerned about the horror and psychedelic films listed, so I spoke to the teacher. She assured me that she'd only show snippets of these films to instruct about camera angles, lighting, and other aspects.

I was satisfied that this was acceptable, but a few weeks later I got a call from the dean that Conrad was skipping class because he felt the films were too scary. We all met, and Conrad voiced his concerns. The dean agreed that the film choices weren't appropriate, and they were removed from the curriculum. However, Conrad was given detention as a consequence of cutting class. Conrad was upset about this. When we got home, I prepared a snack and sat down with him.

"But, Mom, it's all the teacher's fault," he said.

I started by listening to what he had to say. When he was finished, I asked him, "What could you have done about this?"

"What do you mean?"

"I mean, how could you have let the teacher know that you didn't want to watch those films?"

His shoulders slumped and he said, "I guess I could have told her."

"Right. Do you think she would have forced you to watch those movies?"

Conrad shook his head.

"What else could you have done?"

"I don't know."

"Think about it," I said. "It's important."

"I could have called you."

"Right!"

"I could have also gone to the dean."

I nodded my head.

"I could have just closed my eyes during the scary parts."

"Good," I said. "Those are all good solutions. Much better than cutting class, right?"

"Right," he said. At that moment he stopped blaming the teacher and took responsibility for his actions. He understood why he had detention.

I went on to tell Conrad that I was glad that he didn't watch those horrible films. He was, in fact, guarding his mind as I'd taught him long ago, but he just needed to find a better way to do so. Yes, I praised Conrad for guarding his mind and let him understand that at times he might have a consequence for doing what he believed was best for himself.

BE CONSCIENTIOUS ABOUT SPANKING

Spanking is a controversial subject, so I am addressing it directly. There are so many strong opinions. I feel that fear and pain are never good deterrents for bad behavior. In addition, corporal punishment never made sense to me, because it rarely relates directly to the crime. Looking back, I do believe we made a mistake spanking our kids, and I don't recommend it. However, my husband felt strongly that this method could be effective if used correctly. To clarify, Charlie never spanked in rage but did so in a calculated, calm manner.

Still, I cringed. But I showed a united front for our children. That's important. If you aren't in agreement with your partner with regard to your actions and decisions, your children will take advantage of you both. They will drive a wedge between you; *divide and conquer* will be their new motto. So even though I didn't like Charlie spanking our kids, I respected my husband and his strong beliefs on the subject.

For some children, spanking fuels their anger and they rebel. Then you get the opposite of your desired effect. I remember that my brother would laugh whenever my mom spanked him. I think it hurt him (both physically and emotionally), but he didn't want to admit that. So instead he chose to "win" the battle by mocking her. There are times when spanking might seem to work, but does it? A friend told me about how her son wouldn't stop running around the pool. She felt his life was in danger, so she spanked him. It was a very controlled spanking.

"You know, Kate," she told me, "it worked! He never ran around the pool again. I feel like I saved his life that day."

I nodded. "I can see how you'd feel that way. How many times had you spanked him before that time?"

She shook her head. "That was the first time."

"Well, I think it worked because it was so out of character for you. It probably shocked him."

We talked about the situation, and we agreed that she could have succeeded in teaching him that lesson another way also. She decided that spanking might not work as well if she tried it again because it would no longer have the same shock effect.

My husband and I discussed spanking as a form of punishment with our sons when they were young. They knew that it was a consequence of misbehaving. That's an important distinction. Our boys never thought they were going to get hit out of rage. It was discussed calmly. I feel strongly that we made a mistake spanking our kids. I have taken responsibility for the mistake, and I have apologized to my boys for my part in allowing the spankings. I no longer condone spanking, and I advocate that natural consequences that relate to the child's infraction are a much better and more effective alternative to spanking. Let the punishment fit the crime. Parents must spend time figuring out how to reward their kids for good behaviors so we don't even have to have a controversial discussion about spanking.

Chapter Summary:
Creating Benevolent Guidelines

- Routines and rules give your children discipline and predictability in a life that can seem unpredictable.

- If your child breaks a rule or crosses a boundary, be consistent and let them fail. Let your child experience the consequence of their choices.

- Permit your teen to be a part of the decision-making process.

- *No for now, not forever* means that you might not allow your child to do something at this very moment, but in the future that could change.

- All actions have consequences—some positive and some negative.

- Create incentives to encourage the kinds of behavior you want from your kids and consequences for the misbehavior.

- When you are forced to create a consequence, it is best to come up with something that relates to the offense.

- Help your kids learn to recognize their responsibility for their mistakes so they can learn from them.

- It is important to agree with your partner concerning your disciplinary actions and decisions. Yet I do not condone spanking. Natural consequences teach great lessons.

Exercises

Answer all the following questions individually, and then share your responses with your partner and kids when appropriate.

1. Write out your family routines, rules, standards, and boundaries. What are the consequences for breaking a routine, rule,
   standard, or boundary? Think about making the consequences
   applicable to the situation. Write the consequence next to the
   routine, rule, standard, and boundary. Make sure you list the
   unspoken rules and boundaries you wish to teach your child.
   Note: These can be social norms and areas of etiquette that you
   want to make sure your child understands.

2. How can your children be involved in the creation of new
   family routines, rules, standards, and boundaries? How can you
   include your children in the creation of consequences when the
   routines, rules, standards, and boundaries are broken?

3. Have a family meeting. Get everyone to agree to a blame-free
   home, and put a statement to that effect in writing. Ask all
   family members to sign this statement, and post it in a common
   area in the house.

CHAPTER 11

BESTOWING BENEVOLENT REWARDS

REWARD AND RECOGNIZE

Rewards are an excellent incentive, encouraging children to do the right thing. When Carson and Conrad were in kindergarten and first grade, they attended a school in Texas that had a system called the Golden Paws, named after their fearless mountain lion mascot. The children could earn a Golden Paw by putting into action the values and standards set by the school. That is, they followed the rules when others didn't. It was a reward for doing the right thing when temptation and peer pressure were strongest. The effect was that it pointed out the good behavior with praise and reward, which enticed others to follow.

The magic of this system lay in acknowledging students' good behavior linked to a reward for the child at the school. For my sons, it wasn't the glamour of the actual award that was the draw. This award appealed to them because they were competitive, enjoyed the attention, and liked the rewards and the recognition. Each teacher could give out two awards a month and only to someone who wasn't in their class. Conrad received one when a passing teacher noticed that he helped a substitute teacher keep order in his class. Conrad had put his finger to his lips when the other children in his class were becoming unruly on the way to PE one day. The Golden Paw was a recognition of his budding leadership abilities.

Each day, my sons would come home and ask each other if they had earned a Golden Paw that day. Watching them, I realized this system was excellent, so I decided to poach it and made some modifications. As with all aspects of parenting, it's important to know your children so you can help motivate them. Golden Paws worked well with my sons. I called the new reward the Golden Hs (H for Hamilton). I added a new key rule to the ones used in the school: one could never ask for a Golden H. If you felt you did something Golden H–worthy but didn't get the recognition, that's life, and life isn't always fair.

In the beginning, Conrad and Carson would drop some not-so-subtle hints about things they did that were Golden H–worthy. I would always acknowledge the action but would remind them that the act was instantly disqualified because they had basically asked for the reward. I never wavered on this rule, and they quickly learned not to point out their good behavior.

I remember giving out a Golden H when one of my young sons was exceedingly polite to a stranger. He looked the man in the eye and said, "Yes, sir." Another time, I rewarded Conrad and Carson for doing their chores without being asked. I also rewarded them for actions such as holding the door open for a lady or picking up trash and putting it into the trash can. These were all appropriate for my sons when they were in elementary school. It's important to recognize a child for the tasks they perform that relate to their age.

As my boys grew older, my standards grew tougher. In the beginning, I gave Golden Hs out more frequently. Then I made them progressively more challenging to earn, to encourage Conrad and Carson to reach new heights. My husband and I would speak to them about our standards for their behavior. Over time, our standards evolved, and so did what was considered worthy of a Golden H.

Today my sons enjoy helping others even when no one is watching. During the devastating aftermath of Hurricane Maria, they were compelled to help others. Not only did they clear trees from the roads and strangers' yards, but they were also involved in the third-largest relief effort, sponsored by our church. Conrad and Carson unloaded medical supplies from numerous trucks, joined crews to fix roofs, and distributed food to many in need. In addition, they took further steps that included educating single mothers about how to maintain their generators, as it took months for the power to be completely restored to our island. This natural disaster created a sense of loss, despair, and fear in many children and adults, but my boys took it upon themselves to do something about the situation and turned it into an opportunity for personal growth and accomplishment. Doing things for others, even when they weren't directly acknowledged for their good deeds, became a part of who my children are.

REWARD PROBLEM-SOLVING

I made a point of focusing potential rewards around problem-solving. For instance, when they were young, if my sons had trouble reaching a light switch, I'd acknowledge them for seeking out a step stool instead of asking me for help. Or if they spilled their drink but cleaned it up immediately, I'd reward them. The question I'd seek to answer was, did they learn from errors and take steps to change bad behaviors on their own? These are all great Golden H–worthy actions and should be rewarded. After all, we want to encourage children to be independent thinkers.

Jobs today are no longer based purely on education and what you know. Memorizing facts just doesn't have the same value because facts and information are now at our fingertips. It's more important that our children know the right questions to ask and how to use the information those questions produce. Information is available; however, applying the information to one's situation is an important skill. Encouraging problem-solving skills in your children at a young age will be invaluable for their future. When our children get their first job, they'll discover that a boss isn't interested in an employee who always needs direction. That's just annoying. Bosses want their team to work independently and get the job done correctly. Our children need to anticipate problems and create solutions. They need to recognize a problem before anyone else notices it. So that's what we need to teach our kids while they are still young and the stakes are still low.

Golden Hs teach this beautifully. To assist and inspire my sons, I created a cash value for the Golden Hs. When Conrad and Carson were very young, each Golden H was worth a quarter. Later, they maxed out at a dollar. The boys sometimes earned two or three in a day. I didn't place a limit on the number of Golden Hs they could earn; their imagination and hard work were their only boundaries.

Just think of it as a bonus a boss would pay to encourage workers to go above and beyond what is expected. My workers were rewarded with money for solving problems or doing jobs for the sake and betterment of our family and our society. They were praised and rewarded for their actions, reinforcing positive behavior. In our household, we started early with Golden Hs being worth money they could use to buy real, tangible goods they wanted at the store. This was the start of them learning valuable lessons about how to earn, save, and spend money.

GIVE A DAY OF GRACE

We all want our children to grow up to be independent, reasoning adults, able to solve their own problems and thrive in life. To accomplish this, we need to allow our children to fail. However, this brings about seemingly conflicting emotions, churned up because we also feel a strong urge to help, rescue, comfort, and support our children. We all have a strong desire to build them up. As a mother, I feel conflicted when faced with protecting, rescuing, or disappointing my children. I want to rescue them from the pain of their bad actions, but I want to help them discover and learn from the consequences before it is too late (and those consequences become dire).

If your children are anything like mine, they will forget items at home that they desperately need at school. I know I did when I was young. And I'm sure my children's children will do the same. It happens, and we have all learned valuable lessons from those mistakes. These are important lessons, but still, I'm the mom. I'm the one who wants to make sure my sons don't forget things. I want to have their backs no matter what. Shouldn't every child feel like they can count on their mom when they mess up? So, when Carson called me one day from elementary school telling me he'd forgotten his lunchbox, my heart dropped. His young voice sounded so small, crushed, and worried. He knew that he was asking a big favor of me, and I could tell he was aware that he was responsible for the problem.

I had a dilemma. On the one hand, I didn't want this incident to recur on a regular basis. Without any sort of consequence, Carson would learn to rely on me every time he forgot something. However, on the flip side, I didn't want Carson to go through the day without lunch. A starved child doesn't make for a good student; so not only would my son be grateful for his lunch, but his educators would be as well. Deep down, I wanted my son to know that I cared for his well-being, and I wanted to be his hero.

That's when I came up with the concept of the *day of grace*. *Grace* is *freely given kindness*. It isn't something one earns or deserves, but you

218 THE IMPERFECT PARENT

receive it anyway. It's important to understand this concept to understand how my day of grace works. When I give my child a day of grace, I let them know it's a temporary exemption—a reprieve from the consequences of a mistake. I am very clear that this isn't something to expect or rely on. In the case of Carson forgetting his lunch, I was able to bring it to him, and he was extremely grateful. It's especially important that this act not be viewed as simply something I owe him because I'm Mom. No, it's an act of generosity; I'm *graciously* doing it because I can—and because I love him.

My children have learned that my act of grace does not exempt them completely from the consequences. It is a temporary reprieve that helps them through the immediate difficulty; however, it doesn't solve the problem. They know they will need to provide a solution so this problem will not happen again. For instance, I made it clear to Carson that I wouldn't give him a second day of grace if he forgot his lunch again.

Nevertheless, when my children feel like the world is coming to an end, I want to be gracious, even if they haven't done anything to deserve it. Implementing the day of grace, I now had a family policy I could use to help my sons while teaching a valuable lesson. By bringing Carson his lunch, he learned what it felt like to be the recipient of grace. He fully recognized that he'd made a mistake, and he also didn't expect me to fix his problem.

We need more grace in the world today; children need to be taught this early in life. It's important to also note that grace is giving without expecting anything in return. It's done with love and kindness. Once you receive grace, you'll naturally want to give grace, and that attitude will perpetuate. I have always found this to be a beautiful concept. I've seen both Carson and Conrad help one another and others without thought of any sort of reciprocation. I always point it out when they help each other and praise them for these random acts of kindness, as each one makes for a better and happier world.

> We need more grace in the world today; children need to be taught this early in life.

Chapter Summary:
Bestowing Benevolent Rewards

- Rewarding good behavior works far better than punishing bad behavior.

- Create a reward system acknowledging your child for meeting family standards.

- Focus rewards on problem-solving. Encouraging problem-solving from a young age is valuable for your child's future success.

- Children need to know the right questions to ask and how to use the information those questions provide.

- A day of grace is a temporary exemption, a reprieve from the consequences of making a mistake. It's important to note that a day of grace is not something a child can earn.

Exercises

Answer all the following questions individually, and then share your responses with your partner and kids when appropriate.

1. If you feel a reward system is beneficial, create one with your partner for your child. Keep the rules simple and easy to implement.

2. Are there times your child has trouble solving their own problems? Write down questions you can ask your child to help them solve their own problems.

3. Discuss with your partner the circumstances in which a day of grace could be used in your family and when it might not be used. Write down the parameters on how you'll implement a day of grace. Talk to your child about this policy.

PART V

FOCUS ON WISDOM

CHAPTER 12

TEACH FOR LIFE

S ome children will touch the proverbial hot stove even after we tell them not to. It's tough to watch, but sometimes they need to experience the heat before they learn. Lessons learned in a safe environment can be enormously powerful. It's been my experience that some kids will have to learn certain lessons many times over, while other kids can just be told about the heat without the need to touch the stove to find out. As a parent, I always felt it was my responsibility to create a learning environment tailor-made to the child I was teaching.

PROVIDE WISDOM, NOT INFORMATION

Today, with the ability to get any fact or date from a handheld device, getting information is not a problem. Obtaining reliable, trustworthy, pertinent, and appropriate information is more difficult; one must learn to filter out the junk. You filter by using wisdom. The questions you ask and what you do with the information are of the utmost importance. If we teach our kids how to ask good questions, we teach our kids wisdom.

Wisdom involves having experience, knowledge, and good judgment. To help our kids to be wise, we can provide them with experiences and teach them how to cut through the clutter of information to uncover the knowledge they need to answer the question, solve the problem, or get the task done. When my sons were toddlers, they'd ask a host of good questions: "Why is the sky blue?" "Where do babies come from?" and "What happened to the dinosaurs?"

My reply was always a simple, "What do you think?"

Usually they happily shared their ideas, but sometimes Conrad would get frustrated when I didn't offer up an answer. He felt that he had no way to figure it out himself. To help him, I'd ask more questions. Wisdom comes from understanding life and being able to learn lessons that can be used in future situations. To that end, I like to share stories (both the good and the bad) from my past with my boys. This accomplishes a few goals. Not only can I share my experiences so Carson and Conrad can learn from them, but my children can also see that I erred in my youth, so they know they aren't the only ones who make mistakes. We all learn through stories.

For example, I told my sons about a time I almost missed an important and fun event. I was still in high school, and I'd been accepted to a travel and study program where I received college credits. I flew to the destination with one friend and then took a bus from the airport to the hotel. I remember that we arrived much later than expected, so there was a mad scramble. The chaperones provided us with a room key and a detailed itinerary. I didn't even glance at the itinerary but dropped off my bags in the room. By the time I came back to the lobby, the bus had left. I was devastated and shocked that no one had realized I was missing. It never occurred to me that the group would leave without me, but it had. In prior school outings, the adults had counted the kids and knew where everyone was. These chaperones hadn't. I realized at that moment it had been my responsibility to make sure I was on the tour. I hadn't read the itinerary and now I was paying the price.

I realized I needed to adapt quickly; I found out where I needed to be and learned how to use the public transportation system to get there. It was a powerful lesson for me, on many levels. I learned that I was responsible for the situation and that blaming others wasn't going to get me where I needed to go. Sharing this story gave my sons a chance to learn the lessons I'd learned that day without them needing to burn their fingers on the hot stove. They learned a little wisdom that would hopefully help them one day.

USE QUESTIONS TO GAIN WISDOM

To get a good answer, children need to learn how to ask good questions. Their questions will take them to exciting places, but only if they are curious enough to go there. Kids will learn how to ask good questions with practice; parents shouldn't short-circuit this process. I believe that the people who follow their passions, explore the globe, and learn as much as they can are the ones who become the happiest and most productive members of our society. And the journey starts with all those crazy questions they ask as young kids.

I have always encouraged questions, the crazier the better. I am sure it was the inquisitive nature of the greatest innovators that gave us the inventions that made the civilization we have today. Looking forward, it will be our children's questions that will blaze the path for the future. Through intelligent questioning, children will discover how to think logically and work out solutions to their problems. Be patient—kids will ask many, many questions. Remind yourself of the importance of this process, and don't cut them off.

> Through intelligent questioning, children will discover how to think logically and work out solutions to their problems.

When your children are young, answer all their questions to the best of your ability. As they grow older, guide them to resources where they can research on their own. With the internet, it's so easy to get answers to many obscure questions. Just be ready for them to find misinformation and sometimes even stumble upon undesirable sites; guide them away from these.

Another way to encourage good questions is to ask your children lots of questions throughout the day. Help them consider all the facets of their lives. For instance, when my sons came home from school, I asked questions such as "What was the funniest thing that happened today?" I avoided the blatantly obvious "How was your day?" because it usually yielded an answer of "good," which, as I mentioned before, didn't tell me anything.

I liked to check in with my kids often. Sometimes I asked them to give me a short phrase to tell me how they were doing. For instance, Carson might say "frustrated with homework" or "excited for football practice." Or Conrad might say "tired from school" or "annoyed by the lack of snacks in the house." These little snippets would give me a world of information and allow me to plan my actions. For example, before I launched into a heavy topic of conversation, I would find out my sons' emotional state. If they weren't hungry or tired, we could move forward with whatever I had planned.

Questions are powerful. With a correctly phrased inquiry, you can find out a lot about your child's life, their friends (and their lives), what is going on at school, and much more. One of my favorite questions is "What can we celebrate today?" It gets your child talking about the positive aspects of their day and uncovers moments of gratitude. It teaches them to focus on encouraging, happy moments and reinforces the positive memory. As a side benefit, I discovered that this question inspired my sons to go back to school the next day to find another experience to celebrate with me.

Our family enjoys playing communication games at dinner, where everyone has a chance to ask a question that requires more than a one-word answer. The better the question, the more elaborate and passionate the answer. Each person gets to answer the same question, and the person asking can come up with follow-up questions or tweak the original one to make it even better. By asking, tweaking, and listening, Conrad and Carson learned how to formulate better questions. This is a good way to teach kids how to ask good questions.

If you find it challenging to come up with good questions, I highly recommend the game TableTopics, which comes in different versions. The game is a box of cards with questions—it's extremely simple. Players take turns picking a question and everyone answers it, or each person answers the question they chose. There is a family version that is perfect for younger kids, too. It's better than always asking the same kind of questions like, "What did you do in school today?"

Some of the best conversations I've had with Carson and Conrad started with good questions. I separated my children at least once a week and allocated time for each son to fully explore his thoughts and ideas on a variety of subjects. I usually started by telling them facts and sharing stories. Then I asked questions, learning about their developing thoughts and opinions based on what they observed and learned. I was always fascinated. My boys knew that and appreciated that I was truly interested. Start young with this and your children will become accustomed to sharing everything with you. As they get older, your children might become reluctant to open up if you don't have this as a routine. They need to trust you fully and know that you have their backs.

Communication is a two-way street, so make sure to take the time to share your thoughts, ideas, and personal history with your children as well. I promise they want to know about you, too. Be open with them. This process will pave the way for many years of honest dialogue. As you communicate with your child, refrain from telling them what to think or what to feel. Instead, show them that you respect their viewpoint by accepting their words. Now's not the time to correct the way they express themselves. Through this process they learn that children are allowed to have their own thoughts and ideas. This may seem obvious to some, but if you don't encourage this, children might think you disapprove of them if they don't share your exact ideology. They need to know you aren't trying to force your opinions down their throat.

Parents who don't encourage independent thinking and fail to create a safe space for children to share their thoughts will find that their children will learn to tell them only what they want to hear (or what the children think their parents want to hear). They will not give honest answers. We're trying to raise kids who are independent thinkers and problem solvers, right? If you force-feed them your ideology, they'll never learn to think things through for themselves. As your children get older, continue to talk to them, but give them the space and time to figure things out. When they have information, they'll come to a conclusion right for them at that point in time. Still continue to talk and listen to your kids. They will also continue to adjust and rethink their conclusions as life changes and as they gain more information.

Chapter Summary: Teach for Life

- Create a learning environment tailored to each child.

- Kids need to know how to ask good questions; with good questions, kids can gain wisdom through understanding the world.

- Provide experiences to teach kids how to cut through the clutter of information and uncover the knowledge they need.

- Allocate time with each child one-on-one to fully explore their thoughts and ideas.

- Do not tell your child what to think or what to feel; instead provide information and resources.

Exercises

Answer all the following questions individually, and then share your responses with your partner and kids when appropriate.

1. What kind of learner is your child? Does your child learn by listening, watching, or doing? Create a learning opportunity tailored to your child.

2. Write about a time when you found out the answer to your own question without help from another person. Note how that made you feel. Share these stories with your family. Ask your kids if they have a story about solving a problem or finding an answer to a question on their own. Encourage them to tell the family their story.

3. Make a list of ways you can encourage your child to ask questions and be curious.

4. Write a list of questions that you can ask your child to challenge them to give you an in-depth answer about their thoughts and ideas.

CHAPTER 13

TEACH DIFFICULT SUBJECTS

TRY THE EIGHT-YEAR RULE

Most parents teeter on the edge when deciding whether to discuss difficult topics because they aren't excited about tackling unpleasant conversations. This hesitancy creates problems and can, in fact, be a dangerous game of Russian roulette. After all, it's hard to predict when a child will encounter the subject in life. And on top of that, you never know who will introduce it. Guess wrong and there can be long-lasting consequences.

When I considered this dilemma, I talked to many friends and asked for their insights. Most had a complicated system based on ages and developmental stages. I also talked to my mother-in-law, who had a wealth of information on the topic, having a master's degree in child development. However, the more I spoke to her and my friends, the more I felt like I needed a spreadsheet, calendar reminders, and years of education before I could create a plan of attack. It was only when I spoke with my friend Angela that I learned of the *eight-year rule*.

Simply stated, she would introduce any difficult subject eight years before she felt it might come up in life situations. Angela was inspired to create this rule because she always felt she could discuss anything with her mother at any age. In fact, her friends would also go to her mom with personal issues. Angela's mother became a good and trusted source for vital information that was sometimes hard to come by. What impressed me was that Angela's mom had managed to instill her values and beliefs in her kids (and their friends) before other less trustworthy sources could instill theirs. She encouraged her children to never blindly believe without questioning. Instead, Angela's mom gave her kids a foundation of information about each difficult topic, threaded with her morals. Questions were always welcome so that her children could learn more.

No matter the topic, I recommend that you begin talking to your children about these difficult subjects a good eight years before they have to tackle them. Of course, there are no guarantees. Keep in mind that the eight-year rule isn't about counting out eight years; it's about hitting the subject early, way before your children are confronted with the problems in life. Parents need several years to influence and advise their children, leaving enough time for lots of discussions. Your children need this time to form their own viewpoints and figure out what they truly believe about the subject.

> Begin talking to your children about difficult subjects a good eight years before they have to tackle them.

The eight-year rule is an effective tool parents can use with their children to help them make good decisions. Talk to them early and often. Eventually, they will need to listen and take responsibility for their actions. With the proper runway, you have time to influence, advise, and mold your children, as well as teach your beliefs, understandings, and moral code to them. Honestly, this is the right and obligation of every parent. If you are not doing it, someone else is.

TALK TO YOUR CHILDREN ABOUT SEX

I applied the eight-year rule and brought up the sex talk when my kids were five or six. I was very honest and forthright with the information. And I don't mean that I brought it up once and then let it lie until they hit puberty. No, I spoke to them about it often and openly, and I found various ways to discuss sex, puberty, and all the related topics. Unfortunately, with the advent of the internet comes online pornography. No longer is smut regulated to sit behind an obscuring curtain in remote video stores. Anyone searching the web for anything related to sex will hit sites with a plethora of videos that would make a hardened construction worker blush. Trust me, that's not the way you want your children to learn about sex.

I will never forget the time when Conrad was browsing the internet studying worms. I was sitting right beside him monitoring what he was doing. The search started innocently, but because worms have both female and male sexual organs, his search landed on a porn site about hermaphrodites. Honestly, even I would have clicked on the links, as there were no indications that they were inappropriate. Sadly, his natural curiosity gave him a startling education that no one could have anticipated. Because of our previous discussions, Conrad felt comfortable that I was seeing the photos he'd uncovered, which led to a good conversation. Luckily, I was there to explain. But what about those kids who do not have a parent searching the web with them?

Conrad asked many intelligent questions about a woman's body and how it worked. He wanted details and I provided them. I remember him asking some questions that needed more in-depth information. I asked if he wanted more details. Sometimes the answer was yes, and some of the times my son shook his head. When he said no, I told him that we could save the conversation for another day. It's important that your children are ready for the information and willing to receive it when you discuss it.

Having said that, you don't want to postpone the conversation too long. It was my experience that when I started early and didn't make the topic strange, my sons weren't put off learning about sex. It's important to curb any discomfort or awkwardness that you might feel. Whatever you do, don't act embarrassed about the subject. Charlie and I talked about it like any other topic around the dinner table.

When my sons were five and six, I focused on the fact that their mommy and daddy love each other very much and express that love through sex. I stressed that sex isn't a dirty thing but a glorious expression of marriage. I also talked about the difference between moms and dads and how girls develop differently than boys.

When Conrad was in fourth grade, he was helping me with the laundry one day. He noticed blood stains on my PJs and became alarmed.

"Are you okay, Mom?" he asked.

"Yes," I replied. "Do you want to know more?" This was a great opportunity to answer questions about this delicate but natural topic.

He hesitated and then nodded, so I explained about a woman's menstrual cycle. I made sure to include his younger brother in the conversation as well. I let the two ask as many questions as they wanted, and I made sure to answer each one. If I didn't know, I did a little research to make sure my information was accurate. As soon as I could, I broadened the subject of sex to include the effect of raging hormones and the physical urges that the boys would feel in a few years. I also touched on the pros and cons of having sex before marriage. I wanted my sons to fully understand the consequences of this decision and the emotional toll it can take. Of course, we talked about the lifelong obligation involved if the girl becomes pregnant.

I know there are a plethora of viewpoints in the world, and this conversation will vary from household to household with different opinions about dating, marriage, and sex. The important thing is to share your morals and beliefs with your child at an early age. The more information you provide, the more they will understand what they are experiencing as they grow and their body is changing. As Conrad and Carson learned more about sex, I moved into more complex and controversial topics. When one of their favorite babysitters, who was married to another woman, announced they were having a baby, we talked about it. When a popular senior at another school was accused of rape, we sat down and discussed that topic. When sex was in the news, we'd talk about these stories over dinner. It was a perfect entrance to in-depth conversations about this subject.

The main point is that you should feel comfortable discussing the topics that might be considered taboo. Share your thoughts with your children, and allow them to give you their ideas. These may differ from your views, but at least your children are communicating with you instead of hiding their beliefs.

Schools will often broach this subject in their sex education classes, but these classes are offered too late, long past the time the topic should be addressed. I believe if you surveyed the average child, they'd tell you the classes provide too little information too late. Plus, the kids who need the data wouldn't bother asking questions of the teacher. Instead, they'd ask their friends or look it up online. Both of these choices can be disastrous. Their friends might have misconceptions, and the information on the internet is buried among links to pornography. It's far better to get ahead of potential problems by bringing up the subject early.

TALK TO TEENS ABOUT SEX

Even though talking about sex was not taboo in our house, when my sons were in their teen years they weren't always receptive to talking about sex. I remember one time we were having a typical family dinner, discussing a variety of topics. Conrad rolled his eyes and said, "Mom, why are you always wanting to talk about sex and drugs? Do you have a problem you aren't telling us about?"

In Conrad's sarcastic way, he was letting me know that he didn't want to discuss these topics that evening. While I do believe that children need to be ready to hear the information about sex and drugs, they might not be in the mood. That's different. Just because they don't feel like discussing it doesn't mean they aren't ready.

When my kids were young, they spent two years in a conservative area of Austin, Texas, attending a Christian school. The school and their peers provided a biblical influence that I appreciated. One great benefit that came from this was that a group of Christian men and their sons got together a few times to discuss everything a boy is physically, emotionally, biochemically, and sexually going through at puberty as well as the future stages of their life. The dads made the boys feel comfortable so they could ask about anything they wanted. No questions were off the table. My sons found this discussion helpful and enlightening. Because of it, they understood that what they were feeling and the urges they were having were normal. It was a positive experience that left the door open for future conversation with their peers and Charlie.

Now, this occurred when Carson and Conrad were in fourth and fifth grade. I believe that is late if this is your first conversation about sex with your kids. We had been talking about puberty, how the body will change, and sex for several years in our house, so the group discussion did not feel strange to the boys. When Carson started dating, I took him aside to share what it means to be dating from a girl's perspective. Carson was interested and open to discuss this subject in detail. I felt this was the perfect time to explain the emotions of a girl to my son. I also told him that the first sexual experience is quite different for a girl than for a boy. It can be a wonderful preview of a loving relationship in the future if handled well, but it can also introduce harmful ideas and set her on a path for destructive, harmful future relationships if done poorly.

If the first time a girl has sex is because she is pressured to do so, her first experience won't be pleasant. However, if a girl has a good experience with sex her first time, which is easier to have in a committed marriage, she will have a wonderful sex life with her spouse. I'm not encouraging or coaching my son on how to have sex with his girlfriend. More to the point, I'm telling him about the reality and harmfulness of casual sex.

We also have a rule that our sons are never allowed to be in a room with a girl with the door closed. When making rules, we need to understand that boys will have a strong sexual drive; they need to not put themselves in a situation that allows them to act on their impulses. After all, would you give a beer to an alcoholic? So don't leave a teen boy alone with his girlfriend in a bedroom.

I felt it was important for Charlie and me to get to know the parents of Carson's girlfriend. I wanted to partner and ally with them. Fortunately, we were all on the same page. We each had rules for our children, ones we all could respect. For instance, the girl's father told Carson that he didn't want Carson to drive her anywhere. Carson complied but asked if he could become the father's chauffeur for a while so that he could demonstrate his driving ability. Carson quickly proved his responsibility behind the wheel, and the father was impressed and relented.

I am grateful my sons talked to me about intimate and private topics. This didn't happen spontaneously but grew over time as a result of how I talked to them. I made it a priority to have uncomfortable conversations with my boys. I would talk openly about things I saw on TV and on social media that I disagreed with, and I would leave space for my boys to tell me their opinions and thoughts. I made sure to never make them feel that they would be in trouble for telling me anything, and I held our conversations in the strictest confidence.

I broached many topics I think some parents might find taboo. For instance, I discussed teenage pregnancy and the problems having a child when you are young can bring. We talked about the emotions involved with sex, contraceptives, STDs, blow jobs, masturbation, and pleasuring one's partner. We delved into prostitution and human trafficking as well. We also discussed gender fluidity, pronouns, and ways to express ideas. I always tell my boys that we are not God, so we have no right to judge others but that we can show kindness. Jesus was friends with the prostitutes, tax collectors, and societal outcasts.

Some people aren't sure about how to begin talking about sex. I suggest that you start by telling your kids your story. It will let them know that you remember how it was to be a teenager. Share how you felt at their age, what you were doing, and the pressures you experienced. Maybe before you talk alone with them about difficult, uncomfortable topics, bring these topics up at dinner. Yes, all ages can listen. Believe me, the younger kids are watching and learning from the older kids— don't cut them out of the family discussion. If you have these family talks about personal and uncomfortable topics, it will go a long way to demystify these subjects.

Kids will respect you more if you can share your personal story as an example of what not to do, or as an example of what to do, and why you did it. Be brutally honest about why you made your decisions, both bad and good. Children learn by seeing your struggles. They can see the commonalities in the difficulties that they face. I let my sons know that I made choices for my life that I've had to live with, and they are benefiting from my good choices and are enduring the consequences of some of my bad choices. I've shared with Carson and Conrad that I have a great, healthy relationship with Charlie because I made good decisions while dating. I went over many details, including choosing the right clothes to wear.

If I had a daughter, I would discuss her clothing; I wouldn't just tell her that her dress was too short. I would tell her that the skirt being that short will get her attention from the opposite sex and what effect that could have. While it's likely that a teen girl is interested in that attention, she probably doesn't understand what it will yield. So I would ask my daughter if that is the kind of attention she is looking for, and if she insists on wearing short skirts, follow up with her to see how she liked the response she got. I would also suggest asking questions about what other girls are wearing and what type of attention they get. Then find out what she thinks about that. Hopefully, she'll learn that she does not have to be inappropriate to get the attention of the opposite sex.

TALK TO YOUR KIDS ABOUT CRIME

My father was in law enforcement and made a point of taking me to a county jail when I was young. It was incredibly eye-opening. I'll never forget what I saw and how I felt touring the jail. It was smart of my dad to broach that subject directly and early. I suggest that every parent find a way to visit a jail with their children. Also, discuss various crimes, including drunk driving, shoplifting, possession of illegal substances, hit and run, and physical violence.

It's important to point out to children that most people who commit a crime didn't plan to do so ahead of time but did so as a result of making a bad choice that went horribly wrong. Maybe they walked into a store, saw something they wanted, and just took it without paying. Or someone got behind the wheel when they were drunk, thinking they were okay to drive. Sometimes a person gets involved in a crime because they decided to hang out with the wrong people who have a habit of making poor decisions.

One lapse in judgment can change the trajectory of a person's life forever, leading to a crime they never intended to commit. Consider the person who drinks alcohol, drives, and then kills someone. Their life is changed forever. Yet it happens all the time. When I saw news reports about the tragic loss of life because of drunk drivers, I'd point them out to my kids. They weren't easy to watch, but I know that these stories were an effective deterrent against driving while under the influence.

Teaching kids that *a small crime is still a crime* sets an important standard in place for children. For instance, there was a time when our family went to the beach for the day. Carson pointed out a pair of sunglasses on a towel and thought about grabbing them. He didn't see the man in the water and figured he'd "found" them. I pointed out they were on a towel and indicated the man in the water. Carson realized that taking them would be stealing. Although he knew the consequences of the law would be low, especially since they were left unattended, he still wasn't willing to violate his personal integrity. We had a good conversation about this, and we talked about how one crime usually leads to another. I shared a story about a friend I had in high school who liked to shoplift. She eventually got caught, and there were serious consequences for her actions.

We also talked about how a person should take full responsibility for their possessions. When we first arrived in Puerto Rico, Charlie used to keep his keys in the car when it was in the driveway. His logic was that people knew right from wrong and everyone was watching, so no one would steal it. We had a Spanish tutor for the boys who was completely shocked by my husband's viewpoint. He warned Charlie that his car might disappear one day if he kept doing that. We discussed this as a family and realized that Charlie was creating a temptation by leaving the keys in the car, one that might mitigate the crime if it were brought before a judge. Charlie might be seen as negligent in the eyes of the law.

The only defense against crime is a thorough education of our youngsters with lots of discussion. If your kids know about what could happen and examine different scenarios, they are less likely to walk down that path. Applying the eight-year rule to teaching your kids right from wrong is not a guarantee, but it is helpful. Considering these points ahead of time, and armed with information, your children will hopefully be able to recognize a potentially dangerous situation and avoid making a bad decision.

TALK TO YOUR CHILDREN ABOUT DRUGS AND ALCOHOL

The danger of substance abuse is another important subject that can begin early. No matter how clean-cut your child is, they are bound to encounter someone who offers them drugs or alcohol. After all, as of 2022, marijuana is no longer illegal in many states, so it is easy to obtain. In addition, eighteen is the drinking age in Puerto Rico, so some high school seniors can easily purchase alcohol. Unfortunately, young kids are experimenting with other substances all the time. The only way your child will understand the true facts about these drugs on their developing bodies is if you go over it with them.

Many influential people are already talking to your children about these topics, and they may not be telling the whole truth. People on TV, YouTube, social media, movies, and advertisements are pummeling your kids with information, most of which is biased or false. Kids need to understand the true facts and the consequences of taking harmful drugs. Some children might need to see firsthand the harsh reality to understand the consequences of these drugs, while other kids just need to discuss the reality, statistics, and effects of indulging in or abusing various substances.

Make sure to also talk about substances that might be legal but are highly addictive and which can impede one's ability to live a long and happy life. In Puerto Rico, when my sons were each finishing up high school, they could legally buy alcohol and go to bars. I believe not sheltering them from the truth about the consequences inherent in abuse and misuse helped them be aware of the pitfalls of alcohol. They also saw family members who were alcoholics and witnessed people doing crazy things while drunk. As a result, they both became responsible drinkers.

In our modern world, kids are vaping at school and stealing prescription medications from their parents. They have discovered ways to take over-the-counter medicines and alter them into more powerful drugs. The best defense against these temptations is open communication. Arm your kids with the truth, show them examples of the consequences of abuse, share stories that you've experienced or witnessed, and trust them to make the right call. Your kids also need to know about the ugly underworld that goes along with illegal drugs. And the personal prison created by getting addicted, even when the drug is legal.

Kids eventually need to have the full picture of substance abuse. Bring them to various drug rehabilitation programs so they can listen to the stories of real addicts. These kinds of experiences help them understand that very few people started out being addicts; rather, one day they woke up addicted because of a series of small bad choices. Take your children to an AA (Alcoholics Anonymous) or NA (Narcotics Anonymous) meeting. These experiences can leave a lasting impression on your child. I also always keep my eyes open for real-life examples of substance abuse. Unfortunately, they are all around us. In Condado, the section of San Juan where we live, I made a practice of pointing out the homeless addicts to my kids. Yes, some started with mental health issues; however, being homeless led most down the dark path of substance abuse.

Sadly, over time my kids saw one man refuse help and deteriorate. We had many discussions about how this man probably started life with dreams and aspirations, yet his path led him to be homeless. We talked about what the government was doing about the problem and how some help is abused and creates a lifetime of dependency. In addition, we discussed how sometimes people fall through the cracks and talked about our moral obligation to our fellow man.

Sometimes it can be confusing to children when you introduce things like a painkiller when they are ill. They might wonder why one drug is okay but another isn't. Conrad asked me that very question when he was sick and I gave him ibuprofen. He had a hard time understanding this complicated distinction. After we discussed it, Conrad began to understand that some drugs can be used for medicinal purposes, but abuse of any substance is not acceptable.

In my international graduate school, we often talked about the role of drinking in businesses around the world, the games that are played, and the expectations in different cultures. A Japanese friend used to say that to do business in Japan, you must sing karaoke and drink sake. However, he also said that the older businessmen made it look as if they drank a lot but knew how to avoid it. I found this to be helpful, and I shared this tip with my kids.

Have open and frank conversations about alcoholism with your children when they are young. I started talking to my kids about drinking alcohol when they were in second and third grade. I pointed out drunk people at restaurants and parties. I let my kids see what the mistakes look like so that they would know that even though drinking is part of our culture, there are consequences if one overindulges.

I knew that at some point my kids would be in an environment that promotes drinking games. I did my best to teach them about the ramifications of these games because I truly dislike them. One time when Carson and his older cousins were at the ranch, unbeknownst to me, the cousins were playing drinking games. Carson didn't really want to drink, but he wanted to join in the fun. Plus, his competitive spirit was fired up by the idea of the games. He won a few, lost a few, and before he knew it, he was drunk. Looking out for Carson, the cousins stopped the games before he got truly sick.

The next morning, I noticed Carson wasn't moving very fast. I still had no idea that he'd been drinking the night before. However, when I made his favorite cinnamon rolls and he didn't want any, I knew something was up. My husband understood right away what had happened. He told the boys to get their jeans on, and then he gave them chores. Carson was to mow the lawn. This job required him to fill the lawn mower with gas and toil in the hot sun. Carson desperately wanted to come inside and lie down. He wanted to sleep. Charlie and I shook our heads and told him he had to do his chores first. Carson got sick a few times, but he cut the lawn and did all the other jobs Charlie gave him that day. Boy, was he miserable.

It's important to note that I didn't rescue him. Yes, on some level I wanted to, but I didn't give in to that urge. I gave him water and ibuprofen, but I sent him back outside to finish his job. I knew this was a good experience for him. He learned that there are real consequences for drinking too much.

Another fact that I have shared with my sons is that research shows that because the brain is not fully formed until around age twenty-five, alcohol can have negative effects on a developing brain. Although the science on this is always changing, I firmly believe that excessive drinking kills brain cells. I also discussed with my sons the perils of drinking and driving. It's vital to talk about this early on and to keep discussing it. Today, with Uber, the situation is much easier, but as my parents would say, "Drinking and driving kills."

IMPLEMENT A NO-QUESTIONS-ASKED POLICY

My parents had a *no-questions-asked* policy that made it safe for me to extract myself from any situation. If I needed to be picked up from a party, a friend's house, or anywhere, they would come, no questions asked. Why? They knew I was getting myself out of a bad situation before it got worse. They held true to the policy and never gave me a lecture, and I was never grounded. As a child, I knew I had a sacred eject button when I found myself somewhere where I didn't want to be. There definitely were times when I used poor judgment or I was with people who ended up being different than I thought, and I wanted to leave.

I remember a time when I was in high school, I went on a date with a boy from a different school. He was an athlete and popular. This boy had his own car and had always been very polite and gentlemanly toward me. That is, until that night when his friends showed up asking if he'd come with them to a party. It sounded like fun until his friends asked if my boyfriend had a bat in his car. The little hairs on the back of my neck went up and I declined to go.

My boyfriend told me I was being silly, explaining that they always went to parties with bats because it made them look strong; it was just something the baseball team did. He assured me nothing would happen. I was torn. I really liked and trusted this boy, but I didn't feel comfortable about the situation. I called my father and asked him to meet me at the party and pick me up. My father showed up minutes after we got there. I kissed my boyfriend goodbye and left with Dad. I found out later that my instincts were correct. A group of baseball players from another school showed up at the party and a fight broke out. Long story short, my boyfriend ended up in the hospital with a concussion and multiple broken bones. Another boy ended up in traction with a permanent spinal injury. True to his word, my father never questioned me. He just saved me from a dangerous situation.

Children need to understand that bad things could happen at a party. Educate kids not to accept opened bottles or drinks in cups they didn't pour; these could contain dangerous substances. Make sure your kids know that if they find themselves at a party where they feel uncomfortable, you'll pick them up, no questions asked. Have pride in your heart when they call on you, and be sure to share that sentiment with them. After all, your child will only phone if they know you will be happy that they called. You need your children to confide in you no matter what.

Don't lecture them in any way on the ride home from the party. Instead, praise them for having the good sense to leave. Impress on them how grateful you are that they trust you. Of course, if your child wants to talk to you about the situation, be there for them, but otherwise wait until later to talk to them. The important thing is that they trusted you enough to call you and leave the party. Later, when talking about what happened, make the conversation as light as possible. It isn't an inquiry or a trial, and there should be no punishment. When you can, through conversation, lead your child into recognizing how they got there and what they can do to avoid a similar situation in the future.

You could start the conversation with stories from your past, the mistakes you made, telling them how you found ways to resolve the situations. When they realize that they aren't alone, that others have made similar bad decisions, they might be more apt to open up to you. It is always best to listen to your child and their solutions rather than telling them what to do.

TEACH ABOUT BULLYING

I remember seeing a commercial on YouTube that had aired in Europe. It showed how a bully was picking on a younger boy because his hair was red. The bully called him Little Red Riding Hood and announced loudly to the other gathered children, "They better call 911 because his hair is on fire." It was clear that the red-haired boy was affected by the comments. An older child noticed this but didn't say anything. The next day, when the bully tried his antics again, he stopped because he noticed the older boy had dyed his hair red to support the younger boy. At that moment, he realized that it was no longer cool to tease this boy because of a small difference. I was impressed because dying his hair red was such a nonconfrontational way for the older boy to send a strong message that he didn't like seeing the younger kid being bullied.

Bullying is a tremendous problem in schools. What's more, social media makes it easier and more prevalent to torment others. The bully can hide behind a fake social media account and perpetuate lies, gossip, and hatred. It's a dangerous crime. In fact, Charlie has a colleague who lost a son to bullying. Only after his death did the father discover the vicious texts on his son's phone. It was tragic. We need to be aware of this danger and talk to our kids to make sure they don't tolerate bullying. To allow this vicious behavior is ultimately to condone it. Let's teach our children that they have a voice. They can speak up or simply walk away, but they should never put up with cruel behavior.

Bullying can come in a variety of forms. Although hazing is now illegal in most states and not condoned by universities, it still exists. Kids need to learn to stand up to it and say no. I remember hearing about some kids that were pledging a fraternity. They were blindfolded, taken to a place, and told to jump off a cliff into the deep water below before taking off the blindfold. They were only three feet above the water, but the pledges believed what they were told. One broke his legs because he was so frightened that he kept his legs rigid when he hit the ground. Someone should have stood up and stopped this from happening.

Bullying can also start slowly and be subtle. In high school, Conrad and Carson took the same class with a boy who had learning difficulties and behavioral issues. My sons were frustrated by this child because he was often rude. Despite this, all the kids in the class tried to include him. But while doing so, they made jokes at his expense. That was the way these children interacted. They never saw it as bullying. The teacher called them out on this behavior and pulled the parents in for a conference. She pointed out that the behavior was hurtful and mean. I realized that although my sons hadn't considered that they were bullying, they had on some level been doing so. Putting down others isn't right. When I talked to them about this, my sons were defensive. However, after they examined their behavior, they apologized. Conrad and Carson took responsibility and wrote a letter to the kid, acknowledging his good qualities. In the end the boy was grateful and shared some of his struggles with them.

Ultimately, whether you're a kid or an adult, it's not okay to watch someone get bullied or hazed and not do anything. Start teaching your child about this when they are young. Share stories and discuss appropriate ways to stop bullying. One idea is to start by asking your child if they would stand back and do nothing if they saw a friend bleeding. This is a dramatic way to introduce the concept, but it makes the point. After they understand the dangers of bullying, ask your child what they could do if they saw someone being bullied. Then help them formulate a plan for a variety of situations. By keeping an open dialogue with our children about bullying and cruel behavior, we can stop it dead in its tracks. All it takes is one kid to speak up.

Chapter Summary: Teach Difficult Subjects

- The eight-year rule: introduce any difficult subject eight years before you believe it might come up in a life situation.

- Speak often and openly about sex, puberty, and all related topics.

- Make it a priority to have conversations with your kids about uncomfortable topics that might be taboo. This will go a long way to demystify these topics.

- Just because your kids don't feel like discussing difficult topics doesn't mean they aren't ready to talk about them.

- Kids will respect you more if you can share your personal story as an example of what not to do, or as an example of what to do and why you did it. Be brutally honest about why you made your decisions, both bad and good. Children learn by seeing your struggles.

- Arm your kids with the truth about crime and drug and alcohol abuse. Show them examples of the consequences of abuse, share stories that you've experienced or witnessed, visit a jail, or attend a NA or AA meeting.

- Institute a no-questions-asked policy that makes it safe for your kids to extract themselves from any bad situation. If they need to be picked up from a party, a friend's house, or anywhere, come get them, no questions asked. Don't lecture or punish them afterward.

- Keep an open dialogue with your children about bullying and cruel behavior.

- Trust your kids to make the right choice.

Exercises

Answer all the following questions individually, and then share your responses with your partner and kids when appropriate.

1. Create the eight-year rule chart for yourself. Make a list of the topics that you want to be the first to talk to your child about. Indicate the age your child will face each topic and write it next to the topic. Then write the age you need to start talking to your child about the topic, eight years earlier.

2. Write down what you'd like to discuss with your child about sex, puberty, and all related topics. Consider the questions your child will have. Be ready to answer them. If you're uncomfortable about the subject, practice with your partner until it feels natural. Keep it honest, simple, and straightforward.

3. Write down the aspects of crime that you'd like your child to know about. You can look at the news and social media to get inspiration and topics to share with your child. Consider different crimes committed in the world, along with their penalties. Possibly include stories in which the perpetrator didn't intend to commit the crime. Include finding ways to show your child the consequences of crime. You could organize a tour of a local police station or talk to an ex-con.

4. Make a list of the myths and misconceptions associated with drugs and alcohol. Consider the confusions you had about drugs and alcohol when you were young as well as questions you know your child has.

5. Think back to your childhood. Write what you would have needed to feel comfortable talking to your parents about a bad situation. What would have allowed you to call your parents if you got yourself into trouble and needed help? What can you do to provide a no-questions-asked policy in your home?

6. Talk to your child about cyberbullying and in-person bullying. Discuss the effects of verbal and physical bullying. Talk to your child about actions they can do to help stop bullying if they see it.

CHAPTER 14

TEACH LIFE SKILLS

TEACH BEFORE THE FOURTH GRADE

A significant growth and development period for children is from the time they are born to about the fourth grade; this stage is quite formative. While this can be an overwhelming time for parents, I strongly suggest taking a moment to consciously think about what things you want your children to learn. This is the best time to introduce your kids to anything and everything you want to teach them.

From birth to the fourth grade is the golden window when kids are interested in what parents want to share, especially if they think what you are teaching is fun. They are willing to listen to and be influenced by you. This also is a time when kids are uninhibited and curious about the world around them. You still can teach your kids after the fourth grade, but then it typically will be driven by what *they* want to learn or need to learn rather than what you as the parent want them to know.

With your partner, write down the topics you want to teach. Make a list and execute it. Of course, just because you've shared something with your son or daughter doesn't mean that their interest will ignite. Charlie and I believed working on the ranch with the extended family was a vital skill to teach. We brought Conrad and Carson with us every weekend we went there. Being at the ranch always meant work before play. A rancher wakes at the crack of dawn and goes to dinner at dark thirty, that is, thirty minutes after the sun sets. My boys, from their earliest moments, worked alongside their grandfather, dad, uncles, and cousins, doing what they could to help while learning new skills.

One time, when Carson was five and Conrad six, Charlie and the boys had been working all weekend with the cousins. By Sunday afternoon everyone had left, and Charlie and the boys were putting up the equipment and tools. Charlie realized there were three pickup trucks at the lake, all with trailers. One trailer needed to be dropped off at the location with the other equipment, one trailer needed to go to Grandmother's house, and the last one would wind up at our house. There was no other adult around to help him, so it seemed logical to Charlie that Carson and Conrad would each drive a truck to its destination.

Charlie gave strict instructions to Carson and Conrad. "Don't back up with a trailer. If you get into trouble, turn off the pickup and wait for me to come. We will all meet at the front gate after each trailer is dropped off." Charlie had the farthest distance to go, so he left first. Conrad left second and Carson last. Conrad dropped off his trailer and made it to the gate first and waited as instructed. Meanwhile, Carson was driving his truck to the gate and took a right at the fork in the road.

Immediately he knew he had taken the wrong road. Carson stopped and considered his options. He told me later that he thought, "Dad said I can't back up, but he didn't say I can't turn around." Carson started to make a wide turn to go back the right way, but the turn was not wide enough for the trailer on the back. He knew he had a problem when he looked back and saw that the trailer had dented the truck, so he turned off the truck and waited for his father.

When my husband made it to the gate, his first words were, "Where is Carson?"

Conrad looked around and said, "I don't know."

Staying calm, yet feeling nervous, Charlie told Conrad to stay at the gate. Then Charlie went looking for Carson. After a while, Charlie found him, assessed the damages, and drove to the gate with our son. At dinner Charlie let Carson tell the story for my benefit, as I hadn't been there. When Carson started his story, he was beaming with pride as he told how his father had let him drive the pickup with the trailer from the lake to the front gate. When I heard that, I thought nothing of it, because sometimes Charlie put Carson on his lap and let him drive. It was only when Carson got choked up and said that he got into a little accident that I asked for more details. My son explained that he realized he had taken the wrong fork in the road and then tried to get back on the right road without backing up.

"Dad gave me two rules," Carson said. "Do not back up, and if I get in trouble, turn off the truck and wait for him. I followed both rules."

I instantly knew there was something no one was telling me. I asked my son, "Where was Dad?"

"He was in the other pickup," he replied.

"Were you alone?"

"No."

Puzzled, I turned to Conrad and asked him what happened.

Looking sheepish, Conrad said, "I wasn't there."

I then assumed one of the ranch hands or cousins must have been driving with Carson. "Who was with you?"

Carson looked me right in the eye and said, "Maggie."

Maggie is our dog. Charlie could tell I was getting more and more frustrated with each explanation, so he quickly asked Carson, "So what did you learn?"

Carson thought for a moment and then said, "I learned that I need to make bigger turns with a trailer on the back or I will dent the side of the truck."

This is an example of a real-life lesson learned at the ranch. Carson now tells the story as a cautionary tale to anyone he teaches to drive a truck with a trailer. I still like to jest with my husband about how helpful the dog was to a five-year-old driving a truck with a trailer. When Carson turned sixteen and got his driver's license, the family joke was that I didn't need to worry because Carson had already learned from his first accident. All those years of experience driving on the ranch have made both my sons safe, conscientious teen drivers.

I learned later that my sons were willing to spend their weekends doing manual labor with their cousins because they enjoyed being with their cousins, the thrill of being allowed to drive, and the feeling that they were a part of building the ranch. Today, they take great pride in the ranch, especially wakeboarding and jet skiing in the lake they helped build.

FAILURE CAN BE GOOD

Most parents find it hard to stand by and watch their children fail. How many moms and dads have you seen "help out" with a science fair project? However, if parents step in and "save" the child from failure when it really doesn't matter, what will the child do when it does? The fact is these parents are stealing their children's practice time. Failure is not about the outcome; it's about the learning process. It's about taking action and learning from the past so you can change and try again, making different choices, and ultimately making a difference in your life.

John C. Maxwell, a leadership expert, is often quoted as saying, "Fail early, fail often, but always fail forward."[10] I love that phrase and I have shortened it to *fail fast forward*. It's appropriate for any stage of life but is particularly applicable to children. A failure is more beneficial at a

---

10   John C. Maxwell, *Failing Forward* (New York: HarperCollins, 2007), 176.

CHAPTER 14: TEACH LIFE SKILLS

young age because the consequences are less, and the lessons learned can be utilized for the rest of your life. If you do not learn as a child, you can be sure to learn those tough lessons as an adult, when it is often much harder.

There are many life lessons that can be taught through fail fast forward. Buy your first grader an alarm clock and teach them how to set it. Then allow them to go to bed and be responsible for getting up in the morning. They might not wake up on time. Maybe they'll set the clock for p.m. instead of a.m. Don't step in. Let them fail. What's the worst that can happen?

Be prepared that your child might be angry about their failure and blame you. Whatever you do, don't accept any responsibility for the situation. Don't rescue them. They need to fully understand it was their mistake, which caused them to be late. Then follow through and make sure your kid tries again the next night. Be sure they continue until they succeed. Do not let outside pressures influence you to rescue them. Is it going to hurt your child if they show up late for first grade?

If your child learns to routinely set their alarm, get up, get dressed, and be ready for school as a first grader, think how prepared they will be in college. However, if you are the "supermom," waiting on your child, making life easier for them, what happens when you're not there? For instance, you won't be tagging along on your child's first day of college. Wouldn't you like them to be on time for class? It would be tragic if they failed a course because they slept through an exam. And isn't failing in first grade better than getting fired from their first job because they can't show up to work on time? Failing in first grade can prevent future failures.

Allow your children to struggle while the penalties for failure are low. It's first grade, isn't it? As parents, it's our job to *teach*, not *do* everything for our children. If you continually protect your children from failure, you are in fact setting them up to fail badly in the future. It's been my observation that some of the parents who are overprotective end up raising children with huge life problems. Difficult situations can be amazing teaching opportunities for children. When mistakes happen, it's not time to go into protection mode, as so many parents are inclined to do. Mama or Papa Bear need to sit on their hands. It's a great time to show right from wrong, demonstrate good and bad choices, and allow your children to experience consequences in a safe environment.

For instance, if a child cheats on a second-grade math test, they'll encounter consequences if they're caught. But if the child is coddled and not corrected, they're apt to try cheating again. It might even become part of their normal behavior. Do you want your child to get caught cheating on his SAT tests later in life? No, of course not. It's through our children's mistakes that we can teach and raise responsible adults.

I believe that failure points out the practice that still needs to be done. Consistent practice is also part of the equation to become a success. No one ever becomes an expert on the first try. It takes dedicated effort to achieve competence. Do not let your child give up after one try. Competence takes time, and kids need to learn that hard work is what is needed to gain that coveted prize. They will stumble, and it will be messy, but they'll figure it out for themselves if you let them. When Conrad was in fifth grade, he came to me and requested to play the trumpet. I asked if he was willing to put in the time, effort, and energy required to learn the instrument. He nodded with great conviction. It was important that I got that agreement up front. I knew he might want to quit early, but I was determined to hold him accountable.

At that moment, it became my responsibility to help him follow through on his commitment to learn to play a few songs well while completing a full year in the band he joined. Part of the agreement we had was that once he completed his commitment, he wouldn't be required to continue to play the trumpet. It would be his choice at that point.

Another parent might say, "But my son doesn't have the mouth for blowing the trumpet" or "He just lost interest." Honestly, there are an infinite number of reasonable-sounding excuses, but the bottom line is, anyone can reach any goal they set if they don't bolt at the first sign of trouble. I heard loud, jarring sounds coming from Conrad's room each day for a full month, and there were times when he pleaded with me to quit, but I stood my ground. He failed like a champion until one day he played a song—perfectly. It was beautiful, and the entire family celebrated. It was a sweet triumph. I immediately helped my son set a new goal. He chose another song and became determined to learn that one. There were fewer failures, quicker successes, and no further talk of quitting the trumpet. Down the road, Conrad did choose to stop playing, and that was fine. I didn't require that he become a professional trumpet player. That wasn't his aspiration. He just needed to achieve the goal he had set for himself.

Whatever you do as a parent, please don't take the struggle in life away from your children. It isn't always easy to watch your children stumble and flounder because we want to jump in and save them from the pain of failure, but that's a huge mistake. Permit your children to struggle through their problems, and they will

> **Permit your children to struggle through their problems, and they will have their own breakthroughs.**

have their own breakthroughs. And through those breakthroughs, they will achieve a peaceful, unshakeable confidence that no one can take from them.

TEACH PERSEVERANCE THROUGH PROBLEM-SOLVING

Kids understand what they need to do to get what they want. All babies quickly learn that crying helps them get what they need. When they get a little older, they will require perseverance to learn to walk. Some kids take longer than others, but they figure it out through trial and error. Parents, we need to let our kids try and fail; that teaches perseverance. Stop doing things for them. Stop making it easy for them. Let your children figure it out and make it easy for themselves. Let them problem-solve.

I let my children know that it was expected that they do things on their own as quickly as possible. I gave them a road map and taught them how to get there, but it was their responsibility to learn how to do it themselves. I made it clear that Mom will not be by their side forever; they must learn to do it. The first time Carson went on an overnight trip with his school to space camp in fifth grade, I told him to pack for himself. He asked me for a list of items to take along, so we came up with one together. Then he laid everything out on his bed before he put the things into his suitcase. I asked my son if he wanted me to check that he had everything. He said no. I gave a cursory glance to make sure the important items were there and let him pack by himself.

On the first day away, Carson called home. He'd forgotten to pack socks. All he had were the ones he wore. I sympathized with him and helped him come up with possible solutions: wash the socks at night and dry them with a hair dryer, wear the same socks for several days, or borrow a pair from a friend. In the end, Carson came up with his own solution, one which wasn't exactly on our list. He talked a teacher into going to the store so that he could buy new socks. For Carson, having his own clean socks was important.

When I looked over my son's solution, I realized he'd gotten what he needed because he was persuasive, persistent, and knew which teacher to ask. The teacher had already called me, having found out through the grapevine that Carson had forgotten his socks. I had asked her to let him figure it out on his own. At first, this teacher declined to take Carson to the store. Now, she wanted to go, but she respected what I was trying to teach him. However, Carson kept asking and explaining why socks were important. The more he communicated on the subject, the more she wanted to help. In the end, she bought him socks at the store. He'd learned that persistence got the job done. After he returned home, I made sure Carson wrote that teacher a nice, long thank you letter, and he paid the teacher back with his own money.

As my children grew older, they learned to live with the concept of being dedicated to getting things of value. Carson took the SAT five times. His first scores were average. Nothing horrible, but they weren't adequate for the top universities. We approached seasoned SAT tutors, who all basically said the same thing: "We can help raise his scores, but not to the level that Carson wants." This test is actually designed to make getting the top numbers exceedingly difficult. Carson took it all in but was determined to get great scores. One can't always live one's life or make important decisions based solely on the limitations experts put on us.

Carson devoted one week to an SAT boot camp. This helped, but it still wasn't what he wanted, so he hired a personal tutor, with our permission. His next scores actually went down. But Carson didn't give up. He practiced more and then took the test again. His scores went up but still weren't within the range he'd set for himself. So my son studied all summer, taking practice test after practice test. When he took the test again, his scores had improved and were in range of his goal. But he still wanted them to be higher.

By this time Carson had a very respectable result. But he knew that his dream college wanted to see higher scores. He had one more chance to raise the scores before he applied to his college of choice. He threw himself into the challenge and wound up with a combined score that was 270 points higher than his first one. As a result, he was nominated as a candidate for the U.S. Presidential Scholars Program. Carson didn't set out to take the SAT five times. I'm not sure he would have gone down that road had he known how much work would be involved to achieve his goal. However, the truth is that his objective increased over time as he began to see what he was truly capable of achieving.

He adjusted his thinking, determined new goals, and made new plans. Carson set a big hairy audacious goal (a term made popular by author Jim Collins)[11] and made it. He also did not let the so-called experts tell him it was impossible.

To survive and flourish in life, today's kids need to be bold and different. Our children will be called on to draw on their unique talents, ones they've developed as a result of their individual passions in life. After all, we aren't looking for a new generation of assembly-line workers or obedient robots. We need self-sufficient, highly skilled problem solvers. Our children will need to be able to ask the right questions so that they can solve any problem that comes their way.

It's wise to encourage your children to fully assess a problem before searching for a solution on the internet so that they can pose the best question. Kids today are apt to ask the internet a question without completely understanding the problem. This leaves them open to getting information that doesn't apply or solutions that don't work. When breaking down important troubleshooting skills for your kids, focus on getting them to examine the situation and pose and define the problem they want to solve. Then the answers are often easy to find on the internet. The answers are a simple Google search away. However, you must know the right question to ask.

The quality of your life, and especially your kid's life, will be based on the quality of the questions asked. The internet will only provide the answer to the question you type in. Learning to troubleshoot and discover the actual problem is invaluable. The lessons learned might just lead to innovation. This technique applies to many real-world situations. Let's say your child forgets their book at school. I'd start by getting them

---

11 Will Kenton, "What Is a Big Hairy Audacious Goal (BHAG)? Categories and Example," *Investopedia*, August 14, 2023, https://www.investopedia.com/terms/b/big-hairy-audacious-goal-bhag.asp.

to look at and define the problem: "I have a homework assignment to complete and don't have the necessary book to do it." After the problem is clearly defined, I'd invite the child to come up with solutions. I'd start by asking questions like, "What do you plan to do about that situation?" Then, if they don't have a concrete idea, I might ask more leading questions like, "Who else has a copy of that book?" If they pose the correct problem, they will realize it isn't *their own* book they need. They just need *a* book or a way to get the information.

There are multiple solutions that don't require you to drive anywhere or purchase anything, but you might need to walk your child through the steps to solve their own problem. For instance, your child can call a classmate and ask them to take a picture of the pages needed and send them over text or email. That would solve the problem for that day. Some children will respond with a defeatist attitude and give up without trying. That's the time to pull out a good pep talk. The first step will probably be to get them to realize that a solution is possible. You might need to start by getting them to understand that every problem has a solution—and that crazy or wild solutions are acceptable.

We want our children to always come up with multiple options for any difficulty; that way they have a choice of solutions. Settling on one because it is easy to do so is lazy and won't work out well. In my opinion, it's wise not to stop at two choices, because it's limiting and sometimes creates a dilemma. Teach your child to come up with three or more choices so they can truly find the best solution.

I have made it my life's work to figure out why some kids have a life advantage over others. I have observed and interviewed many people and have concluded that those parents who provide opportunities for their children, but take a hands-off approach, usually wind up with children who are good problem solvers. As you teach your kids these skills, you need to make sure they don't consider you, the parent, the answer to their problems. If you solve everything for them, your children will depend on you for the rest of their lives. We need independent thinkers.

TEACH HOW TO HANDLE PROBLEMS WITH OTHERS

In Puerto Rico, Conrad had a teacher who called him her *token privileged white male*. The teacher was a single Latino mom who was struggling after the hurricane. I wasn't happy with this label, but Conrad asked me not to say anything. He knew she was hurting, and he wanted to win the teacher over and show her that the stereotype was false. If I waltzed in there complaining, I would be proving her right.

As a result of this situation, Conrad and I talked about the inequalities in the world, racism, the differences between men's and women's salaries, and how the hurricane could be making life even harder, especially for single moms. Conrad understood how much it cost to run a generator and how time-consuming it was to stand in line for gas, groceries, and potable water. As a family, when we went to the grocery store after the hurricane, we divided and conquered: one person stood in line while the other two got the groceries. Since this teacher was on her own, Conrad knew everything took her much longer.

In the end, he worked out for himself that his teacher might just be frustrated. He decided he could win her over because he realized she didn't know him very well. So Conrad took it upon himself to allow the teacher to see a different side of him by sharing his interests and helping her. He brought her ice, offered to do laundry for her, and brought her food from the relief distribution center where he volunteered. Through this experience, my privileged white male son got to experience a glimpse of racism. He was judged and labeled based on his skin color, gender, and socioeconomic background. He learned how to combat it, and he showed that *with great privilege comes great responsibility*. Looking back, if I had sat down and talked to the teacher, I would have been correcting the teacher. Most likely she would have politely nodded while cementing her opinion about why privileged white males were a burden to us all.

As parents, we want to have our kids' backs, and we want our kids to know that. But what are we teaching our kids if we fight their battles? So there needs to be a balance. Your child does want to know that you are on their side. You need to be compassionate toward your child and their feelings, yet make sure your child knows that this is *their* conflict. Conrad's experience with his teacher taught me that. As a parent we want to jump in and protect, yet by talking to Conrad I learned that he understood the situation for what it was and didn't make it personal. From the beginning, Conrad understood that regardless of what the teacher said, he had an obligation to treat her with respect because she was the teacher. He also knew he was a privileged white male and it was his responsibility to show her a different perspective, compassion. Today Conrad has a lasting friendship with that teacher. They shared an amazing growth experience. My son turned things around on his own.

TEACH EMPATHY

Both my children are very empathetic. In the preceding story, Conrad's empathy with his teacher helped him solve the problem in a meaningful way. But it was not always this way. When Conrad was little, I don't think he always understood what he was feeling. In kindergarten, there was a boy who picked on Conrad. No one liked this boy, so Conrad let this child pick on him and didn't tell anyone. He knew the boy was sad and was having a tough time. I think he hoped the boy might change if Conrad was nice to him. If I had taught Conrad to understand empathy at that point, he probably wouldn't have let the boy pick on him. Instead, he might have realized that he could feel for the child without accepting the bullying. As it was, Conrad's compassion for the boy caused him to not defend himself.

Part of empathy is the emotion that we feel as a result of another person's experiences. We can teach children to understand when they are taking on and experiencing the feelings of another person. It can be difficult to tell the difference between feeling another's emotions and our own. By understanding where the emotions are coming from (and that they are making the other person's emotions their own), our children might be able to better understand why they are reacting the way they are. When that is achieved, our children will come closer to understanding empathy.

Some kids will understand this concept but won't be able to put it into words. We can help them find the words to explain what they are feeling and why they are feeling it. Other kids will not understand why they start crying in a room full of other people crying. There will also be kids who have no strong emotions when others are expressing strong feelings. That is okay too, and they need to learn they are naturally less empathetic. By understanding what is going on around them, the feelings that they are feeling or not feeling, kids will be better able to navigate life.

Empathy can be used to teach kids to understand what it would be like to live in another person's situation. My kids were born into a family that is educated and affluent and lives in a country in which they can prosper. When Conrad volunteered at the hurricane relief center, he learned what it could be like to walk in someone else's shoes; he experienced some of the struggles, disappointments, and problems that others experience every day. He heard many stories about families with no potable water or with holes in their roofs. He also learned firsthand about the dire situation in the hospitals because we had friends who were in that situation. When children catch a glimpse into someone else's life, I believe that glimpse can make an impression that will last a lifetime.

One way to teach empathy is by showing your children that you are empathetic to their problems and feelings. Showing empathy with actions and words helps kids to understand. They can learn a lot through life experiences and build on this understanding. Start early and speak about the subject often. Read stories and find news articles to talk about.

It's important to note that feelings can be biological, based on gender and size. When we traveled as a family, there were times I felt unsafe, especially when we were in a new place. My boys rarely felt what I felt, so I shared with them the details of what I felt so they could empathize. They often responded with suggestions. By acknowledging my feelings and talking to me about them, they were being empathetic. Conrad and Carson did not have to feel what I was feeling. They just needed to understand and acknowledge the emotions I was experiencing. Stepping into my footsteps has helped them gain empathy with me and other women.

TEACH KIDS RESPECT FOR EARNING MONEY

Although I believe that volunteering is work, it doesn't provide the same experience as earning money. When a child volunteers, they should do so with the intention of giving their talents to help others without expecting anything in return. Giving to those who cannot help themselves is altruistic and noble. However, it's also important to teach our kids that earning money is a vital need in life.

Some parents will say that children need to focus on school, not on earning money. Why not make earning money part of a child's education? Knowing how to earn money is another life skill they will need along with reading, writing, and arithmetic. If kids don't understand how to make money, they won't survive well without their parents. I'm not talking about allowance because that isn't earned money. Children will learn to spend at the level of what they are given, waiting for the next dole. That just sets them up to expect welfare for the rest of their lives.

I paid my children for the work they did above and beyond the expected household necessities. I wouldn't pay them to make their beds or clear away their dishes when they were young; I would compensate them for picking up leaves or washing the car if they wanted to earn money. I *hired* my sons for these special jobs only if they had completed their regular chores as expected. If they hadn't, there were consequences.

When one of my sons completed a special job, he brought me an invoice that stated the agreed-on pay for the job. That invoice went into a jar and was paid at the end of the week. We had set rates for some jobs, but I allowed room for negotiation if my sons felt that more was due to them. In addition, if I needed the job done faster and couldn't find anyone else to do it, the pay went up. This system taught my sons about supply and demand.

My husband's family did not have a lot of money, so he needed to earn his own spending money as a kid. Charlie's father helped him do so by putting him to work at a young age and always paying for the labor. Since his family owned a farm, my husband was hired to do many different jobs, like building a barbed wire fence at the age of ten. I can tell you, working in the West Texas heat is hard work. When Charlie turned thirteen, he needed braces, which wasn't in his parents' budget. My husband really wanted straight teeth, so he paid for the braces from his savings. If you talk to him about it today, he'd probably get a faraway look on his face and describe the feel and the sound of the check ripping from the checkbook. To Charlie, it felt as if the braces cost all the money he earned from working outside in the brutal sun.

Since money was so tight and he was paying for the braces, Charlie always brushed as the dentist instructed him to do. There was one hundred percent compliance. I love that story and was inspired to encourage my children to be interested in their teeth. My husband and I wanted that same level of commitment from our sons, so we asked that they help pay for their braces, and it worked.

This technique could be applied to any major purchase that involves your kids. Consider that just because you can afford to pay for things for your children doesn't mean you should. Instead, allow them to invest in their own lives. Your kids will feel like they are in control of their own destiny. This builds strong, self-reliant children that will not blame others for their problems. They will know that they have the power to make decisions and take responsibility for themselves. It's been my experience that when children have their own money, especially when they've pushed through various obstacles to earn it, they learn to value it. Money looks different when it is truly yours.

When I told my sons they could buy a toy with their own money, the truly miraculous thing to me was that my children didn't get upset when they didn't get the toy they'd been begging for. After the first time this happened, a light bulb illuminated in my head. Now that Conrad and Carson had their own money, the decision was theirs and they thought hard about the purchase and decided they didn't want the toy anymore. Why? Because their money had value—whereas mine didn't. It was interesting to me how frugal my sons became. What a great life lesson.

As my sons grew up, their requests became more extravagant. For instance, one day when Conrad was about thirteen, he told me he really wanted a pair of expensive sneakers. My son researched why the sneakers were so much better than normal sneakers and why he thought they were worth the extra money. The cost was about double what I had allocated to spend on shoes, so I let him know that he'd need to pay half the price if he really wanted them. Without hesitation, he agreed, and he was thrilled with his purchase.

Conrad took care of those shoes better than any other pair I'd ever gotten him. One day, we prepared for a hike that promised to get our feet muddy, sandy, and wet. Conrad looked down at his feet and realized his shoes would get dirty. Since these sneakers were his pride and joy, he decided to change into his old sneakers.

"I saved my old shoes for an outing like this!" he said.

It was the first time I hadn't had to caution him that his shoes would get dirty. Why? Because he'd invested in them, and he valued them. Kids who don't want to earn money don't have any incentive. If your children ask to go to a movie with friends, I suggest that you ask how they are going to pay for it. This would be a great incentive for them to earn some money. Otherwise, what's the point of earning this useless commodity? When you require that your child chip in to get the things they really want, they'll start to see the value of hard work and the rewards it can offer.

Discussing the value of things should be an integral part of a child's education. Lead by example. I can tell you that when I waste money, my kids pick up on it. However, when I'm frugal, they notice it, too. It's good to remember that wealthy people are wealthy because they know how to earn money—and, more importantly, they know how to save it.

What do you do when your child doesn't have the money to go to a movie when their friends are going? I handled this situation as if I were a bank. My sons could get a loan that they had to pay back with interest (which was always a dollar to keep things simple) later. If done correctly, this system can increase the child's incentive to earn money; no one likes to pay interest. I clearly remember the first time I loaned money to Carson. He was so happy at first because he could go to the movie with his friends. It cost fifteen dollars, and he only had five. I told him that, like at a bank, he would have to pay me back the ten dollars plus one dollar in interest. His jaw dropped. There was no Bank of Mom; instead, these boys had Loan Shark Mom.

I explained to Conrad and Carson that banks make money from the interest people pay on their loans. That is their business. I also explained that banks pay a small percentage to people with savings accounts because they use this saved money to loan out to others. I'll never forget the wide-eyed look they gave me that day when they learned about the concept of interest. They both wanted to earn interest on their money. We opened bank accounts and they learned firsthand how a bank works.

START EARNING YOUNG

As I've mentioned a couple times, my sons' first business together was a lemonade stand. Conrad was six, getting ready to start first grade, and Carson was beginning kindergarten at five. Just a few months prior, they had asked if they could set up a stand in front of our house. I shook my head no because it wouldn't do well there; they hadn't considered several important problems.

Even though they were very young, I sat them down and taught them about the four Ps of marketing: product, price, place, and promotion. I asked my sons to create a business plan before I'd sign off on the lemonade stand. I didn't hear anything more about the lemonade stand for a while. But when I began planning the back-to-school night at their school, the boys came to me with the solutions for the problems I had presented with the four Ps. In fact, they had created a whole new plan: They wanted to stake out a spot in front of the school and give a share of the profits to the PTA. I was impressed. How could I say no to that?

Their plans weren't what you might picture, small and unassuming. They hit the ground running with big hairy audacious goals. They each used their unique skills to tackle all the issues that arose with the energy of a locomotive. I could see Conrad's logic and organizational skills peeking through, along with his quiet leadership abilities. He was the one who predicted that there would be many thirsty people at the school event. Carson came up with the idea to donate part of their profits to the PTA, which would help motivate parents to buy their lemonade. We had a lot of fun trying out various lemonade recipes, which resulted in my kitchen floor becoming a sticky mess. In the end, they came up with a tasty mixture that they were confident would be a success.

Figuring that the principal would be thrilled by the idea, I set up a meeting with her for the next day. Then I sent the boys in alone to pitch their idea. The meeting was over in five minutes. To my surprise, the boys came out with sad faces.

"She said no," Carson mumbled.

I was shocked. What? Why? The principal joined us and explained that parents and students couldn't sell anything on school property.

We walked out of the school, both boys terribly upset. I didn't blame them. I was a little perturbed as well. Just then we heard the jingle of an ice cream truck rolling up in front of the school. The boys each gave me a look and I laughed.

I raised a brow. "Want some?"

"Yes!" they chorused, their moods immediately improving.

As we munched on our treats, Conrad looked up at me. "Mom?"

"Hmm?"

"Why doesn't the ice cream man need the principal's permission?"

I was stunned by his insight. What a good question! "I think it's because he's on the street. He isn't technically on school property."

Carson and Conrad both jumped up excitedly. "We can do that too!" they said at the same time. "We could sell from the street."

They were completely rejuvenated. We raced home and prepared for the evening's event. The boys decorated our golf cart with streamers.

We parked the cart where the ice cream truck had been, at the curb in front of the school. The boys sold their ice-cold lemonade with a tiny piece of lemon and a sprig of mint in each cup. The drinks were immensely popular.

I can tell you that those two little engines worked and worked and learned a lot. So did I. Since I learn best by watching others and testing what I have learned, I can tell you that I've become a better parent by raising these two magnificent boys.

Chapter Summary: Teach Life Skills

- Don't steal your children's practice time. Let them do their project even if they will fail.

- Make failure just another subject to discuss, something that happens routinely in life.

- Life is about learning, trying new things, and knowing that when you fail you can learn by continuing to move forward.

- Consistent practice is part of the equation to becoming successful.

- A parent's responsibility is to hold their children accountable for the goals they set for themselves, whatever they may be.

- Don't take the struggle in life away from your children. Anything in life worth having is worth working for.

- Praise your children for their accomplishments.

- Encourage your children to follow their passions in life.

- Teach your child to live a productive, independent life.

- Give children the power to invest in their own lives.

Exercises

Answer all the following questions individually, and then share your responses with your partner and kids when appropriate.

1. Make a list of all the things you'd like your child to learn before the fourth grade. Put the list in order of importance to you. Identify who is going to teach each topic on your list to your child and when it will be taught. Talk to your child about the list you want to teach them and take action.

2. Write down some examples of times when failure motivated you to become better at a skill. Note how failure was a part of your learning process.

3. Write about a time you persevered. Note why you worked hard to achieve the goal and how you felt at the end. Make sure to include the obstacles you overcame.

4. Have your child participate in Lemonade Day. Go to lemonadeday.org and start your child on the path to earning money.

QUESTIONS ON FOUNDATIONAL PRINCIPLES

Ask yourself the following questions to determine your foundational principles.

1. Create a list of values your parents passed on to you. Of those values, cross off what is not important to you and add the values that are important to you. Read over the list and write why each value is important and on the list.

2. Describe what a successful family looks like to you. What are the keys to making it successful? What is not happening and what is happening in this family?

3. What family traditions do you want to continue from your childhood and why? What family traditions do you want to start and why?

4. Describe how you were disciplined. How will you discipline your children? How and why is your disciplinary approach similar to and different from how you were disciplined as a child? Share this with your partner, and make sure you are both in agreement on your disciplinary process.

5. What role did your parents play in your education and extra-curricular activities? What role do you want to play in your children's education and extracurricular activities? Why?

6. What does work-life balance mean to you, and how will you apply it to your family? What do you want to model for your children? What is more important, sacrificing your career for your family or your family for your career? Why?

7. Who is the primary breadwinner in the family and why?

8. What does financial stability mean to you? Who is responsible for the family's financial management? How do you want to teach financial literacy to your children? How did you learn financial literacy? What was helpful and what was not helpful in your learning process of financial literacy?

9. Describe the roles your parents played in your family when you were growing up. How could those roles have been different? Why? What roles do you want to play in the family? Why are you the best person to take on those roles? Is there one head of the family and who is it?

10. What roles do you want your parents to play in your family and why? What roles did your grandparents play in your life?

11. What role does extended family play in your life, your family's life, and your children's life? Why is extended family important or not important?

12. How did your parents handle conflict or disagreements? How would you do it differently and why? Who has the final say in your family and why?

13. What are your views on spirituality or religion? Describe your spiritual journey. What do you want to pass on to your children? How important is religion versus spirituality?

14. What are your views and hopes for your community involvement and your social life?

15. What are your short-term goals and your long-term goals?

16. What do you believe keeps a couple together? What is essential in a marriage? What was the underlying value that kept your parents together, or what was the underlying value that led to their split-up?

17. What significance do you give to adaptability and openness to change in your family life? What significance do you give to routine and structure in your family life?

18. How do you demonstrate love and affection in your family, and why is it important? How was it demonstrated to you as a child and what did you like or dislike? Why?

19. What does it mean to be a family? Why is family important to you? How do you show that you prioritize family?

20. What legacy was left to you by your parents? What legacy do you want to leave to your children? What is important to you about family history and ancestral heritage? What role did family history and heritage play in your childhood? What role do you want family history and heritage to play in your family?

ADDITIONAL READING

Bandler, Richard, and John Grinder. *Reframing: Neuro-linguistic Programming and the Transformation of Meaning.* Moab, UT: Real People Press, 1982.

Baumrind, Diana. "Child Care Practices Anteceding Three Patterns of Preschool Behavior." *Genetic Psychology Monographs* 75, no. 1 (1967): 43–88.

Baumrind, Diana. "Effects of Authoritative Parental Control on Child Behavior." *Child Development* 37, no. 4 (1966): 887–907.

Chapman, Gary. *The 5 Love Languages: The Secret to Love That Lasts.* Chicago: Moody, 2009.

Cloud, Henry, and John Townsend. *Boundaries with Kids: How Healthy Choices Grow Healthy Children.* Grand Rapids, MI: Zondervan, 2001.

Ferriss, Tim. "Marriage Is Never 50/50." TikTok post, June 5, 2023. https://www.tiktok.com/@timferriss/video/7241204908203003142.

Miniño, Arialdi M. "Mortality among Teenagers Aged 12–19 Years: United States, 1999–2006." *NCHS Data Brief*, no. 37 (May 2010). https://www.cdc.gov/nchs/data/databriefs/db37.pdf.

Reckmeyer, Mary, with Jennifer Robison. *Strengths Based Parenting: Developing Your Children's Innate Talents.* New York: Gallup Press, 2016.

Rogers, Carl Ransom. *Client-Centered Therapy, Its Current Practice, Implications, and Theory.* Boston: Houghton Mifflin, 1951.

Voss, Chris, with Tahl Raz. *Never Split the Difference: Negotiating as if Your Life Depended on It.* New York: Harper Business, 2016.

INDEX

ABOUT THE AUTHOR

KATE HAMILTON has been married to her husband, Charlie, since 2000 and is a mother of two independent and confident young men in college. Some might say she is an unlikely writer because of her dyslexia, yet her life experiences compelled her to write this book. She earned an MBA in international business and is a former corporate executive turned mother and entrepreneur. When Kate is not coaching parents and their children, you will find her volunteering with Lemonade Day, a youth entrepreneurship program; planning the next family adventure; or working with Charlie in San Juan, Puerto Rico.

You can contact Kate with comments
or questions at kate@caprockpartners.com.

.